*Digital*
*Scrapbooking*
FOR
DUMMIES®

# Digital Scrapbooking FOR DUMMIES®

by Jeanne Wines-Reed and Joan Wines, PhD

WILEY

Wiley Publishing, Inc.

**Digital Scrapbooking For Dummies®**

Published by
**Wiley Publishing, Inc.**
111 River St.
Hoboken, NJ 07030-5774
www.wiley.com

For general information on our other products and services, please contact our Customer Care Department within the U.S. at 800-762-2974, outside the U.S. at 317-572-3993, or fax 317-572-4002.

For technical support, please visit www.wiley.com/techsupport.

Wiley also publishes its books in a variety of electronic formats. Some content that appears in print may not be available in electronic books.

Library of Congress Control Number: 2005924623

ISBN-13: 978-0-7645-8419-0

ISBN-10: 0-7645-8419-7

Manufactured in the United States of America

10  9  8  7  6  5  4  3  2

1B/SQ/QZ/QV/IN

WILEY

# About the Authors

**Jeanne Wines-Reed,** often affectionately called "Scrapbooking's Ambassador of Good Will," promotes the scrapbook industry on many levels. The Great American Scrapbook Company (GASC) that Jeanne founded in 1997 now hosts annual scrapbook conventions around the U.S. Jeanne's commitment to her company's mission ("Encouraging the Preservation of Personal and Family Histories") propelled her into many new endeavors, including her founding of the International Scrapbook Trade Association (ISTA) in1998 and the launching of *Scrapbook Retailer* magazine in 2002, an extremely successful publication in which scrapbook industry manufacturers and retailers exchange information and expertise.

Jeanne likes to emphasize scrapbooking as a powerful vehicle for achieving understanding and peace in our world communities. Recently (the past 5 months), Jeanne has been working with the Photo Marketing Association (PMA) to promote scrapbooking in England, Australia, New Zealand, and Japan, as well as putting on her conventions in the U.S. and co-authoring scrapbooking titles for Wiley with her mother, Dr. Joan Wines. You can contact Jeanne at jeanne@scrapbookretailermagazine.com or (801) 627-3700.

**Joan Wines,** an English professor with a PhD from the University of Southern California, has worked on publications and other facets of her daughter Jeanne's scrapbooking enterprises since 1996. As a mother, grandmother, and member of a large extended family, Joan has an avid interest in scrapbooking personal and family histories. As a professor who teaches literature, writing, and multimedia, she has an equally avid interest in narrative — and thus the stories that scrapbooks tell.

Dr. Wines became interested in digital technologies in the late '80s when she was teaching at the University of Southern California (USC). She took advanced training in digital design at IBM (CA, NC), Harvard, and at various software manufacturer seminars, conferences, and workshops — then co-founded and developed a Multimedia program at California Lutheran University (CLU). Currently, besides teaching, Dr. Wines directs a Center for Teaching and Learning and the Writing Center at CLU. She writes and presents papers on teaching and learning at national and international conferences and is particularly keen on ensuring a more systematic integration of digital literacy into the higher education curriculum.

# Dedication

To the scrapbook industry's manufacturers and retailers — who have made possible so much for so many.

# Authors' Acknowledgments

We need first to thank Wiley for their interest, questions, suggestions, and expertise; all of which helped us shape and complete this book on digital scrapbooking. Thanks to Joyce Pepple (acquisitions director), Tracy Boggier (acquisitions editor), senior project editor Alissa Schwipps, and copy editor Jennifer Bingham. We also want to thank technical editor Kathy Samoline for her careful reading of the text and all of the product manufacturers who patiently answered our many queries.

We could not have written this book without the help of the staff of *Scrapbook Retailer* magazine and the Great American Scrapbook Company — more specifically without the research work and tech know-how of Ray Cornia (one of the star players in this collaborative effort) and the diligent attention of Jennifer Williamson to the placement, accuracy, and quality of the book's black-and-white and color images.

## Publisher's Acknowledgments

We're proud of this book; please send us your comments through our Dummies online registration form located at www.dummies.com/register/.

Some of the people who helped bring this book to market include the following:

**Acquisitions, Editorial, and Media Development**

**Senior Project Editor:** Alissa Schwipps

**Acquisitions Editor:** Tracy Boggier

**Copy Editor:** Jennifer Bingham

**Technical Editor:** Kathy Samoline

**Senior Editorial Manager:** Jennifer Ehrlich

**Editorial Assistants:** Hanna Scott, Nadine Bell

**Cover Photos:** © Brian Twede

**Cartoons:** Rich Tennant (www.the5thwave.com)

**Composition Services**

**Project Coordinator:** Erin Smith, Jennifer Theriot

**Layout and Graphics:** Joyce Haughey, Barry Offringa, Lynsey Osborn, Heather Ryan, Julie Trippetti

**Interior Photographs:** *Scrapbook Retailer* magazine

**Proofreaders:** Leeann Harney, Carl Pierce, TECHBOOKS Production Services

**Indexer:** TECHBOOKS Production Services

**Publishing and Editorial for Consumer Dummies**

   **Diane Graves Steele,** Vice President and Publisher, Consumer Dummies

   **Joyce Pepple,** Acquisitions Director, Consumer Dummies

   **Kristin A. Cocks,** Product Development Director, Consumer Dummies

   **Michael Spring,** Vice President and Publisher, Travel

   **Kelly Regan,** Editorial Director, Travel

**Publishing for Technology Dummies**

   **Andy Cummings,** Vice President and Publisher, Dummies Technology/General User

**Composition Services**

   **Gerry Fahey,** Vice President of Production Services

   **Debbie Stailey,** Director of Composition Services

# Contents at a Glance

**Introduction** ...................................................................1

**Part I: Getting the Lowdown on Digital Scrapbooking**......7

Chapter 1: A Bird's-Eye View of the Digital Scrapbooking Scene .......................9

Chapter 2: Gearing Up to Scrapbook Digital Style.....................................23

Chapter 3: Exploring Your Software Options ............................................37

Chapter 4: The Digital Design Process in Brief .......................................49

Chapter 5: Exploring Popular Digital Scrapbook Styles ................................65

**Part II: Brushing Up on the Basics**..............................83

Chapter 6: Mastering Basic Digital Photo Processing ..................................85

Chapter 7: Exploring Layout and Design Options ......................................103

Chapter 8: Enhancing Your Pages with Digital Graphic Elements .......................121

Chapter 9: Making a Statement with Basic Text .......................................135

**Part III: Taking Your Digital Scrapbook
to the Next Level** ....................................................147

Chapter 10: Tackling Advanced Photo Correction ......................................149

Chapter 11: Getting Creative with Advanced Effects ..................................161

Chapter 12: Trying Your Hand at Artistic Text Techniques ............................185

Chapter 13: Incorporating Sound and Video ...........................................199

**Part IV: Getting Creative with Fun Projects** .................211

Chapter 14: Creating a Digital Wedding Scrapbook in the Classic Style ................213

Chapter 15: Putting Together a Digital Family Album Using the Heritage Style.....227

Chapter 16: Celebrating the Here-and-Now with a
Pop-Style Digital Reunion Scrapbook ................................................243

Chapter 17: Working with Digital Theme Projects .....................................255

Chapter 18: Sharing Your Scrapbooks .................................................265

**Part V: The Part of Tens** .......................................283

Chapter 19: Ten Tips for Every Digital Scrapbooker ..................................285

Chapter 20: Ten Digital Scrapbooking Pitfalls to Avoid..............................293

Chapter 21: Ten Creative Ways to Integrate Digital Techniques
into Traditional Scrapbooks ........................................................299

Chapter 22: Ten Fun Ways to Involve Kids in Digital Scrapbooking ....................305

Appendix: Web Resources..............................311

Index ..........................................................319

# Table of Contents

*Introduction* ..................................................... *1*

About This Book.........................................................................1
Conventions Used in This Book ...............................................2
What You're Not to Read...........................................................2
Foolish Assumptions ................................................................3
How This Book Is Organized.....................................................3
    Part I: Getting the Lowdown on Digital Scrapbooking......................3
    Part II: Brushing Up on the Basics.................................................4
    Part III: Taking Your Digital Scrapbook to the Next Level ..............4
    Part IV: Getting Creative with Fun Projects....................................4
    Part V: The Part of Tens...............................................................5
Icons Used in This Book............................................................5
Where to Go from Here..............................................................6

*Part 1: Getting the Lowdown on Digital Scrapbooking ......7*

**Chapter 1: A Bird's-Eye View of the Digital Scrapbooking Scene . . .9**

Considering the Advantages of Going Digital ............................9
Finding the Tools You Want and Need.....................................11
    Handling the hardware issues ....................................................11
    Choosing beginning-level software ..............................................14
Exploring Popular Digital Scrapbook Styles ...........................15
Saving Your Work....................................................................16
    Organizing and saving individual photos as you take them ...........16
    Saving work in progress .............................................................17
    Storing your digital images .........................................................17
    Preparing your printed images for storage....................................18
Sharing Digital Files ...............................................................19
Get Ready, Get Set . . . Scrap!................................................20
    Creating a comfortable and functional workstation .......................20
    Preparing for action ...................................................................21

**Chapter 2: Gearing Up to Scrapbook Digital Style . . . . . . . . . . . . . . .23**

Acquiring the Essentials..........................................................24
    Calculating your computer needs ................................................24
    Scoping out scanners.................................................................27
    Pondering printing possibilities ...................................................29
    Deciding on a basic digital camera ..............................................31

Adding Extra Tools over Time................................................................33
Upgrading computer capabilities..........................................33
Enhancing your scans..............................................................34
Experimenting with specialized printing.............................34
Enhancing the functions of the digital camera..................35

## Chapter 3: Exploring Your Software Options ....................37

Identifying Your Operating System.......................................................38
For PCs.......................................................................................38
For Macs.....................................................................................39
Scoping Out the Scrapbooking Software Scene..................................39
Outfitting beginners.................................................................40
Stepping up to intermediate software...................................42
Scrapbooking on a whole new level with advanced software.......43
And the winners are . . ............................................................46
Investing in Software Extras..................................................................46
Forging ahead with far-out fonts...........................................47
Grabbing great graphics...........................................................47

## Chapter 4: The Digital Design Process in Brief ..................49

Creating a Digital Design Library..........................................................49
Looking after photos.................................................................50
Keeping an eye out for embellishments................................51
Creating color palettes.............................................................52
Exploring other design resources...........................................52
Setting Up a Digital Scrapbook Project................................................53
Deciding on a topic...................................................................54
Selecting materials from your design library.......................54
Deciding on page size...............................................................55
Sketching tips for your pages..................................................55
Writing the story.......................................................................56
Working with photos and images...........................................57
Creating the Digital Layout....................................................................58
Starting with a base or a template page................................58
Layering......................................................................................59
Positioning items on the page.................................................59
Keeping Your Computer Happy: Discarding
or Relocating Leftover Files..............................................................62

## Chapter 5: Exploring Popular Digital Scrapbook Styles ..........65

Looking at the Major Scrapbooking Styles..........................................65
Getting a digital handle on the heritage style......................66
Using digital tools to concentrate on the crafty style.........68
Putting some pop into your digital layouts..........................70
Finding ways to digitize shabby chic......................................72

Using digital tools that help you achieve the
exacting standards of a classic style..............................73
Making digital pages in the modern style .....................................75
Analyzing the digital artist style.........................................76
Surveying Other Scrapbooking Styles ...............................................77
Styles for baby ...................................................................77
Designing with favorite fantasies .....................................77
Experimenting with the eclectic style ............................78
Tying in to specific time periods.....................................78
Fooling around with fashion .............................................79
Focusing on vocation.........................................................80
Designing for sports lovers ..............................................80
Even more scrapbooking style ideas ...............................82

*Part II: Brushing Up on the Basics* ................................*83*

**Chapter 6: Mastering Basic Digital Photo Processing** ...........**85**
First Things First: Taking Great Digital Photos...........................85
Shooting at maximum resolution .....................................86
Creating your own interesting photos.............................87
Planning your photographic time table............................88
Taking Advantage of Your Digital Equipment's
Built-In Processing Features...................................................89
Looking into your digital camera's picture viewing program........89
Cultivating the camera cropping habit............................90
Enlisting the help of your scanner's
hardware and software settings...............................91
Utilizing Editing Programs to Improve Your Digital Images....................92
Adjusting size and resolution ...........................................93
Cropping.............................................................................96
Changing your photo's position with the Rotate tool .....................98
Finding the Flipper .............................................................98
Selecting brightness and contrast....................................99
Reducing red-eye................................................................100
Sharpening your photo images..........................................101
Repairing Scanned Photos ..........................................................102

**Chapter 7: Exploring Layout and Design Options** ................**103**
Brushing Up on Visual Design Principles.....................................103
Balance ...............................................................................104
Harmony ..............................................................................105
Unity....................................................................................105
Rhythm ...............................................................................105
Positive and negative space..............................................106
Color....................................................................................107

Applying Design Principles to Your Digital Scrapbook Pages ...............108
Marking out a grid ...................................................................108
Creating balance .....................................................................109
Finding your focal point ........................................................110
Using lines and shapes to create structure,
depth, and dimension .........................................................111
Creating emphasis...................................................................113
Enhancing Your Design Strategies with Digital Operations...................114
Using scanners and cameras to prepare
unusual design elements ....................................................114
Descreening printed photos ..................................................115
Making your photo a background ..........................................117
Tiling your images and photos ..............................................118
Texturing your photos ...........................................................119
Collaging or montaging your images and photos .................119

## Chapter 8: Enhancing Your Pages with Digital Graphic Elements

First, a Few Technicalities......................................................121
Understanding digital graphics types....................................122
Reviewing the importance of resolution for digital graphics .......123
A word about copyrighting .....................................................124
A cautionary tale about the Internet ....................................125
Manipulating Clip Art .......................................................................125
Looking for printed clip art....................................................126
Gathering clip art from the Internet......................................127
Using clip art ...........................................................................127
Incorporating Illustrations and Drawings ......................................128
Using Photos from the Internet ......................................................131
Downloading issues ................................................................131
Stocking up on stock images..................................................132

## Chapter 9: Making a Statement with Basic Text

Translating Text Terms.....................................................................135
Working with Fonts ..........................................................................137
Going over some font basics...................................................138
Exploiting the design possibilities of body and display fonts ......139
Understanding how your computer stores and copies fonts ......140
Forestalling font problems .....................................................140
Finding fantastic fonts ...........................................................141
Incorporating Text into Your Scrapbook .......................................142
Keying text into your digital layout ......................................143
Using handwritten text in digital scrapbooks......................144

## *Part III: Taking Your Digital Scrapbook to the Next Level* ................................................ *147*

### Chapter 10: Tackling Advanced Photo Correction ...............149

Making Sure Your Photo-Editing Software Is Up to the Challenge .........150
Introducing Cloning and Healing ...............................................................151
    Attack of the Cloning tool ..................................................................151
    Healing damaged images ...................................................................152
Adjusting Color ...........................................................................................152
Retouching with Digital "Painterly" Tools ...............................................154
    Dodging and Burning tools ................................................................154
    Playing with the "brush" tools ..........................................................155
    Breezing through airbrushing ...........................................................155
    Pushing the Pencil tool ......................................................................157
    Practicing with the Pen tool ..............................................................157
Cutting Out Unwanted Objects ..................................................................158
    Eraser tool ...........................................................................................158
    Magic Wand .........................................................................................159

### Chapter 11: Getting Creative with Advanced Effects ...........161

Enhancing Your Page Design ......................................................................161
    Making the most of montage ..............................................................162
    Creating a panorama layout ..............................................................163
Trying Out Some Commonly Used Color Variations ................................166
    Converting color images to grayscale images ..................................166
    Saturating and desaturating images .................................................166
    Tinting an image .................................................................................166
Creating Special Effects with Filters and Plug-Ins .................................167
    Working with filters ...........................................................................168
    Applying a Gaussian blur ..................................................................171
Making Exciting Embellishments ...............................................................172
    Making hand drawings to use as embellishments ...........................172
    Creating embellishments from found objects ...................................173
    Scanning with 3-D embellishments ...................................................173
    Making your embellishments look more "real" .................................174
Creating Unique Backgrounds ....................................................................176
    Using your own photos as backgrounds ...........................................177
    Texturing page backgrounds .............................................................179
    Concentrating on background color ..................................................181
    Finding other ways to create impressive digital backgrounds .....182

**Chapter 12: Trying Your Hand at Artistic Text Techniques** . . . . . . . . **185**
Souping Up Your Software ........................................................185
Wrapping Text .......................................................................186
Wrapping text automatically.............................................187
Wrapping text manually....................................................188
Creating Curvy or Wavy Text Lines...........................................189
Stretching and Skewing Text Boxes and Letters ........................189
Outlining and Filling Letters with Patterns and Colors................191
Outlining around a letter in whatever color you choose ...........191
Filling the letter with a pattern or with a photo ...................192
Rotating Text.........................................................................192
Changing Text from a Horizontal to a Vertical Format.................193
Shadowing Your Text ..............................................................194
Applying Filters ....................................................................194
Designing Your Own Fonts .......................................................195
Waxing Poetic: Incorporating Long Journal Entries .....................195

**Chapter 13: Incorporating Sound and Video** . . . . . . . . . . . . . . . . . . . **199**
Looking At Multimedia Merchandise...........................................199
Keeping it (relatively) simple with presentation programs..........200
Over the top with authoring programs ................................202
Creating a Multimedia Album ...................................................203
Organizing your elements .................................................203
Adjusting sizes of digital images .......................................205
Adding sound and video....................................................205
Sharing Your Album ...............................................................207

**Part IV: Getting Creative with Fun Projects** . . . . . . . . . . . . . . . . **211**

**Chapter 14: Creating a Digital Wedding
Scrapbook in the Classic Style** . . . . . . . . . . . . . . . . . . . . . . . . . . . . **213**
Sketching Out Your Story.........................................................213
Incorporating a journaled story into the album's overall design ...214
Finding the right font for your story....................................214
Making a quick mock-up for your wedding album ....................216
Choosing Photos for Your Classic Album ....................................216
Creating your own classic photos and images .......................217
Classic embellishments .....................................................218
Altering your photos to suit your design ..............................218
Collecting classic photos and images from other sources ..........219
Selecting Your Wedding Album's Color Palette............................219
Designing the Classic Wedding Layout with Digital Tools .............220
Lining up classic page items with the Snap To Grid feature.........221
Using the Sizing tool for balancing your classic composition......221

Assembling Your Wedding Album ..........................................................222

Deciding on your page size ........................................................222

Bringing in your digital backgrounds ......................................223

Putting on the finishing touches on
your digital wedding album ..................................................224

**Chapter 15: Putting Together a Digital Family
Album Using the Heritage Style** .........................**227**

Telling the Heritage Stories ..........................................................227

Focusing on a single ancestor, place, event, or time period ........228

Tracking down the stories ..........................................................228

Using digital tools to enhance your writing ...........................229

Choosing Your Photos ...................................................................230

Finding family photos ................................................................231

Repairing photos .......................................................................231

Aging your photos to get a uniform look ................................232

Creating the Color Palette .............................................................234

Choosing your colors .................................................................234

Using digital tools to get the colors you want .......................235

Designing Digital Heritage Layouts .............................................236

Adding memorabilia and accessories to your heritage pages .....236

Using and resizing embellishments and other items
to fit your layout designs ......................................................237

Assembling a Heritage Album ......................................................238

Finding the right page size for your journaling ......................238

Creating heritage-style backgrounds ......................................239

**Chapter 16: Celebrating the Here-and-Now with a
Pop-Style Digital Reunion Scrapbook** ....................**243**

Figuring Out Your Pop-Style Story ..............................................244

Incorporating current pop trends ............................................244

Short stories? Long stories? ......................................................244

Choosing Your Pop Images ..........................................................246

Creating pop photos and images ..............................................246

Drawing on pop publications and characters .........................249

Creating the Color Palette .............................................................249

Using your photos to "find" a color palette ............................249

Getting your main color elements from your backgrounds ..........250

Designing Pop-Style Layouts .........................................................250

Creating pop page backgrounds ...............................................250

Using the "non-art" pop style ...................................................252

Incorporating memorabilia, accessories, and
embellishments into your pop design ..................................253

Completing Your Digital Pop Album ............................................254

**Chapter 17: Working with Digital Theme Projects** . . . . . . . . . . . . . . .255

Choosing a Theme .................................................................................255
Gathering Scrapbook Theme Materials..............................................257
Designing Theme Layouts.....................................................................258
Exploring Popular Theme Page Ideas..................................................259
School scrapbooks......................................................................259
Friend themes.............................................................................260
Family scrapbooks......................................................................261
Pet scrapbooks ..........................................................................263
Vacation scrapbooks .................................................................263
Business scrapbooks .................................................................263
Hobby scrapbooks .....................................................................264
Remodeling projects ..................................................................264
Public building projects.............................................................264

**Chapter 18: Sharing Your Scrapbooks** . . . . . . . . . . . . . . . . . . . . . . .265

Printing Your Digital Pages .................................................................265
Resizing and saving....................................................................266
Adjusting your printer settings ...............................................267
Binding your pages ....................................................................267
Digitizing Your Traditional Album Pages ...........................................268
Using your scanner ....................................................................268
Using your digital camera .........................................................272
Transmitting Your Pages Electronically ............................................275
Preparing your pages for e-mail by using PDFs.....................275
Publishing your pages on the Web............................................278
Burning Your Books on CDs and DVDs................................................280

*Part V: The Part of Tens* . . . . . . . . . . . . . . . . . . . . . . . . . . . . .*283*

**Chapter 19: Ten Tips for Every Digital Scrapbooker** . . . . . . . . . . . .285

Pinpoint the Kind of Digital Scrapbooks You Want to Create.................285
Work with the Hardware You Already Have.......................................286
Select Software That Meets Your Needs and Skill Level ...................286
Master Your Hardware and Software...................................................287
Keep Your Computer Healthy...............................................................287
Set Up a Workable File System ............................................................288
Take Advantage of Your Digital Camera .............................................289
Back Up Your Files .................................................................................290

Manage Your File Sizes and Resolutions ................................................291
Share Your Scrapbook Pages ..............................................................291

## Chapter 20: Ten Digital Scrapbooking Pitfalls to Avoid . . . . . . . . . .293

Don't Rush to Replace Equipment ........................................................293
Don't Put Too Many Programs on Your Computer ...............................294
Don't Forget to Bring Your Camera.....................................................294
Don't Forget to Create a Morgue File....................................................295
Don't Ignore Copyright Laws ..............................................................295
Don't Start Too Many Projects .............................................................296
Don't Print on Colored Paper ...............................................................296
Don't Abandon Traditional Scrapbooking ............................................297
Don't Get into a Rut ............................................................................297
Don't Give Up......................................................................................298

## Chapter 21: Ten Creative Ways to Integrate Digital
## Techniques into Traditional Scrapbooks . . . . . . . . . . . . . . . . . . . . . .299

Print Out Digital Images ......................................................................299
Customize Special Background Papers ..................................................300
Support Your Embellishments..............................................................300
Print Stickers ......................................................................................301
Make Your Own Headers .....................................................................301
Scan in Handwriting or Drawings.........................................................302
Make Iron-Ons.....................................................................................302
Replicate Letters and Documents .........................................................303
Use Digital Tools to Share Traditional Scrapbooks ...............................303
Catalog Your Images ...........................................................................304

## Chapter 22: Ten Fun Ways to Involve
## Kids in Digital Scrapbooking . . . . . . . . . . . . . . . . . . . . . . . . . . . . . . .305

Give Your Child a Digital Camera ........................................................306
Help the Kids Download Free Clip Art...................................................306
Scrapbook School Assignments ...........................................................306
Scrapbook a Special Event....................................................................307
Create a Child's Family Tree ................................................................307
Photograph and Write about Favorite Possessions ...............................307
Make Gift Scrapbooks..........................................................................308
Avoid the Doldrums..............................................................................308
Make a Group Scrapbook .....................................................................309
Teach Scrapbooking at Your Local School ............................................309

## Appendix: Web Resources ..................................311

Exploring Scrapbook-Specific Web Sites ..................................311
Locating Clip Art and Images on the Web ..............................314
Finding Fonts Images on the Web ..........................................316
Checking Out the Chat Rooms ................................................316
Posting Your Pages ................................................................317
Specialty Programs ................................................................317

## Index ..................................................................319

# Introduction

* * * * * * * * * * * * * * * * * * * * * * * * * * * * * * * * * * * * * * * * * * * * * *

*T*empted by scrapbook-friendly hardware and software computer programs, increasing numbers of scrapbookers are testing the digital waters. And once immersed, they find that they can easily cruise the Internet for advice, training, resources, storage space, and all other things relevant to digital scrapbooking.

Although *Digital Scrapbooking For Dummies* has much to say to beginners, it speaks as well to experienced scrapbookers (both traditional and digital). Remember that you don't have to chose *between* scrapbooking digitally and scrapbooking traditionally; traditional scrapbookers use digital elements in their handmade scrapbooks and digital scrapbookers add traditional elements to their digital pages. Mix it up! Experiment! And, most of all, have fun with the exciting new options that are out there waiting to make your most innovative and elaborate creative dreams come true.

## About This Book

This book is designed much the same way scrapbooks are designed. We lay out a background in Chapter 1 and then go over the specifics in the chapters that follow.

You don't have to read the book straight through from cover to cover. Read Chapter 1 to get an idea of which sections you want to explore first. Choose what most interests you. Skip around in the pages, and then zoom in on the details of your focus. (We help you navigate by referring you to other chapters, and to other books, where you can find more information about your individual interests.)

*Digital Scrapbooking For Dummies* is intended to make you comfortable with digital scrapbooking programs, tools, and techniques. We give you lots of information in language that even the greenest novice can understand — information that puts you on the inside track in photography, graphic design, and special effects.

Use the book as you will. Dip in and out as you please. Explore some of the Web sites we list for you — but come back to us often. We want you to try at least a few of the tips and tricks we've picked up from professional artists and graphic designers, so that you can make *wow* pages — and keep on making them!

# Conventions Used in This Book

We use the following conventions throughout the text to make things consistent and easy to understand:

- ✔ New terms appear in *italics* and are closely followed by an easy-to-understand definition.

- ✔ **Bold** highlights the action parts of numbered steps and other important information you should know.

- ✔ All Web addresses appear in `monofont`.

- ✔ We use the terms *digital page* to refer to a computer-generated page and *digital layout* to refer to a computer-generated two-page spread.

- ✔ *Tic-tac-toe grid* is our term for a fabulous design trick that you (and everyone else) will want to use to create balanced pages and layouts.

- ✔ We use standard computer terms for digital processes (such as *crop, resize, dodge, burn,* and *scan*), even though not all programs use these terms. For example, *skew, stretch,* and *distort* are different terms that all describe the same function. Which of these terms you become familiar with will depend on which program you use.

- ✔ A *file* is a saved document. It can be a text document, a graphic document, or a scrapbook page.

  In the program instruction books, the program's different functions are called tools, so we use this terminology, except when we refer to the icon or symbol that "pictures" the tool on a toolbar, or when we're talking about *features* (such as the Sharpening feature), which aren't referred to as tools in instruction manuals.

# What You're Not to Read

You don't have to read the *sidebars* — the text in gray boxes. Our sidebars usually provide details about the history and processes of digital technology and other interesting but nonessential aspects of digital scrapbooking.

You also don't have to read the paragraphs accompanied by a Technical Stuff icon unless your mind gravitates toward computer lingo or you feel better when you're as completely informed as possible.

# Foolish Assumptions

We made some assumptions about you the reader. Look at the following list and see if we got it right:

- ✔ You like efficiency.
- ✔ You have some experience creating traditional scrapbooks.
- ✔ You like to keep up on new trends in scrapbooking.
- ✔ You don't want to spend a lot of money on digital scrapbooking until you know whether or not you enjoy it.
- ✔ You're busy, but want to balance your life by connecting (meaningfully) with family and friends.
- ✔ You're computer literate, but still like step-by-step instructions.
- ✔ You hope that scrapbooking digitally will help you organize and share the photos scattered throughout the house and/or the digital photos on your hard drive.
- ✔ You like things simple, and you like them simply explained.
- ✔ You want a clear overview of digital scrapbooking, even though you realize equipment, tools, and techniques are constantly changing.

# How This Book Is Organized

*Digital Scrapbooking For Dummies* is divided into five parts. The following sections explain what information you can find where.

## Part I: Getting the Lowdown on Digital Scrapbooking

In this part, we explain what types of equipment and programs are available for digital scrapbooking and make suggestions about the ones that may best fit certain individual profiles. Then we briefly cover the main points of digital design and recommend design processes and procedures that work well for digital scrapbooking. We also tell you about the most popular scrapbook styles and how you can incorporate their techniques and conventions into your own albums.

# Part II: Brushing Up on the Basics

In this part, we give you a preliminary understanding of the digital scrapbooker's tools. We discuss basic digital photo enhancing techniques as well as page design considerations and typesetting options. We also share some secrets about digital graphics that you can use to enhance the look of your digital scrapbooks.

If you have limited computer experience, you may feel a bit overwhelmed at first — after all, digital scrapbooking is a multifaceted as well as a many-splendored thing. Just approach it as you would anything you want to study. Read over a few times the sentences or passages you don't quite understand. The dawn will come!

# Part III: Taking Your Digital Scrapbook to the Next Level

Part III builds on the basics covered in Part II. We demonstrate how to fix damaged photographs and how to do those cool texturing and watermarking special effects. Plus we show you all of the following: how to make montage images, how to take and use panoramic photos, how professionals use certain image filters to create extraordinary effects, and how to use tricks such as wrapping and skewing to create awesome layout text.

The chapters in Part III discuss advanced digital techniques that can transform your scrapbook pages into beautiful works of art. (Not that you want to use them all the time in every album you make. But it's nice to know these techniques when you want some very special effects.)

# Part IV: Getting Creative with Fun Projects

In this part, we give you the lowdown on the techniques that separate the artists from the beginners. Find out how to make those special style pages and get some ideas on choosing themes that will unify your scrapbooks. Then learn about how you can share your finished pages on CDs, DVDs, or over the Internet.

We suggest you select a set (or sets) of photos you want to get into an album *before* you start reading this part of the book, because you may have so many great ideas you might have trouble deciding where to begin. Your photo sets will surely "connect" with something you read in this section, and you can work on your project with those photos as you read.

## Part V: The Part of Tens

All *For Dummies* books have a Part of Tens section that gives readers sets of ten tips related to the book's subject. The first set included in *Digital Scrapbooking For Dummies* contains ten tips for digital scrapbooking beginners, and the second warns about ten pitfalls to avoid.

Then we tell you ten ways to use digital techniques with traditional scrapbooking. The final Part of Tens chapter provides ten easy-to-implement and specifically described ways to involve kids (especially bored kids) in digital scrapbooking.

A handy dandy appendix of Web resources rounds out Part V. These sites, used in conjunction with the information in the book, should get you up and going in the digital world in no time.

# Icons Used in This Book

We refer to the symbols in the margins of *Digital Scrapbooking For Dummies* as icons. Keep an eye out for them — they mark items of importance.

We use this icon for concepts we hope you'll keep in mind as you're doing your digital scrapbooking.

This icon highlights technical information. You can skip it if you want to, but you certainly don't have to.

Tip icons note information that can save you time or money.

The warning icons direct you away from common scrapbooking mistakes.

# *Where to Go from Here*

Digital scrapbooking opens up some new possibilities for the scrapbooker/ storyteller in you. How you choose to use these possibilities is totally up to you. If you love all things digital and are happy spending hours at the computer, you may want to go all out for digital scrapbooking right away. If not, you might limit your digital involvement — at least initially.

Either way, we suggest you read Chapter 1 first because it can help you decide where you stand on the digital scrapbooking spectrum — a decision that will strongly influence the way you use all the rest of the information in the book. Then let the Table of Contents and the Index determine your next steps.

If you're really interested in photography and in what you can do digitally with your photos, read Chapter 6 in Part II and all of Part III. In those chapters, we give you a series of how-to's: how to organize film and digital photos, how to fit them into your designs, how to do advanced photo manipulation, how to enhance your photos, and how to create special photo effects.

We also include project sections for those of you who like to jump into hands-on work immediately. Part IV keeps you busy! You can choose to begin making a heritage (or another scrapbook style) album or to start a themed scrapbook with a set of photos you've been itching to put together — the ones you can't wait to incorporate into pages and send out as e-mail attachments. We inspire you, show you the procedures, present you with the options, tell you how to use the tools — and everything else you need to satisfy that get-it-done urge that keeps you so active and makes you so successful.

You may want to pop in on the Part of Tens chapters in Part V when you open the book. They offer some interesting insights into digital scrapbooking — insights that may serve as touchstones when you journey into the how-to's and how-not-to's and the whys and wherefores of this fascinating hobby.

Wherever you begin, be sure to swing by the color section in the middle of the book and check out a few of our favorite finished products. The captions direct you to the chapters where you can find out how to use the featured techniques in your digital scrapbooks.

# Part I

# Getting the Lowdown on Digital Scrapbooking

The 5th Wave                    By Rich Tennant

"It's very popular with the more traditional scrapbookers."

# In this part . . .

In this part, we give you an overview of digital scrapbooking, introduce you to the basic equipment you need, and give you a first taste of the variety of styles available to the digital scrapbooker. As you poke around, exploring and discovering what's going on in digital scrapbooking, we encourage you to assess *your* budget, *your* schedule, *your* digital equipment, *your* goals, and *your* style. Only then can you begin to balance the various elements in ways that make the most sense for you.

# Chapter 1

# A Bird's-Eye View of the Digital Scrapbooking Scene

*In This Chapter*

▶ Discovering what's great about digital scrapbooking

▶ Figuring out what you need

▶ Taking a look at some styles

▶ Making sure your work stays with you

▶ Sharing digital pages

▶ Getting down to digital business

**D**igital scrapbooking is a fantastic fit for today's fast-paced society — and its tools and techniques are easier, quicker, and more economical to use than ever. Plus, as busy scrapbookers take advantage of the latest generations of printers, computers, and software programs, they're *completing* many more of their projects in record time!

This chapter includes a brief introduction to some of digital scrapbooking's most important features — features we explore more specifically in other chapters: navigating the equipment and program minefields, digitizing scrapbook page elements, choosing a scrapbook style or styles, and saving and sharing pages digitally.

## Considering the Advantages of Going Digital

The new equipment and programs adopted by digital scrapbookers have transformed many former skeptics into believers (and users). Even the most technology-shy scrappers are overcoming their hesitations and trying various aspects of digital scrapbooking — especially after they tune in to the Internet and see the spectacular Web pages digital scrapbookers are producing.

Of the many reasons for the increasing popularity of digital scrapbooking, the following are *a few* you may want to remember when people ask you why you've decided to go digital:

✔ Digital scrapbooking's strongest selling point is that it saves you time — you can produce and distribute multiple copies of your work quickly and easily.

✔ You can also produce easy-to-read text very quickly — and get those stories that have been left untold for too long into digital format. The upshot is that much more of an important story gets recorded than otherwise would have been the case. (For specific info on creating well-designed text to tell the stories that support a scrapbook's images, see Chapters 9 and 12.)

✔ Not many can resist these great conveniences and options for sharing their scrapbook pages: printing out digital scrapbooks, e-mailing them as attachments, posting them on the Web, or burning them to CDs and DVDs.

✔ Correcting mistakes, editing, moving things around, and revising are much easier and quicker to do digitally than they are by hand. For example, you can size and resize your backgrounds with a few simple mouse clicks.

✔ Digital scrapbook pages can include and take advantage of a mix of materials including audio and even video clips (see Chapter 13).

✔ Just because you decide to go digital doesn't mean you have to give up the social aspects of traditional scrapbooking (which, like the old quilting bees, have provided a communal creative outlet for thousands of women — and men!). In fact, digital scrapbooking broadens social circles. Many digital scrapbookers get together to share their digital sources and resources — as well as info about how they use their editing programs. They attend scrapbook conventions, go to crop parties, and powwow with all of the other scrappers (digital and traditional). *And*, they talk up a storm in online digital scrapbooking chat rooms (see the appendix for the addresses of Web sites that offer these features).

You don't have to choose between traditional and digital scrapbooking. Digital artists still make traditional (sometimes called *paper-and-scissors*) albums and/or they print hard copies of their digital work. And, conversely, traditional scrappers experiment with digital scrapbooking. In fact, they've been adding digital techniques to their repertoires at ever-increasing rates, especially as it's become obvious that incorporating these techniques can do so much to enhance handmade projects (scanning images, home-printing photos and pages, making original digital background papers, and so forth).

# Finding the Tools You Want and Need

Starting a new venture that involves expensive equipment usually calls for caution and restraint — and digital scrapbooking is such a venture. If you want to try it, be sure to look both left and right before crossing "the digital divide."

We offer you a conservative set of guidelines to start you on your way — guidelines based on *experience*. We think that beginning your travels at a reasonable pace ensures that you get the most for your time, effort, and money. The digital extras you decide to purchase (or not) will largely depend on how elaborate you want your digital scrapbooks to be and how digitally "savvy" you are (or become).

To begin a journey into the world of digital scrapbooking using outdated equipment may actually not be such a bad idea when you're "just looking." Do remember, though, to make allowances for your finished products should you opt to go this route. The results you can achieve with today's best hardware and software far surpass those you get with older equipment and programs.

## Handling the hardware issues

Things in the digital world move so rapidly that what's impossible to accomplish digitally today may be easy-as-pie tomorrow. That's one reason you don't want to spend too much money before you know more about the digital direction you want to take.

Explore the digital scrapbooking hardware scene one step at a time. If you evaluate the benefits of digital scrapbooking as you test drive new equipment and try new techniques, you can gain enough skill and confidence to make decisions that are right for you.

### Taking a realistic look at your computer

The most expensive piece of equipment you'll *eventually* purchase is a new computer. If your computer isn't the newest or best on the market, *don't* give it away just yet. Look first at some of the detailed considerations for using the computer you currently own — as well as those that may prompt you to look for a newer model (see Chapter 2).

The level of digital scrapbooking you can achieve with your current computer depends on the computer's processor, its operating system (OS), and the amount of random access memory (RAM) it has. For instance, say you have an older computer with a 200 Megahertz processor, a Windows 98 operating system, and 64 megabytes of RAM. This isn't a "bad" computer, but it limits the programs you can run (most of the newer programs aren't made for this type of system). Still, you *can* use this computer to get a feel for digital scrapbooking and what it can offer.

When and if you feel the time is right for a computer upgrade, you may want to spend a little extra for a laptop model. Laptops have become the convenient choice for many of today's on-the-go scrapbookers.

### Deciding about printers

Improvements in color printers (especially inkjet printers) have had a primary role in ratcheting up the importance of digital scrapbooking. And that happens to be one decision you *can* make at the get-go — *do, yes for sure, do* purchase a good, quality printer! Here's why:

- ✔ Not only do you need a good quality printer to print out digital photographs for your scrapbooks, you also need it when you want to digitize and print out an occasional traditional scrapbook and of course to print out your digital albums.

- ✔ You need your home printer for "proofing" your work — even when you intend to have it printed at a high-quality photography store later on.

- ✔ You or someone else will always want copies of digital pages for one reason or another — and it's great to have a printer handy when you need one on short notice.

## Digital scrapbooking in Microsoft Word

You can use Word (Microsoft's basic word processing program) to make scrapbook pages. If you want to try this before buying special scrapbook software, just do the following:

1. Under File choose Page Setup and set all margins to 0 inches.

2. Go to Insert and choose Text Box, then draw the box to fit your page.

3. Add colors, lines, textures, and/or images to create a background.

4. Then go to View, choose Toolbars, and select the Drawing Toolbar to find the drawing tools to create fun scrapbook pages.

You can send your pages as e-mail attachments (see Chapter 18) or print them. To print a page, simply go to File and select Print then Properties and click on the Paper tab. Find the Document Size menu and choose the Custom Paper Size or User Defined option to set your paper size for the printer. Piece of cake!

Before you buy a new printer, consider these shopping tips:

- ✔ If your printer is more than two years old, take a few of your files to a discount printing service and have a page printed out to judge printout quality. This will give you a good idea of what kind of quality you can expect from today's digital printers. Comparing these pages with pages printed on your old printer will help you decide how soon you want to handle your printing needs.

- ✔ When you're ready to purchase a new model printer, make sure you choose one that comes with quality papers and pigment-based inks — and check out our information on printers in Chapter 2.

Many digital scrapbooking converts keep their old printers to use as an inexpensive way to print and proof pages.

### Making up your mind about digital cameras

Some digital scrapbookers still like to use film for certain occasions. When they get their prints processed, they scan them and then use them as digital images. If you don't have a digital camera, and want to approach digital scrapbooking in small steps, you can do the same thing. If you have your film images put on a CD, you can slip the CD into your computer and save yourself the hassle of having to scan your pictures to get them into digital format.

In the meantime, borrow a digital camera to see how you like it. If you decide to buy a digital camera, *don't* get a super-high-quality model at first. Find a regular digital camera (3 to 5 megapixel model) instead. As is true with many pieces of equipment, it's best not to purchase an expensive version if you've never owned one before. For more on what to look for in a digital camera, see Chapter 2.

Even if you have a wonderful film camera that you love, we encourage you to give digital cameras a try. After you start using that small, easy-to-carry little picture taker, capturing those unexpected and priceless shots, and saving all the money you once spent on film processing, you may wonder why you didn't buy this newfangled gadget sooner.

### Sizing up the scanner situation

If you don't have a scanner, have a friend show you how to use one or go to a store that sells scanners to find out what's out there (refer to Chapter 2 for tips on evaluating scanners).

Scanners are available in a wide range of styles and prices. Pick one that fits your budget, but remember to look at the power of the scanning software that comes with the equipment. You want the scanner/software combination that gives you the most features — one that has descreening and easy *scaling* (sizing) of finished scans, for example.

A good quality scanner doesn't have to be pricey. It *does* need the right software. Many people don't tap a scanner's potential because they've previously used a poor scanner/software combination, were disappointed by the results, and don't realize what a quality scanner can do.

## Choosing beginning-level software

There are several types of software created specifically for scrapbooking (see Chapter 3 for more information on the options). Some software programs work better on low-end equipment than others, so keep in mind that your choices in software are usually determined by the kind of hardware you're using.

In general, Mac users have an easier time getting their computers to work with scrapbooking software than PC users (this is because Macs are made for graphic applications); *however,* fewer scrapbooking programs are available for the Mac.

Our suggestions in this chapter are for the beginner who wants to conduct low-cost digital scrapbook trial sessions using older computer equipment. Before you spend the big bucks, try the free trial downloads that many of these programs offer. You have only 30 days to decide whether you like a program, but that's usually enough time to give it a try.

You may notice that we suggest different programs in Chapter 3 than the ones we suggest in this chapter. The programs we list in Chapter 3 require a properly configured computer with lots of RAM. You may want to upgrade to those programs later if you decide to work seriously with digital scrapbooking.

### Beginning digital scrapbooking software for the PC

We recommend that PC users who want to check out digital scrapbooking get Perfect Scrapbook Maker by Cosmi. At a cost of about $10 plus shipping, this is an inexpensive way to find out whether you like digital scrapbooking.

HP Creative Scrapbook Assistant — which costs about $20 — is an additional possibility. Another good choice would be Scrapbook Factory Deluxe by Nova, although the cost of this program is closer to $40. There are other software programs available, but most of them only work with newer computers that have more RAM (see Chapter 3).

### Beginning digital scrapbooking software for Macs

Mac users can get their feet wet with HP Creative Scrapbook Assistant — which costs about $20. If you decide you love digital scrapbooking, you may eventually want the pricier Adobe's Photoshop Elements. This program sells for $90 to $100.

# Exploring Popular Digital Scrapbook Styles

When a certain way of scrapbooking gets used and emulated enough, it becomes a recognizable style with its own common conventions and techniques. We list some of the most popular styles and their characteristics in Chapter 5 — and show in Chapters 14, 15, and 16 how to make complete albums using the classic, heritage, and pop styles.

Scrapbook style categories are arbitrary — that is, scrapbookers have made them up or borrowed them from other disciplines and applied them to scrapbooking. You can follow the conventions of a style or mix-and-match as you please. You can also create your own unique styles.

The following bulleted list shows you where to go to get more information about scrapbooking styles — including the classic style, the heritage style, the crafty style, the pop style, and so on:

✔ You can discover a lot about scrapbooking styles from scrapbooking magazines. Most of these publications offer suggestions, include examples, give detailed instructions on how to make the digital pages illustrated in the articles, and provide the *URLs* (Internet addresses) of leading digital scrapbook artists — who sometimes respond to your e-mails personally.

✔ Many digital scrapbooking sites feature a gallery where you can look at examples of how scrapbookers have handled various styles. If you find something you like, you may decide to purchase a CD of digital resources — which gives you a place to start when you begin working with a particular design style.

✔ Online digital scrapbooking chat groups are another good resource (we recommend some groups in the appendix). Just take a gander at what topics are being discussed to see whether any of them interest you. When you find one that does, you may also discover a whole new group of helpful friends.

✔ You can also tap in to Web training programs, find out about classes that are being held in your area, and get book references. Many of these books give you step-by-step instructions for creating albums in your favorite scrapbooking styles.

✔ In the appendix of this book, you can find several Web sites that feature examples of various digital scrapbooking styles.

When you decide what style you want to use for a particular scrapbook project, you can pencil sketch or make a mock-up for your planned album. We describe the design process in Chapters 4 and 7, including how you decide what the focus of your project will be, how to choose a color palette, and how to create an overall design scheme (take a quick peek at the color insert section of this book to see what possibilities digital design holds in store for you).

In Chapters 6 and 8, we show the best methods for handling, gathering, digitizing, and manipulating your photos and embellishments. We also help you decide how you want to develop your stories and integrate the texts with your album design (see Chapter 9). If you plan to get fancy with some of your graphics and designs (and what scrapbooker doesn't?), we show you how to kick your digital scrapbooking up a notch in Part III (Chapters 10 through 13). You'll love the way these tricks and special effects put *you* and your digital pages in a class with the pros.

# Saving Your Work

Although digital enthusiasts continue to argue that storing scrapbooks in digital form makes infinite sense because you can reprint them whenever you want, others counter that no one really knows just how long computer files will actually last on archival quality disks.

In the old days, we thought the information on floppy disks would last for as long as the disk did, but we soon found out that although some disks lasted for years, others went bad after a few weeks. Hard disks aren't totally secure either — especially when you're doing graphics work. Even laser written CDs can go bad and won't last forever. There was a general hope that this data storage system would last longer. It does, but not by as long as we'd hoped. The lesson is that you need to make several copies of your files.

One of the best reasons to take up digital scrapbooking is that it's so easy to *save your work in many different formats* (see Chapter 18 for more details about different formats). In the following sections, we give you valuable info about saving your work. We also give you tips on the following: organizing and storing photos as you take them; saving your work *while* you're working on it; and printing out your pages and projects.

## Organizing and saving individual photos as you take them

Once you start taking digital photographs, your computer will be filled with great photos almost overnight. Before this situation gets out of control, you need to develop an image file system. You also need to work out a way to put these images onto CDs or DVDs so you can find them again (see Chapter 4 for our suggestions).

A digital photo album program is a good option for organizing and saving your photos. These programs come in many different configurations, but they all allow you to easily view your images and select which ones you want to use. You can download a variety of photo album programs for little or no cost from the Internet on sites such as tucows.com. Or you can buy a program that is specifically designed to interface with your photo-editing software. Some photo-editing programs come packaged with a photo album program (yours may!).

## Saving work in progress

Experienced computer operators know how important it is to save their work frequently. Power surges, program freezes, computer overheating, crashes — all of these sudden surprises can result in lost files. If you make a habit of saving often (or see if your program can be set to save changes automatically), you won't have to redo much if you happen to experience a computer problem.

Save your sometimes hard-won filtered images in a special file (see Chapter 11 for more info about filtering). Just because you know how you created the image doesn't mean you can do it exactly the same way again. If you like the result you achieved by applying one or more filters to an image, save it.

## Storing your digital images

Store your images on your computer but *also* store them somewhere else as well. Computers break — and when you're working with graphics and graphics programs, they seem to crash more often than they do when you're using the computers just for word processing or other types of work. You don't want to lose your graphic images in a computer crash disaster.

Store your photographs and scrapbook files on a CD or DVD as a backup to your computer hard drive. When selecting a CD or DVD writer choose one that can *write in sessions.* That means you can keep adding to the CD or DVD disk until it's full.

There's a difference between a CD or DVD player unit and a combination CD or DVD player/writer. It's a good idea to have a professional install a CD or DVD player/writer unit because not all aftermarket CD/DVD player/writers are compatible with all types of computers. You need to buy one that's compatible with your system. CD/DVD drives write at different speeds: 8x, 16x, and so forth. If you purchase 16x for an 8x system, you won't be able to write data to it using your computer. Also, be aware that just because your system has a CD/DVD installed doesn't mean that it's a drive that can burn disks. To verify that your specific drive has the ability to burn disks, look on your sales ticket for these letters: CD/W or CD/RW *or* DVD/W or DVD/RW.

Back up important information onto several distinct brands of CDs or DVDs and then store these various copies in different locations to protect them from fires or other disasters (keep one extra set of backups somewhere other than your house). Most experts say we should refresh or reburn our data disks about every seven years — onto the next generation of (better and/or *new and different*) digital storage media.

## Preparing your printed images for storage

You may want to print images for storage or in order to use them more immediately in your traditional scrapbooks. Either way, you want to make sure that you create the best possible prints by keeping the following points in mind.

### Flattening your image

It's important to flatten an image before you print it out. When you *flatten* an image onto one layer, you transfer all of the layers you used to make the image onto just one layer (see Chapter 4 for more info about layers). You can save the other layers in case you want to move things around separately again, but when you're going to print, make and save a flattened file for that purpose.

First of all, a flattened image prints faster — a lot faster. Secondly, you can't save the page in most file formats until it *is* flattened. If you think you may want to use the image in different ways in the future, save it in the *native format file* (the file format your program typically uses) of your photo-editing program, and then also save it (flattened) in a format that's easy for your printer or your friends to use.

Personal printers used to do a little better with TIF images than they did with JPEG images. Recently, however, most programs have upped the quality of the JPEG images they produce. Today, the high-quality JPEG images printed out from the new generation of photo-editing programs usually are every bit as good as the high-quality TIF images — which have long been the yardstick for image quality.

### Setting the resolution of your image

In the past, most good home printers could only handle about 150 to 200 pixels per inch (ppi) resolution — even though the printer box text often claimed to be able to handle 600 to 1200 ppi. If you ran an image at 150 ppi and the same image at 200 ppi, you couldn't see a lot of difference. If you printed out an image at 300 ppi, the only difference you would notice is that it took longer to print. In some cases, the image may look a little darker, but not much.

Today, the story is a little different. The higher resolution images from the new photo printers really are better — providing you use the matching brand-name high-quality glossy photo paper (though the highest cost doesn't *always* equate exactly with highest quality). If you use regular plain paper, or even super white inkjet paper, the old 200 ppi rule still holds.

### Archiving your printed pages

Saving and conserving a printed digital scrapbook page is the same as preserving a traditional scrapbook page. You need to protect the page from harsh light (especially sunlight), place the work in page protectors, and shield your scrapbook pages from excess heat and humidity — see *Scrapbooking For Dummies* (Wiley) for more on archival issues and concerns.

As a scrapbooker, you may wonder if a printed scrapbook page is as achievable as a traditional scrapbook page. If you print your pages on your home inkjet printer and use the brand name paper that matches your printer and your printer ink, the page should be reasonably permanent. If you have your scrapbook page printed out at a quality photography store, the image should be as long lasting as any other photographic print.

# Sharing Digital Files

Digital scrapbooking has this advantage over conventional scrapbooking: After a digital file is saved, it can be digitally duplicated countless times. If you print out your scrapbook and then spill coffee on it, you can print it out again. You can copy the file and send it to your sister in Detroit. If she loses it, you can easily send her a new copy. If you have 27 friends who want copies of your scrapbook, you can make 27 inexpensive copies in short order — one for each of them. For a more detailed explanation of digital sharing see Chapter 18.

Even traditional scrappers go digital when it comes to sharing their material with others — partly because there are so many ways to do it:

✔ The most basic way to share digitally is to scan and print out your pages at home or at a photo store — or, you can use both methods if your purposes call for that.

✔ Some people share their scrapbook creations via e-mail to be viewed on a computer monitor. You can use one of several computer file formats for this, but the PDF format is probably the most universal, the most flexible, and the most preferred.

✔ Another method for distributing your scrapbook pages is to save and share them on disk. A PDF file doesn't print out very well, so if printed copies are wanted, send a CD to accommodate the higher resolution files.

✔ You can also create and share your files on a Web site.

# Get Ready, Get Set . . . Scrap!

A proper workspace is essential for digital scrapbooking. You may have all the right tools, but if you can't use them effectively and effortlessly, they don't do you any good.

You don't have to dedicate your working space exclusively to scrapbooking — but space does need to be available when you want to use it for your digital scrapbooking projects.

Look at the area you have in mind for setting up a designated scrapbooking "station" with these questions in mind:

- ✔ How can I maximize the space?
- ✔ How can I get the most out of my equipment?

## Creating a comfortable and functional workstation

Scrapbooking takes space and this doesn't change just because you've chosen to do it digitally. You need a flat, level surface for your computer, printer, scanner, and computer supplies so you can effectively spread out your materials when you're working. Go through the motions of preparing a project to get an idea of how much space you need and how to place your equipment pieces strategically.

The following tips will help you buy equipment that meets your actual needs:

- ✔ Purchase a good computer stand. It won't matter what it looks like, but *what it does* is crucial. You need to know where everything is when you're working (and it has to be out of the way when you're not). The stand lets you store your equipment compactly, protect it from damage, and use it safely and easily).

   One major purpose of your computer stand is to organize and contain the rat's nest of cords that lie in wait to trip you and break your connections, plugs, and receptacles.

- ✔ Consider getting a rolling computer platform. Its mobility adds some useful options to your working environment and can minimize the distances between individual pieces of equipment.

> ✔ Another important consideration is the chair(s) you have to sit on. No matter how comfortable a computer chair is, it will become uncomfortable after long hours of use. Plan periodical breaks, and swap chairs to give your back a rest.

## *Preparing for action*

To create a great workspace, walk yourself through the following steps. Take them one-by-one until you've checked out each item on this activity list. When you're ready to go, you'll know you've done everything possible to make your digital scrapbooking experience a great one!

1. **Identify what space you have available for digital scrapbooking.**

   You probably want to center this space around your Internet connection.

2. **Decide what types of equipment you *eventually* want to have and determine how big (or small) a space you need for all of it.**

   Make a detailed sketch of how you want to connect your equipment. If you have new equipment, you can connect everything through USB connections: USB 2 connections are fast, expansion hubs are cheap, and it's simple to borrow cables or purchase more cables for new connections. Another popular connection system uses wireless connections — not quite as fast, but you eliminate most cord problems. Another plus: You can place your equipment throughout your house and it all still works together.

3. **Plan your proposed work area to determine how and where you will perform various digital operations: scanning, printing, typing, and so forth.**

4. **Shop for appropriate computer furniture and compare prices.**

   This step can save you money. And you may find some new designs that can increase the usability and functionality of your scrapbooking workspace.

5. **Find out what other digital scrapbookers like in terms of equipment and workspace.**

   Try to do this after you have already gathered some information on the topic so that you can recognize a great idea when you see one.

6. **Purchase as much of your digital work station equipment at the same time (or close to the same time) as possible.**

   Include your computer and your peripherals (scanner, printer, digital camera, and so forth). If you buy these items years apart, they may not work well together — although you won't run into as many conflicts as we used to encounter with older equipment.

# Chapter 2

# Gearing Up to Scrapbook Digital Style

*In This Chapter*

▶ Getting the hardware you need

▶ Focusing on a few extras

*I*f you're a scrapbooker who's decided to "go digital," you may feel a little intimidated by the technical aspects of integrating digital images and techniques into your work. Knowing that you have the "right" digital equipment and tools gives you a boost in confidence, and we want to help you figure out exactly what "right" means for you.

You want the set-up that meets *your* needs. You may be planning to use digital materials and tools only for printing your traditional, hard-copy scrapbook albums. If so, some of the digital equipment and tools we refer to may not interest you at present. One warning here though: We've talked to *many* scrapbookers who began using digital processes solely to streamline the work for their traditional albums. Most of them, as they become comfortable with digital processes, have eventually opted to create more fully digital and fewer handmade albums. We mention this because it's a factor you may want to consider when you're getting yourself ready for digital scrapbooking.

In this chapter, we give you information about the essential equipment you need to make dynamic digital scrapbooks (we assume you already have enough low-tech scrapbooking tools and materials!). We also show you how you can add extra tools to your digital repertoire over time, tools that can help advance your scrapbooks to a whole new creative level.

# Acquiring the Essentials

A full-fledged digital scrapbooker uses a computer, a scanner, a printer, and a software program to edit the digital materials that go into the albums. (See Chapter 3 for information about scrapbooking software.) As you begin working in the digital world, you may soon see the wisdom of buying a good digital camera. The benefits include eliminating film processing costs, getting your photo images into your designs and printed more rapidly, and being able to share pictures more easily. You can also print hard-copy photos of your digital images.

In the following sections, we cover each piece of digital scrapbooking equipment separately, so that you can make informed choices about what you want, what you need, and how many dollars you plan to spend.

Use the connector type you feel most comfortable with. Although we feel that USB connections are the easiest to use for connecting cameras, printers, scanners, and other peripherals to your computer, some people (based on their equipment and expertise) opt for wireless connections or other types of cable connections.

## Calculating your computer needs

The following essentials can help you navigate easily through the digital and technical world.

If you already have a computer — either a personal computer (PC) or a Macintosh (Mac), laptop or desktop — make sure it's adequate for the digital scrapbooking you plan to do. We help you evaluate your current computer system and determine what upgrades you may need in this section. If you don't own a computer or are in the market for a new system, this section can serve as a guide so you're sure to get a computer that meets your scrapbooking needs.

IBM named its first personal computer the PC, and PC became the term that differentiated IBM or IBM-compatible personal computers from other personal computer types — like the Macs. The term is now usually applied to personal computers based on Intel or Intel-compatible microprocessors. A computer's other components, including the operating system, may be varied, but they can all be considered under the PC umbrella term. For more information, take a look at the latest editions of _Macs For Dummies_ by David Pogue and _PCs For Dummies_ by Dan Gookin (both published by Wiley).

## Maintaining a clutter-free computer

Some computers just work well; others seem to crash no matter what you do. If your machine is continually crashing, you may be astonished at how much better it will run when you get rid of the clutter:

✔ Take off all the games.

✔ Get rid of programs you're not using.

✔ Clean up your hard drive.

✔ Run the defragmentation (or *defrag*) and the optimization programs for your hard disk. This will reposition digital information to save space and help make your computer run

better. Instructions on how to defrag are usually included in your system user guide or instruction book.

And anticipate a crash! Adopt a Murphy's Law attitude and assume that, at one time or another, whatever computer you buy is going to go down. To prepare for disaster, you can buy the extended warranty when you purchase the computer (we always do), back up your work (often) on CDs, and consider the advantages of the laptops (see the info in the "Deciding whether a laptop or a desktop model best suits your needs" sidebar).

Most computer software related to scrapbooking operates on the PC and Macintosh platforms. If you're comfortable with one of these platforms, you may want to stick with it, and choose your scrapbooking software accordingly. Even if, after reading this chapter, you decide you need a new computer, it may be easier for you to stay with the environment you've become accustomed to.

The computer you purchase today will be outdated in short order, and the fact that it's difficult to know what you're going to need or want a few years down the road complicates matters even further. But you can make the best of the situation by doing a little homework. One of the best sites for researching computers (and digital cameras as well) is http.pcworld.com. This easy-to-navigate site creates great comparison charts that are simple to understand and use.

### Taking stock of your hard drive and memory

The *hard drive* is your computer's main storage device; *random access memory* (RAM) is the memory your computer draws on to perform its processing functions. Because there is only so much memory on your hard drive and images can be easily lost or misplaced, be sure to print out a hard copy of all your digital images.

# Deciding whether a laptop or a desktop model best suits your needs

If you're in the market for a new computer, take a minute to weigh the pros and cons of laptop and desktop models. For more information on laptops, take a look at *Laptops For Dummies* by Dan Gookin (Wiley).

A laptop (PC or Mac) costs almost twice as much as its desktop counterpart, but there are definite advantages to purchasing a laptop:

✔ You can work anywhere (outside, in the car, in another country, in airplanes, and in airport waiting rooms!).

✔ You can show your work to anyone, whatever the purpose and wherever you happen to be.

✔ If your computer crashes, it's much easier, and in many cases cheaper, to fix a laptop than it is to fix a desktop model.

How, you may ask, is this possible? After all, laptop parts are two to four times more expensive than similar parts for a desktop model. Well, most computer crashes are software- or operator-related rather than a result of defective parts. Laptops are easy to pick up and take in to repair shops, where the computer gurus usually charge only a minimum fee to perform their formatting magic. Laptops are also easy to ship for repair (another good reason to purchase the extended warranty). Contrast this with the cost of having a computer repair person come to your home to fix your computer, or with the hassle of lugging your desktop into a repair shop and back home again after the repairs have been completed.

Many people prefer desktop computers because

✔ They cost much less than laptops.

✔ The desktops feel more substantial than laptops — the keys, keyboard, and monitors are significantly larger, for one thing.

✔ Those who give a high priority to *safety and security* factors tend to opt for the desktops — it's much easier to lose or damage a laptop than it is a desktop.

You should have at least 500 megabytes of RAM and a 60 gigabyte hard drive (storage memory) to scrapbook properly. If your current system doesn't have enough oomph, or if your computer just doesn't run as well as you like, you may need to upgrade by installing more RAM or perhaps getting a new hard drive.

Even though upgrading is usually an easy and productive fix for a problem computer, be sure to look at your computer holistically. Get the big picture! Figure up what upgrading will cost (with labor) and decide whether it really makes sense to spend money on the old computer. Many times, people pay to upgrade their RAM only to find they also need a new hard drive or a better monitor or a new video card. In the end, they realize it would have been cheaper to purchase a new computer. So be sure to weigh the options.

If you decide it's smarter to buy a new system, check into just buying the computer and using your existing monitor, keyboard, and mouse rather than buying all new equipment.

### Running a compatible operating system

An *operating system* (OS) is a computer program that tells your computer what it's supposed to do and how to do it. Almost all new computers come with an operating system already installed. Technically, your computer's OS is also a software program (we revisit this topic in Chapter 3) — though some argue that it's really more like hardware, because without the OS, your computer couldn't schedule tasks, allocate storage, or interface with peripheral equipment (scanners, cameras, and so forth).

For now, we'll just point out that the OS is *the* most important program on your computer and that compatibility issues almost always relate to it. Think of things this way: If your OS can't work with your peripheral hardware *or* if it can't work with your software, you have compatibility problems.

The scrapbooking software options we give you in Chapter 3 will work fine with Windows XP (for PCs) and Mac OS X operating systems. For more information on the particular operating system you're using, just check out the latest *For Dummies* book on that particular release.

## Scoping out scanners

Scanners are simply amazing — and we love using them. A scanner is really a specialized digital camera, which converts real items such as photographs, cloth, and paper into digital form. For more information on scanners, check out *Scanners For Dummies* by Mark L. Chambers (Wiley).

If you feel the need to wade through all the consumer information regarding the various brands of scanners and to educate yourself about their wide assortment of features — please! — be our guest. But be aware of "scanner hype" — which contains a full load of useless information and advertising gobbledygook. The fact is that most scanners do a fair to good job, and that the big difference in scanners relates more to the scanning software than it does to the hardware. That being said, you still have to figure out how much you need to spend and what you should look for in a scanner.

In the following list, we go over what you can expect to find in each price range:

- **Bottom-of-the-line (under $80) scanners:** You may find, in short order, that scrapbooking requires more features than these low-end scanners provide. However, they *are* cheap and easy to use.

✔ **Scanners in the $85 to $120 price range:** These scanners serve you well if you're going to limit yourself to reflective scanning — that is, if you're just going to do simple scanning tasks like scanning photo prints, magazines, books, and other print sources. Unless you want to scan slides, transparencies, or film, this is probably the kind of scanner you want.

Microtek and Epson scanners give you the best software/hardware package for the price. Of these two brands, Epson has a reputation for working better with IBM-compatible computers. Microtek scanners are usually rated as being better for scanning true color (though the difference in color quality isn't appreciable). Other scanners (including Canon, HP, Visoneer, and Mustek) are working hard to upgrade their software to match the function standards of Microtek and Epson, and some scrapbookers already prefer these scanners to the ones we've recommended.

✔ **Transparency scanners at $150 to $350:** Invest in a transparency scanner with a light lid if you want to scan slides. These scanners work better than most other types of transparency scanning devices. Epson and Microtek each make true light lid transparency scanners in the $150 to $350 price range. If you want one of these scanners, you can special order it or buy it online.

Beware of the scanners that come with transparency adapters. These adapters don't usually work well. The images they produce are generally blurry and the color quality tends to be poor.

✔ **Low-end professional flatbed scanners in the $400 to $500 price range:** These scanners give you even more scanner muscle. They also include software that helps you process your photos automatically. It's easy to enlarge your images because the software features an *image interpolation program,* which means that the software manages the pixels in your photos so that you don't get a blocky look when you enlarge the images. The software that comes with these scanners also helps you control your color and contrast levels.

✔ **Specialty scanners:** Get one of these if you want to spend some big money. But ask yourself this question first: Why pay for an expensive photo print or transparency specialty scanner when the general-purpose ones work as well as they do?

One scanner issue that's rarely discussed is *generational loss* — the loss of quality every succeeding time an image is duplicated. It happens on every image you scan, so always try to use the first scan of the original image. Generational loss takes place even if you purchase a very expensive scanner. One big reason for using photo-editing programs is that they make it possible to adjust the image using tools that help reduce the generational loss factor — by using the Brightness/Contrast feature or the Sharpness filter, for example. You can also clean up the image by cloning out the dust spots and scratches and maybe even repair any tears or cracks with the healing brush.

# Pondering printing possibilities

The quality of photo prints, like the quality of other things, is judged differently by different people (quality is relative, in other words). Some scrapbookers judge the quality of a printed image by preservation criteria — that is, how long the image will last. Papers and inks make a difference here. Scrapbookers look for photo papers and inks sold by reputable companies and advertised as long-lasting. Printers make a difference in the quality of printed images too, although again, quality is a relative term. One scrapbooker's definition of a quality image from a printer may not be another's.

## Buying branded ink and photo paper

Most printers do a great job of printing out material that does *not* have to be long-lasting. But partly because preservation has become so important in scrapbooking and other fields, many printer manufacturers are now focusing on improving archival quality printing. Industry and advertising standards have tightened since the days when manufacturers claimed their inks and papers would "be good" for 75 to 100 years. When some of those inks faded in just two or three years, more science and less advertising hype changed the industry's attitude toward the question of printing longevity.

Although the wild claims for archival printer quality have died down significantly in recent years, we're still only *guessing* about how long printer inks and papers will last. Most experts say about 15 to 20 years, but no one really knows how many years today's materials could last with proper document care. Improvements are being made every day.

The bottom line: To extend the life of your scrapbooks, buy branded inks and match those inks with brand-appropriate papers. After-market inks can be used in most printers, but these inks don't provide the higher archival quality the branded products provide. The difference between branded and after-market is simple: *Branded* products are sold together under a well-known trade name (Epson, Kodak, and so forth), whereas *after-market* products are sold separately and under generic or less well-known names.

For example, Epson brand ink on Epson brand paper works great (actually, the current consensus is that Epson high-quality paper and ink lead the pack in terms of quality and longevity). But if you apply one brand of ink onto some other brands of paper, the ink may not dry for days.

Purchasing the same brand of ink and paper is an expensive proposition, and some scrapbookers have found that taking their disks or memory cards to their favorite local photo store (or one of the discount superstores) and having their photos commercially printed is far cheaper than printing their images on a home printer. But do the low prices at these discount stores mean that quality suffers? Many experienced scrapbookers who think it does choose to have their images printed at professional photography outlets. The price is usually high, but the quality is superb and the images seem to be reasonably long-lasting.

### Selecting a home printer

No matter what decision you make about getting some of your photos printed commercially, you still need a home printer for your digital scrapbooking work — so you can proof your images and pages, produce them at any hour of the day or night, and save money by home printing a certain percentage of your work. Your personal scrapbook design preferences can help you decide which printer is best for you. We recommend getting a trusted brand name printer and using long lasting, matching brand, photo quality inks. Here are some choices:

- ✔ **The 12-x-12-inch format:** Not too long ago, no affordable printers (or printer papers) could accommodate this scrapbook layout size. That's changed, and now there are a few consumer printers available that will print to this format. Your best bet in our opinion is an Epson 1280 or R1800. Or check out scrapbook stores that are now able to print true 12-x-12-inch pages thanks to Epson scrapbook central workstations.

- ✔ **The 8½-x-11-inch format:** If you scrapbook in this format, you have a much wider range of printer choices. Though the Epson printer gets the highest marks because it comes with the best inks and papers, you can find many other good models. In the regular printer line, a printer costing about $80 is just as good as those costing more. The higher priced printers do print faster, but the quality of the images is about the same.

- ✔ **Photo printers:** These printers are designed to print photos. As with the regular printers, the higher priced ones will print faster but not necessarily better — but in this case *faster* is a relative term. Photo printers are notoriously s-l-o-w. You can probably live with a slow regular printer, but spending a few extra dollars for a faster photo printer is a wise investment. Can you really tell the difference in the quality of images printed on a regular printer and images printed on a photo printer? Yes! You can also feel the difference when you buy the inks, although it's painful to see how quickly the ink gets used up: An 8-x-10-inch full color image can cost as much as $1.50 to $2 when you figure the cost of paper and ink.

Most inkjet printers output better color than laser printers because the inkjet market has demanded this type of development whereas the laser market has focused more on printer speed and quantity. When looking at color inkjet photo printers, one indicator of image quality lies in the total number of inks used in the printer. Basically, the more colors of inks, the better the image quality. Naturally, more inks can lead to greater costs, but the high-quality printers put the different colors in individual cartridges so you only need to replace the color cartridge that is empty and not a whole color set.

# Deciding on a basic digital camera

Digital cameras, just like so many other consumer commodities, are constantly changing. Every 6 to 7 months, the technology improves. What's "new and in" this year will be replaced by a "newer and cooler" model in no time at all. This sounds ominous, but it can work to your advantage. To check out this topic in greater depth, take a look at the latest edition of *Digital Photography For Dummies* by Julie Adair King (Wiley).

Camera stores usually have a stockpile of out-of-date cameras because camera models are often improved before the store has a chance to sell off the original models. You may be able to get a good deal on an excellent digital camera by waiting until a new model comes out and then snapping up one of its older (but still extremely useful) counterparts.

Before you run out to pick up a digital camera, do yourself a favor and:

- ✔ Corner everyone you know who has a digital camera and ask them what they think are important features (preferably over lunch or dinner so you have time for a long conversation). Keep a little notebook handy to jot down some of the details you hear (and you'll hear plenty). Listen for repetition. If four out of five of your friends think the carrying case is a "must have," it probably is (they'll tell you why!).

- ✔ Check with a few of the experts in your local camera shops, and talk with them about what digital camera model is likely to be the best one for you.

- ✔ Look at the digital camera evaluations on *Digital Photography Review's* Web site (www.dpreview.com).

- ✔ Do some reading on your own (we suggest the *Digital Photography For Dummies* book).

You can start right here with this list of things to consider about digital cameras:

- ✔ **Lenses:** As with a film camera, the heart of a digital camera is in the lens. Choosing a camera with a good lens will give you the sharpest possible images. Check with a knowledgeable camera expert and find out which brands have the best lenses. We find that Canon, Minolta, Nikon, and Olympus digital cameras generally have the best optics. We discuss removable lens cameras later in the chapter.

Quality lenses are molded or ground so that there is very little distortion in the way they bend light to fall on the image area of the camera. Because various types of lenses use different specs, it is usually easier to indicate brands rather than specs to help someone choose a camera. Even many photo store "experts" don't know about lens quality specs.

✔ **Megapixels:** *Megapixels* measure how many pixels a camera can record. The more pixels a camera can capture, the larger and the better quality image it can produce. In today's market, a 3-megapixel camera is the minimum size a digital scrapbooker should purchase. The 5-megapixel models are starting to get more affordable, and the 6-megapixel models are about the maximum size most scrapbookers need to use.

As a general rule, the more megapixels your camera has, the larger you can make your images. One caution, however: If you don't shoot your photos on a high enough resolution setting, you're not taking advantage of your camera's capability. Many people reduce their resolution so they can take more pictures before uploading their images. A better strategy is to purchase an extra memory card or two and swap the cards out as they fill up. Or you can bring along your laptop and upload your images onto your computer's hard drive.

✔ **Camera size and durability:** Biggest isn't always bestest! Who wants a camera that's too big to lug around? A smaller, more inexpensive camera may serve you better than a large, expensive one because you may be more apt to carry it around with you. The Canon digital Elph is an example of a very compact camera that's small enough to fit into your pocket — but it has enough capability to take some great images that can be made quite large.

Olympus digital cameras are built to withstand rugged treatment, *and* they have an excellent lens cover system as well (see Figure 2-1). A panel slides over the lens to shield it from bumps and dirt and makes it easy to tuck into a pocket or purse. If your lifestyle (or your personality) requires this kind of durability, look at the Olympus line — or at Fuji, which also makes some very durable digital cameras.

✔ **Color quality:** Overall, the digital cameras made today do a very good job of getting the color right. This is one area that has greatly improved over the last few years. Unless you choose a digital camera that costs less than about $75, you shouldn't have to worry about color quality.

✔ **A picture viewing program:** One of these for your computer is a must. These programs, sometimes called *album* programs, help you quickly view and choose the photos you want for your scrapbook pages.

✔ **Battery life:** Digital camera battery life is an issue you should carefully consider. Some cameras eat batteries at almost twice the rate of others. The good news here is that you can find many Internet sites that compare digital cameras — and battery life is one comparison category these sites tend to follow closely. Many people wonder about using rechargeable batteries in digital cameras. Some cameras specify that only alkaline batteries should be used. Those who use digital cameras with rechargeable batteries quickly discover that these batteries need to be changed often.

Always keep an extra charged battery on hand. When it's cold, the batteries sometimes don't work — so keep the extras warm in your pocket for a quick switch.

*Courtesy of Olympus*

**Figure 2-1:** This Olympus digital camera is small, compact, and durable.

# Adding Extra Tools over Time

Sometimes, as you advance in digital scrapbooking, you just have to ignore your frugal side and purchase new equipment and new tools. But be careful. If you decide to buy something new, look for a solid piece of equipment rather than the one that's the newest and the "best." Tech salespeople love to sell cutting-edge technology, even though it has a reputation for being *buggy* (having a bunch of small problems or quirks that make it frustrating to use). When you want the most bang for your buck, look for a piece of equipment that's current in its features, but make sure its components have been well-tested and have good track records.

## Upgrading computer capabilities

Adding more RAM memory or installing a bigger hard drive are two upgrades that pay big dividends. Other upgrades need to be carefully considered because they don't always result in big improvements. As the price for computers continues to drop, it's often easier and more cost effective to just purchase a new system (provided it comes with adequate RAM).

Another upgrade that makes a huge difference in your scrapbooking experience is a large-screen monitor (17 to 22 inches). Because you're working with art-related materials, a large, good-quality monitor makes it easier to visualize how your scrapbook pages are going to look after they're printed out.

Most people justify the purchase of a large new monitor because the image quality is better and the images on the screen are easier to see — however, the bigger monitors are so colorful, users sometimes get frustrated because the printed material they output doesn't look as good as what they see on the screen.

With experience, you'll be able to accurately guess how the printed colors on your scrapbook pages will vary from what you see on your monitor. You can use your photo-editing program to adjust the colors and the contrast until you get the colors on the monitor and the printouts more in synch.

You also can increase the capabilities of your computer by upgrading your scrapbooking and/or photo-editing programs. Most computer program manufacturers upgrade their programs about once a year. Often the improvements made to the upgraded programs increase productivity and/or ease of use. And you may find that you want to add new, more sophisticated programs as your skill levels increase — always keeping in mind that the difficulty of mastering new programs translates into fantastic rewards!

## Enhancing your scans

After you're sure you've taken care of the basic setting tasks on your scanner (see Chapter 6), it's time to think about scanning-enhancing programs. Many of today's midpriced scanners come packaged with a program called Digital Ice. Digital Ice can improve some aspects of scanning, including enlargement, color levels, and scratch repair. Digital Ice and programs with similar functions (such as Photoshop) not only help with overall scan quality but can also, to a limited degree, overcome poor scanning habits — although, naturally, they give the best results when used in concert with good scanning practices.

## Experimenting with specialized printing

First, a caveat on experimentation when it comes to printers! Scrapbookers are famous for combining things in strange and wonderful ways, a tendency that can take the digital scrapbooker to new and glorious heights *or* turn their equipment into undignified heaps of metal and plastic. Scrapbookers who try to run various kinds of papers through their printers may be inviting such a catastrophe. Printer reliability is based on the use of a certain range of paper style and weight, and violating these parameters isn't a good idea. Printer feeding mechanisms are very unforgiving — you *don't* want to hear the outraged sounds they make before they bounce their various parts across your floor. To avoid this situation, consider the following options:

- ✔ **Use specialized papers in your printer:** Fortunately, a wide variety of papers *can* be used safely in the average printer. You can even print on specialized sugar paper and by so doing, put a scrapbook page on the top of a sheet cake!

- ✔ **Commercial printing:** As mentioned earlier, digital scrapbooking has opened up the possibility of getting your scrapbook projects printed at a conventional printing establishment.

# *Enhancing the functions of the digital camera*

Some people like taking pictures. Others don't. If you're one who likes photography, you may be interested in several items that can enhance your digital camera experience.

For starters, digital cameras have finally arrived at the point where some affordable models have removable lenses. This is exciting news because now you can use close-up (macro) lenses, telephoto lenses, wide-angle, and even fish-eye and other specialty lenses. These cameras can also do a good job for short video clips.

We like the Canon line for digital SLR (removable lens) cameras — other people are very loyal to other brands. Those who have lenses for SLR film cameras will probably choose to stay with the same brand so they won't have to purchase new lenses.

Some top-end digital cameras ($800 to $1,200 — or more) have Adobe Photoshop color profile plug-ins which make for much improved color-balancing possibilities. These digital cameras have built-in light meters and several focusing and lighting options.

Enhancing your digital camera doesn't have to cost a fortune. Figure 2-2 shows you some of the best and least expensive digital camera accoutrements.

**Figure 2-2:**
Check out these digital camera extras including a tripod, memory cards, a camera case, and extra batteries.

*Courtesy of Omega Satter*

The following list offers more detail on a few of the add-ons pictured in Figure 2-2:

- ✔ **A small writing pad:** This little item is one of the most inexpensive, lowest tech, yet most necessary accessories you can buy. Use it for listing your shots. It's amazing how much you forget about your pictures between the time you take them and when you download them into the computer. You may want to list when you took the picture, who was in the shot, what settings you used on your camera, and any notes about what happened before and after the shot.

- ✔ **Additional memory cards:** Another memory card is pretty affordable and allows you to take more shots without uploading images. Having more than one memory card also helps when you need to print out photos at the store.

- ✔ **A camera case:** Another inexpensive, but valuable, purchase. The case not only protects your digital camera, but also holds your supply of extra batteries. If you travel a lot and/or often take outdoor shots, we recommend a hard case to protect your camera and lenses.

- ✔ **A CD or DVD burner:** Use this valuable tool for storing your images someplace other than your hard drive. Burn backup CDs or DVDs. When (not if) your computer crashes, you'll be glad you have these backup copies.

- ✔ **An inexpensive, but sturdy tripod:** Tripods help you get sharper images in all types of lighting situations.

- ✔ **Photo-grade fill lights:** If you see yourself taking a lot of interior shots, some photo-grade fill lights complete with stands really pay for themselves. Using these fill lights eliminates the flash-burning-a-hole-in-the-middle-of-your-shot problem.

# Chapter 3

# Exploring Your Software Options

*In This Chapter*

▶ Taking a look at your operating system

▶ Getting a broad view of the digital scrapbooking software scene

▶ Looking at some fun extras

*M*ost computers come with "bundled software." The bundles usually consist of a basic word processor program, a simple database program (not always though), a Web browser, and a selection of media players. Scanners usually come with good software programs that allow you to make some basic photo corrections. And digital cameras almost always have some sort of photo viewer or album program that organizes images.

All of these software programs are useful, but very few (mainly only word processing programs such as Microsoft Word) take you to the point of actually making a scrapbook page. To *really* scrapbook digitally, you need to invest in some additional software.

Most scrapbook-specific software is written for the PC only — because about 87 percent of computer software users have PCs (this figure varies depending on who you're talking to). Many Mac users, who tend to be more professionally graphic-oriented, already use the upper-end graphics programs. But there are a few digital scrapbooking programs for Mac users who aren't graphics pros.

In this chapter, we help you select the software *you* need to start scrapbooking digitally. We include specific info for the beginning, intermediate, and advanced digital scrapbooker; for the PC and the Mac user; and even for the "just curious" scrapbooker who wants to sit on the sidelines for a while and wait to be convinced that digital scrapbooking will "really" expand her creativity and capabilities.

# *Identifying Your Operating System*

To talk about computer software programs, we first have to talk about computer operating systems — at least a little!

Don't have a clue what OS has been installed on your computer? You're not the only one! Many, many people, even those who use their computers heavily and for a wide variety of different purposes, don't know anything at all about their operating systems. Sometimes the OS name is on the monitor when you first turn on your computer — right there — big as life! If it isn't, click on My Computer, then Properties, and then System to find out what system you're working with.

## *For PCs*

The term PC is actually an abbreviation for personal computer. This term is most often used to indicate a computer that is IBM-compatible — one that works with the old DOS operating system or, in recent years, a computer that runs some version of Microsoft Windows.

The operating system questions with IBM-compatible computers are more complex than with the Macintoshes (Macs). Windows 98 is a good PC operating system, but like the older Mac operating systems, it's beginning to have some serious software-related problems — problems due mostly to its age and the lack of support from many hardware developers.

Windows Me, 2000, and all the other flavors of consumer windows operating systems prior to Windows NT and XP also have compatibility issues in one form or another. How serious these issues are really depends on the specific computer and the particular pieces of equipment you choose to use with it. Windows XP will work well (is compatible) with most peripherals and with the PC scrapbooking software we introduce in this chapter.

## Peeking into the history of digital imaging

Digitized images snuck almost unnoticed into standard computer software. Originally, word processing programs just handled words, but the programs were gradually enhanced and expanded to include clip art and then digital photographs and other digital images. Still, the word processing programs couldn't do it all. If they could, there'd be no need for drawing programs, photo-editing programs, and scrapbooking programs. As word processing programs improved, these other programs were also developing and finding ways to do very interesting things. The scrapbooking software that we review in this chapter took their image and text manipulation ideas from these predecessors.

## *For Macs*

A Macintosh computer has a graphical interface that appeals to graphic artists and designers. This specialized computer, made by the Apple company, is most often used by digital designers, video editors, and/or print-oriented computer operators.

If you own a Macintosh, we recommend that you use OS X (that's a Roman numeral 10, by the way, not a letter). If you're running on a system lower than OS X, you're likely to have problems when you start your digital scrapbook projects. This doesn't mean you have an inferior computer. It just means that almost all of the Mac scrapbooking software you want to purchase is designed for OS X. If you bought your Mac computer after 2001, you're probably (though not necessarily) running on an OS X system.

If you want to, you may be able to update the operating system on your Macintosh to OS X — although only if certain variables apply. Consult a Mac expert if you plan to give this a try, because some computers don't accept upgrades gracefully. For more on Mac OS X, see *Mac OS X For Dummies* by Bob LeVitus (Wiley).

You *can* purchase good used computer software, but using older software will be an exercise in frustration if it doesn't work well with the newer Windows and OS X operating systems. In order to use the older versions of software on the Macs, you have to run two operating systems on the same computer — switching back and forth from one system to the other as you work.

# *Scoping Out the Scrapbooking Software Scene*

Acquiring the digital scrapbooking software you need doesn't have to cost a fortune. To find some good, low-cost programs, read this chapter and then type *digital scrapbooking* into Google or some other search engine. After you find some scrapbooking software, check it out by doing the following:

- ✔ Find out what's being said about today's scrapbooking software programs so you can figure out what suits you best.
- ✔ Comparison shop by checking prices on the Web and in scrapbook and computer stores.
- ✔ *Try* these programs before you purchase any of them:
  - Go to those sites that offer freeware and shareware programs, where you can often find a program written by some genius software programmer at a fraction of the cost of commercial programs.

Freeware and shareware are two different categories of software, but they're often listed on the same sites. With both freeware and shareware, you can try out the software, but with shareware you're supposed to pay a fee to use it if you want to keep it.

- Look for scrapbooking software programs that offer trial versions (usually the trial period lasts anywhere from two weeks to 30 days).

  *Trial software* is a special type of software; a temporary version of some commercial software that only lasts two to four weeks before it quits working and you have to purchase it or quit using it. Sometimes trial versions will not allow you to save your work until you purchase the software.

In both the PC and Mac environments, you find three basic types of programs for the digital scrapbooker: beginning, intermediate, and advanced. In the following sections, we give you some examples of scrapbooking software in these categories so you can weigh the options after considering your needs and experience level. We recommend our favorites later in the "And the winners are . . ." section.

Print a copy of all product license numbers you receive after you purchase a program online. These numbers are important if you ever have to reinstall the software, or if you need to put it on another computer.

## *Outfitting beginners*

Much scrapbooking software on today's market is targeted at the digital scrapbooking beginner. These programs are great for experimenting and practicing. They typically come with prebuilt pages, plenty of clip art (pre-made art that's ready to drop into your design), and may even include stock photographic images (general-use photos).

The best beginning programs also offer photo-editing software and allow you to build a page from scratch. As you advance, though, you'll find that the features of these basic programs can't match those of a good quality graphics or photo-editing program — and you'll want more.

Just to give you an idea of what to expect from the beginner's software, we list a few of the more popular scrapbooking programs (most are PC-only) and comment briefly on the benefits of each of them.

### Art Explosion Scrapbook Factory Deluxe 3.0

This PC-only program by Nova Development was created especially for the beginner, but intermediate-level scrapbookers might choose to use this program as well. The many pluses of this program include the following:

- The four CDs provide over 5,000 page templates, more than 1,000 fonts, and upwards of 40,000 graphics. This program is moderately priced at about $40 and is easy to master.

- Most of the page designs and graphics can be classified as "cute," but you can easily add graphics or clip art from other sources to make pages in any style you like. Art Explosion Scrapbook Factory Deluxe 3.0 even includes a simple photo-editing program that allows you to remove red-eye, crop photos in unique shapes, and apply special effects.

- As with most scrapbooking programs, you can use the software to make journals, cards, envelopes, labels, T-shirt designs, slide shows, and so forth.

The balance between ease-of-use and advanced editing features has been carefully thought out and nicely implemented.

### Perfect Scrapbook Maker

This PC-only program targeted for the beginning digital scrapbooker is currently undergoing a major overhaul. The new version is scheduled to be released in the final quarter of 2005. We include Perfect Scrapbook Maker here for two reasons: It's one of the few programs that can save a scrapbook page to PDF format; and the Cosmi marketing team indicates that the company is firmly committed to meeting the needs of digital scrapbookers. Pre-release notes indicate that the program includes 2,500 or more ready-made templates, 380 creative fonts, 35,000 quality images, and 1,500 artistic accents.

### My Scrapbook 2

Priced at $25 to $30, this Ulead product is strictly a PC program. It has a different feel and structure from the other scrapbook programs (you'll either like or you won't) in that it offers fewer page templates and fewer images. But it does have more workable file formats, giving you greater flexibility in downloading images from sources such as digital cameras, memory sticks, and so forth. Other benefits of My Scrapbook 2 include the following:

- It makes greeting cards, diaries, photo frames, posters, and T-shirt designs.

- It has a special feature that can make panoramic images or stitch together a large image that's been scanned in two parts.

### Creating Keepsakes Scrapbook Designer Deluxe

This Broderbund product, a PC-only program that costs about $20, is designed especially for scrapbookers. Considering its low price, you can hardly go wrong. It's an easy-to-use choice if you want to explore digital scrapbooking before fully committing to it. The pluses include the following:

- ✔ It can save to PDF format.
- ✔ You can use it to make greeting cards, calendars, flyers, tags, invitations, and so forth.
- ✔ In addition to 4,500 templates; 25,000 images; and 700 fonts, it contains a basic photo editor and a basic drawing program.

### Creative Scrapbook Assistant

This program from Hewlett-Packard is the entry-level scrapbook program for Mac users (it also works with PCs). The program costs about $20 and comes with a nice demo and a good instruction booklet (though the program is so simple and well-laid-out, you probably won't even have to read it).

This program was made to use on average computers without lots of random access memory, or RAM. The images and templates included in this program have a resolution of 150 ppi to accommodate these computers. The program has a feature that automatically helps the scrapbooker organize the elements used for each page.

## Stepping up to intermediate software

Digital scrapbookers at the intermediate level often opt for clip art programs, which offer a huge selection of images and some page-editing tools as well. These programs may include a few templates you can work from, but in large part, you build your pages from scratch. Once again, the advanced digital scrapbook artist will want more.

We mention the two preferred by digital scrapbookers here — one program for the PC and one for the Macintosh.

### The Print Shop Deluxe

This Broderbund PC-only program costs about $40. This desktop publishing solution has a wide range of *applicability* (it's useful for many different kinds of projects). Its pluses include the following:

- ✔ It boasts 310,000 images and 16,000 project templates (though none of these are scrapbook templates). You can start with a blank page or use one of the program's templates (though you're limited to an 8½-x-11-inch or smaller page size).

✔ You can create quick-and-easy greeting cards, labels, calendars, newsletters, and much more — and then print your projects out or share them electronically with family and friends.

✔ You can make a Web presentation complete with video and audio clips.

### Print Explosion Deluxe

Nova's Mac-only program (compatible with OS X) comes on three CDs. It can create all sorts of printed material; scrapbooks are just one of many possibilities. It's priced between $55 and $60 and comes with 8,800 ready-made designs and 90,000 graphics (including 5,000 photographs, 2,500 fine art images, and 500 fonts). It has a good instruction manual and pictures for all the graphics available on the CDs.

## Scrapbooking on a whole new level with advanced software

Photo-editing software wasn't originally intended for making scrapbooks, but scrapbookers have found photo-editing programs very useful for creating their digital pages — even more so after manufacturers improved the programs and included additional features scrapbookers could use.

Adobe's Photoshop is the photo-editing program against which other photo-editing programs are measured. Although this type of program offers the most flexibility, it's also the most difficult to master and there's not much template help to get you started with your scrapbook page.

Adobe's Photoshop Elements and the other photo-editing programs we review in this section do include some of the special Photoshop features that allow you to do advanced scrapbooking design. Veteran digital scrapbookers may miss a few of the filters, editing tools, and special effects that they would get in a true photo-editing program like Photoshop, but the programs that follow work very well for most scrapbookers who want to produce advanced digital scrapbook pages.

### Photoshop Elements

This Adobe product is an unusual program; made to be as easy-to-use as possible. Offered in both PC and Mac formats, it costs about $100, much less than the $650 you'd spend for the regular Photoshop program. Photoshop Elements has different features than Photoshop. Its capabilities are staggering, and it's so well-designed that a digital scrapbooker can get results right away. (Adobe sells the more expensive Photoshop program to professionals who need that program's high-end features.)

For those who want to go deeper into the program, it comes with an excellent instruction manual (and a whole new vocabulary!). You may want to purchase the latest edition of *Photoshop Elements For Dummies* by Deke McClelland and Galen Fott (Wiley) to help you master this great program — which has the following desirable features:

- ✔ It edits and manipulates your digital text and images better than most other programs.
- ✔ You can import and export material in most popular file formats (including PDF).

### Paint Shop Pro 9

This PC-only Corel product is popular with digital scrapbookers and costs about the same as Photoshop Elements — though it's often offered with a rebate that brings the price down to the $50 to $60 range.

The good points of this program include the following:

- ✔ Paint Shop Pro handles type a little better than Photoshop Elements does, and it also offers a nice Pen tool that allows you to draw and to easily adjust your drawing. This Pen tool is a big plus, because it's the tool you need for tracing when you have to improve a low-resolution clip art image.
- ✔ Two especially attractive aspects of Paint Shop Pro for scrapbookers include the specialized scrapbook CDs (pre-made background papers and templates plus embellishments) and the scrapbooking instruction manual entitled *Scrapbooking the Digital Way*. These materials are so good, you may want to check into them no matter what program you use.

### Corel Draw Essentials 2

Here's another PC-only program that gives consumers a lot for their money. This package has both a drawing and a photo manipulation program. It's extremely versatile and only costs $70 to $80.

The best features of the program include the following:

- ✔ This program can import and export in a wide variety of formats (including PDF).
- ✔ There's an excellent texture section you can customize to fit your needs.
- ✔ This program gives you all the text management tools that are missing in most other programs.

For users looking to graduate to the next level, CorelDraw Graphics Suite 12 is a great product to explore.

### *Picture It! Premium 10 and Digital Images Suite 10*

These two Microsoft products operate similarly. Picture It! Premium is the simplified version. It retails for about $50 and comes with a $15 rebate. Digital Images Suite costs about $100 but offers a $30 rebate. Both products are PC-only, and both are superbly designed programs that come with well-written, easy-to-use instruction manuals. (New versions of these programs were released just before publication. The names for the new products are Digital Image Suite 2006 and Digital Image Standard.)

It's evident that these programs were made for people who want to edit their photos as simply and easily as possible. Because both programs work in a similar fashion, purchasing the more feature-rich Digital Image Suite would seem wise. Here are the pros of these two programs:

✔ Digital Images offers an extra CD with a collection of templates, clip art, and photos. Most of the images are contemporary in design.

✔ Both programs offer an album function you can use to catalog your digital images, a worthwhile feature that makes your digital scrapbooking work easier.

✔ These programs let you make animated flipbooks and Web animations. The instructions don't go into detail about how to set up the program to make a 12-x-12-inch page, but it's not difficult to figure out (the key is to set up a 12-x-12-inch canvas).

### *ACDSee PowerPack*

This basic PC-only photo-editing program by ACD Systems is priced at about $80. Packaged in three parts, it does about the same things as Microsoft Digital Image does, but is a little harder to understand and use. The advantage of this program is that you can download a trial version from the Internet and try it before buying, which tells you that ACD is confident of the quality of its product. If you purchase the software, you get a 30-day money-back guarantee. Like many other programs, ACDSee PowerPack doesn't save into the PDF format.

### *PhotoImpact 10*

Ulead's PC-only photo-editing program is priced at about $90. This full-featured editing program compares favorably with Photoshop Elements in terms of the number of features it offers. It has a well-thought-out user interface, but you need some time to master it; the ten-chapter video tutorial helps users get up and running

Ulead also offers a scrapbook-specific program (My Scrapbook 2), so PhotoImpact doesn't have scrapbooking templates. However, many of its features (such as those found in the type gallery) will serve the scrapbooker well. You can also download additional images from the Ulead site (most are low-resolution images). We suggest that you take Ulead up on its 30-day trial download offer to test it out.

## And the winners are . . .

In this section, we help you select the best program for your scrapbooking needs — basing our recommendations on your level of computer expertise:

### If you're a beginning PC user and have little or no digital design experience

We suggest you try Nova's Art Explosion Scrapbook Factory Deluxe 3.0. It comes with a good instruction manual, and the clip art and photo images look great on your scrapbook page. Another good option is the HP Creative Scrapbook Assistant.

### If you're a PC user who has some computer experience

We recommend you choose either Adobe Photoshop Elements or Microsoft Digital Image Suite 10. Digital Image gives you some nice clip art and photos and it has a good instruction book. Photoshop Elements also has a good instruction manual and, in addition, has better photo-manipulation tools.

CorelDraw Essentials 2 is another good choice, especially for those people who can draw with a mouse. If you choose this program, get a good aftermarket instruction book so you can take advantage of all it can do.

### If you're a Mac user

Here, the choices are between Creative Scrapbook Assistant, Print Explosion Deluxe, and Photoshop Elements. Beginners will probably like Creative Scrapbook Assistant or Print Explosion better, but computer-savvy scrapbookers will no doubt want to use Photoshop Elements.

## Investing in Software Extras

Beginning digital scrapbookers find that as their personal styles and sets of preferences emerge, they want to incorporate new digital resources. Some scrappers need more typefaces to work with; some want more clip art; others prefer photographs or are very interested in cool backgrounds and unique embellishments. Manufacturers have collected and/or developed software for each of these needs. (Please see Chapter 8 for further information concerning graphics.)

In this section, we tell you where you can find some of the extra software that would be just right for your scrapbooking style.

Many programs don't save files as PDFs, the preferred format for sharing your scrapbook pages with family and friends (see Chapter 18). However, you can get a *PDF conversion program* by going to a Web location such as tucows.com, where you'll find shareware and freeware available for this purpose. Try the PDF-converter program out before you buy. If it doesn't work well, or is too hard to use, look for something else. PDF converters are made for both PC and Mac systems and you should find something you like for $40 or less. Converting your files to the PDF format will eliminate the frustration of e-mailing scrapbook files that bounce back or take three hours to download.

## Forging ahead with far-out fonts

We talk a lot about the importance of fonts in creating text and incorporating text in overall design (for more information on text techniques, see Chapter 12). Perhaps the best sources for a wide variety of reliable and interesting scrapbooking fonts for your designs are the font ads in scrapbooking magazines.

*Display fonts* (fancy title fonts) are a special breed of type. True display fonts don't usually have many different versions (such as the bold and italic versions of regular fonts). Many display fonts are so unique, they come in only one version (or occasionally in two). You can find them on the Internet, but be careful about these offerings — some are very strange.

Beware of the CDs available for $4.99 at your local office supply store — the ones that advertise 1,000 creative fonts. In most cases, these CDs give you the same fonts you got when you purchased your computer. Because a font is technically comprised of one style of type, when you have a regular Times font, an italic version of Times, a bold version, and a bold italic version, you have a total of four fonts. See how easy it is to get to 1,000 fonts in a big hurry?

You can often find display font CDs in the same discount bin with the 1,000 font CDs. The 50 to 100 different fonts offered in the display font CD are usually a much better deal for the scrapbooker.

## Grabbing great graphics

You can get a collection of CDs that will give you 50,000 to 90,000 clip art images for about $50. Although not all of these images are usable, there are often enough good ones to justify the purchase price. But be aware that many of these various collections contain some of the same images and that a graphic "bargain" isn't always a good investment — because many of these "great deals" offer only low resolution images or poorly designed cartoon images.

Look for clip art that comes with a printed reference book so you can see the images printed out on a page. It's frustrating to have to search through a stack of CDs, clicking repeatedly as you try to find a project-appropriate image.

Good sources for finding quality image collections include the following:

- ✔ Try the scrapbook magazines and the graphic software producers, who offer clip art or photo collections at reasonable prices for use with their programs. Scrapbookers have been known to purchase these scrapbooking programs just to get the clip art.

- ✔ Search the Internet for free high-resolution graphics. Most of the images on the Web are 72 ppi and very small, but you *can* find the higher resolution images you need. For instance, www.freebyte.com/clipart_images_photos_icons is a must-visit, and you'll find some nice clip art at www.barrysclipart.com. Some of the photographic images at www.morguefile.com are royalty free and copyright-authorized-to-use for noncommercial purposes. Images at www.imageafter.com can be used even for commercial purposes.

- ✔ Ask any of the various travel bureaus in your area (or in places you visit) for images. These people *want* you to use their photographs. When you ask about copyright restrictions and permissions, you'll find that the bureaus are usually quite accommodating.

# Chapter 4

# The Digital Design Process in Brief

*In This Chapter*

▶ Collecting and cataloging digital design materials

▶ Setting up the project

▶ Making your digital pages

▶ Clearing the deck

**D**igital scrapbooking is fast, efficient, and clean. These qualities lead to one very important result: *You can actually complete scrapbooks!* The authors of this book know that (as much as we'd like to), we're never going to get *all* of those photos into beautiful handmade scrapbooks. But the digital revolution has given us hope. We really think now that we'll make digital copies of every photo in our archives and organize them into meaningful digital albums.

The digital environment doesn't change the design "rules" of traditional scrapbooking, but it does make applying them easier and faster. In this chapter, we show you how scrapbooking digitally affects your design process: gathering materials, setting up a project, laying out your photos, journaling, and other page elements. We also give you some tips for cleaning up when your project is completed.

## Creating a Digital Design Library

To jumpstart your creativity, you may want to create a *digital design library* — a collection of digital materials you can access easily when you're working on your various digital scrapbook projects. Always be on the lookout for digital design materials — including photos, embellishments, and even color combinations that appeal to you. Scan materials that aren't yet digitized to get them into digital form.

Digital tools make saving your design materials easy. Just organize the design samples into folders on your hard drive or CDs: textures, colors, images, patterns, embellishments, and so forth. Before long you may start subcategorizing — into color shades, types of images, and whatever else your design mind dreams up. These folders will soon be a wonderful personal library of great design materials that have special appeal to you.

As this digital library grows, it may become difficult to remember every item in your collection. It's a good idea to make a thumbnail of each of these items and then print them out so you can see what you have at a glance. Many of the album programs that help you organize your digital images will also allow you to print out thumbnail versions.

The following sections suggest places to find design materials and ways to organize the materials for easy access.

## *Looking after photos*

Good photos help build the backbone of every scrapbook. Organizing your photos so you can easily find and use them is an important key to frustration-free digital scrapbook projects. Scrapbookers generally have two organization systems: one for their hard-copy printed images and another digital organization system for their digital images. Remember that often these are identical images or photos in two different formats — printed and digital.

### *Organizing hard-copy photos*

Many traditional scrapbookers have hard copies of their photos. Even those people who take digital images often make prints of their images — just in case they somehow lose them in a computer crash or other unfortunate incident.

When you pick up hard copies from a printer or photo processor, take the time to write the date and event on the photo envelope — even if you don't have time to catalog all the images right then. Keep your pictures in the envelope and place them in a protective box. (When you do get the time to properly catalog your hard-copy photographs, divide them by event, place them in a protective envelope, date them, and store them in chronological order.)

You can also save your hard-copy images digitally by scanning them, putting them into appropriate digital file formats and folders, and burning them to CDs or DVDs.

If you take digital pictures, you may want to use the following convenient service offered by many photo stores: The store uploads your images to its Web site, and you then pick up your hard-copy prints the next time you visit the store.

### Cataloging new digital photos

Many people have a hard time creating a good filing system for their digital images. Keep these two guidelines in mind as you're deciding how to organize your new digital photos: File the photo images as soon as possible after you take them so you remember the important details, and create a plan for filing your images that will help you know exactly where to place the new images and where to find them when you need them later.

Your plan should complement your individual thought processes and unique way of approaching organization tasks. People use many different strategies for filing digital images. We give you a sample here, but suggest you adjust it to fit your own favorite modes of structuring, categorizing, and organizing:

✔ Create several general categories such as parties, vacations, hobbies, relatives, work, home, and so forth. Try to make enough of these categories so that any picture you take will fit into one of them, but don't make so many that you're confused when you return to look for your images.

✔ When you place a new image into a general category folder (such as *vacations*), create a new folder (within or "under" the vacation folder) and name it using the date you photographed the image. We find that dating really helps us find the files we want to use.

✔ As you place the images in the dated folder, rename each image to help you remember what it is. This is very important. Most digital cameras name images with a number. If you don't rename your images, then you may end up going through every numbered image until you find the one you're looking for. (Although if you use a photo album program that shows you a thumbnail image of each photo, you may decide to skip the renaming step.)

See Chapter 1 for specific advice about archiving digital photos and completed projects for the long term.

## Keeping an eye out for embellishments

As all scrapbookers know, *embellishments* are little extra items used to "dress up" scrapbook layouts. Be on the lookout for such items. They're everywhere!

Keep your eyes open not only for images, but for especially interesting objects, colors, shapes, and textures — the building blocks of embellishment design. Take digital shots of design elements you like and may use in your albums and incorporate them into your digital design library.

One design advantage to purchasing a small digital camera is that you can carry it with you wherever you go. This means you can collect design ideas *and* digital materials from all kinds of different sources: publications, gardens, walls, museums, and so on — and on.

As you become more sensitive to color, pattern, and texture, life seems to get more and more interesting. Even waiting time becomes productive — as, for example, when you flip through magazines in the doctor's office to find new combinations of pattern and texture (just snap digital photos of the ones you like and save them for your design library).

## Creating color palettes

A *color palette* is a selection of a few colors (often three basic colors) that go well together in a design scheme. For traditional scrapbookers, many of whom hold colors next to each other to see if they look good together, this is a straightforward process. For digital scrapbookers, the process is a little more complicated.

In fact, color selection is probably the aspect of digital scrapbooking that's most different from its counterpart in traditional scrapbooking. That's because the colors you see on the screen are different from the colors the printer will print out. And colors aren't consistent on all printers either. Colors from the same file will look different depending on what printer you use. The color discrepancies bother some people more than they do others.

In general, printers produce darker looking colors than those you see on the screen, so if you want bright colors on a printout, you may need to adjust them so that they look unusually bright on your screen. If you hold the colors you choose up to the screen and match them the best you can, they usually look good together when you print them out.

One digital trick that works well is to use your editing program's Eyedropper tool (color picking tool) to select a major color from a photo on your digital scrapbook page. Then use this color for your title or headline. Because the color coordinates with your photo, the headline usually matches the photo nicely.

You may want to use the color wheel made by EK Success (it comes in two sizes). Or try a less expensive option — paint chip cards from a local hardware or paint store.

## Exploring other design resources

Scrapbookers don't create in a vacuum. The more you see and study other people's designs, the more creative you can become with your own. Expand upon (rather than simply copy) the ideas that appeal to you (see Figure 4-1). Ask other scrapbookers what they think about in terms of texture and patterns — most are glad to share their secrets when you're interested in their work.

**Figure 4-1:**
You can borrow design ideas from another source without actually copying the original design.

*Courtesy of* Scrapbook Retailer *magazine (Designed by Michelle Guymon)*

Get in the habit of collecting design materials with your digital camera. *You are the artist when you approach scrapbook design in this matter and you don't have to worry about copying other people's work* (refer to Chapter 8 for a discussion about copyright issues).

You may also want to use other sources to get digital design materials. These materials proliferate on the Internet (see our appendix for Web sites that feature downloadable design elements). You can also get CDs and DVDs that offer interesting design ideas and materials. Or you can scan both actual and digital design elements you like. Put all of these resources into your digital design library folders.

It has long been a practice of commercial artists to create *morgues* — collections of images, designs, patterns, and textures that the artist thinks have been well done or might be useful. When searching for ideas, the morgue can yield inspiration. Taking one idea from one source and another idea from a different source has helped many a designer achieve new creative heights. For more on this topic, see Chapter 20.

# Setting Up a Digital Scrapbook Project

Creating a digital scrapbook is really not much different from creating a traditional scrapbook, but some people have trouble starting when they can't touch the paper and physically move the pictures around. The following guidelines may help you get more comfortable with beginning the digital scrapbook-making process.

## Your stories enhance your photos

The better the story you tell, the more impact your images have. This little exercise will prove it: Have a friend or relative show you a stack of old photos you've never seen before. Select an image and analyze your response to it. Then have your friend tell you something about the people in the photograph. Look again at the photo and note how your response to it has changed. Even though the story behind the image may not be totally engrossing, it affects the way you respond to the image.

## Deciding on a topic

Make a list of the scrapbooks you want to put together. Add to this list whenever you get an idea, and then prioritize which ideas are most important to you. In this way, you can keep track of all your good ideas and focus on the most important projects first. We think that older photos and stories should have priority because they've been deteriorating and fading in memory longer than the new photos and stories. But others don't see it that way. They want to record every important detail and image of what's happening now!

Whatever your method, determine to plunge in to the number one project on your list — immediately! If you already have a style in mind, great! If you don't, check out Chapter 5 for descriptions of some of the most popular scrapbook styles. You can be sure to find one that has your name on it.

## Selecting materials from your design library

You probably already have a general idea what photos you need to scan for your project and what story you want the digital album to tell. You may even have a vague idea of what you want to see on one or more of the layouts. But perhaps you can't quite picture the exact sizes, colors, or patterns of the elements.

Most people have difficulty visualizing their albums and they have to put page elements in place before they can begin the adjusting process. Often, looking through the thumbnails in your design library sparks some great ideas — because it gives you access to all the possible design materials you've previously collected.

Just browse through the folders and select the elements you think may complement your photos and your story. Try a few of them and do several sketches until you get a good combination of pictures, titles, embellishments, and other elements.

Even though you plan carefully, most of your pages eventually turn out differently than you imagined they would. Always, though, they'll be much better looking because you went through the sketch step — and, the more often you go through this process, the better able you are to envision the end result accurately.

## Deciding on page size

Unlike traditional scrapbooking, your decisions about page sizes in digital scrapbooking are based on the very practical consideration of whether or not you'll be printing out your work. If you want a hard copy of your digital album, you have to look closely at your printer and its size capabilities.

What's important in relation to the page size of your digital album is what page sizes your printer can handle (see Chapter 2 for information about printers and page sizes). If you have an abundance of photos and journaling, you may want to use the larger page sizes — but if you plan to print out your album, your printer's capabilities may dictate that you need to use a smaller page size. In that case, you need to rethink your design to fit smaller pages. (You can see why it's a good idea to determine your scrapbook's page size before you create your page and layout mock-ups or sketches.)

Set the page size for your album by opening a new document in your digital editing program. When it asks you what page size, specify the size of your full scrapbook page (or at least the maximum page size for the printer you're using). If you do this on a base page that you then set up as a template for the whole album, your work goes much faster.

## Sketching tips for your pages

Sketching out your pages gives you a rough idea of what size you want your photographs, what space is available for any memorabilia and embellishments, and how much room there is for journaling. You'll be surprised how helpful this rough sketch will be. Figure 4-2 demonstrates how to sketch out your pages.

As you add page elements, you get a feel for how to organize and place your items. You figure out which fonts fit and which ones are either too small or too large. You also get ideas about the background images or patterns you want on your page (see Chapters 7, 8, and 9 for basic design tips).

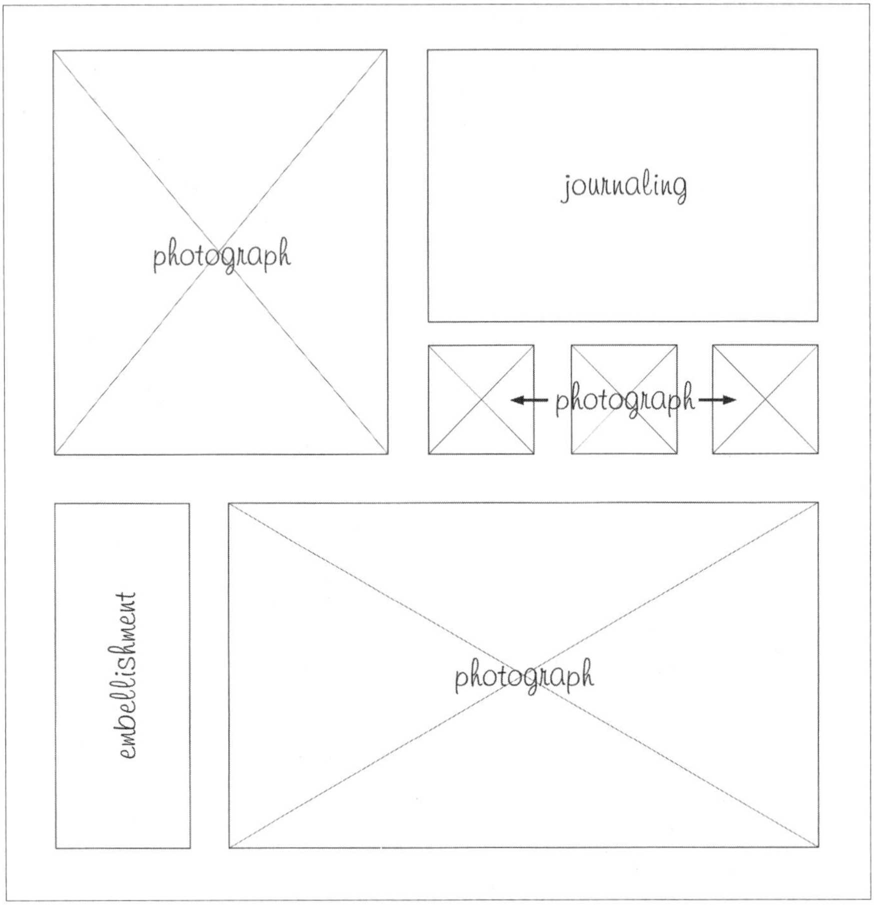

**Figure 4-2:**
Creating a sketch of your scrap-book album pages should help you envision the style, look, or mood you want to achieve.

*Courtesy of* Scrapbook Retailer *magazine (Designed by Michelle Guymon)*

## *Writing the story*

The quality of a scrapbook comes, in the last analysis, from the story it tells. Look at every photograph you have that relates to your scrapbook project — even if you know you won't use all of them in your album. These photos give you ideas about story details. In most cases, it's best to write your story first and then include the images that support the story (although when you make heritage albums, you usually do things the other way around — see Chapter 15).

After you find your images, see what embellishments are available, and sketch out some possible page designs, your original story idea may change. This is fine. The changes are part of the creative process. So even though you write your story before you begin designing, keep in mind that it will change as you work to integrate it with the other elements in your layouts.

You don't have to be a great writer to tell your stories. Just start explaining the photos and other elements on your pages. Keep in mind that you're recording these stories. You're an archivist, a preservationist. At the most basic level, you're creating a compelling story for your future self, one that will interest you when you're old, gray, and lucky enough to have the leisure to revisit your memories.

Incorporating *journaling* or story telling into digital design can really be fun (see Chapter 12 for detailed information on journaling). Generally, you can tell "small" stories on a page, balancing your journaling with the page's images. Or you can follow a page full of journaling by a page with very little text and more pictures or graphic elements.

But many times, your story goes beyond the design limits of a page. It begs to be told — and you must tell it! In such cases, go ahead and do entire pages of journaling consecutively — maybe including some small consistent design element throughout the whole album on these fully journaled pages. For example, you could put a small picture of your grandmother in the center of every page or a clip art flourish between various sections of the narrative.

## *Working with photos and images*

When you can get your images to speak, your journaling says more too. Images and text should complement each other. The interplay between the images and the text will add interest and charm to your scrapbook pages.

Make sure you select images that say what you want them to say. The following bulleted list will help you choose the best images for an album:

✔ **A large image indicates importance.** Viewers take extra time to see what the largest image has to say.

✔ **An image stands out if you make sure it's different from the other images around it.** A colored image on a page filled with black-and-white images doesn't just stand out; it screams for attention. A single *duotone* (two colored) image will also catch a viewer's eye.

✔ **A cropped photo sends an intensified message.** To crop, select the key part of an image and throw the rest of it away. You get the same kind of effect when you leave the key area of a photo in full color and screen back the rest of the image — or show the entire image and then copy and enlarge the key part of the photo so you see the image plus the best part of the image again.

✔ **Fill-in images can help with visual gaps.** Use other photos, clip art, or drawings to illustrate selected points of your story. For example, if you don't have a picture of Uncle Arnie falling into the river, just use a picture of the river at the location where the incident occurred.

You can place text on the images by using the layer function in your editing program (see the "Layering" section later in this chapter). Place the text on its own layer so you can position it on the image (you can then move the text and image separately before you flatten and save — see Chapter 1 for more information about flattening images).

# Creating the Digital Layout

Remember that you're seeking to create a framework for your story that will draw readers in and keep them interested. To do that, a good page designer juxtaposes and balances contrast and consistency, using unique design elements to add interest and variety and balancing those with the expected and predictable.

Attention to consistency gives unity to the scrapbook. Use the same type font and the same sized letters throughout the album, for example. Consistent margins on all your pages are usually a good consistency choice, too, as are similar picture placement on each spread, repeated color combinations, and the repeated use of selected embellishments.

Good designers exploit the interplay and tension between contrast and similarity, stirring things up and surprising the reader with the unexpected. (Just don't let the surprises weigh more heavily than the consistencies in your overall design!)

For each scrapbook you create, make a separate project folder so that all elements used in that project can be saved in one easy-to-find place. List the consistent design elements of each project and save the list and formats in a text file in your project folder. If you have to stop working on the scrapbook for an extended period of time, this list of design parameters will help you quickly get back up to speed when you return to it.

Simple page design is usually a safe approach for beginning digital scrapbookers. If you do choose to include some detailed pages, alternate them with simpler ones. This concept of alternating the busy with the simple should also apply to your text.

## Starting with a base or a template page

One way to create consistency in a project is to use the same basic format for all of an album's pages (a great time saver!). When you start a new page for the album, you just call up the template without having to reselect all the page specifications — and you can still adjust variables on every new page you create according to your design requirements.

To make a base page you can use as a template, do the following:

- ✔ **Choose the resolution you require.** (See Chapter 6 for detailed information about resolution.)

- ✔ **Specify the background page color.** Choose white from the White or Transparent menu.

- ✔ **Call for rulers to be displayed and set up a grid.** Rulers and grid buttons are found under View on the Menu bar. Grid size can be adjusted from the preference button found under Edit or under View on the Menu bar.

- ✔ **Save the page as a template so you can access it again and again.**

## Layering

Digital scrapbookers create their pages in a way that mimics the process of making handmade scrapbook pages — by "layering" the page elements. Most editing programs have a layering function that allows users to create any number of layers on a page.

Scrapbook designers are continually using the Layer or New Layer commands on their programs as they work. They place different page elements on different layers and can then move and reposition each of the layers independently. In addition to the background layer, you may have one photo on one layer, another photo on a second layer, accessories and embellishments on other layers, and different pieces of text on additional layers. You then use your cursor to easily place the elements where you want them to go.

Different programs handle layering commands differently, so check your program manual or online index for instructions. Remember, too, as explained in Chapter 1, that you need to flatten all of your layers as a final step before sharing them electronically.

## Positioning items on the page

The story being told by the scrapbook page is all-important. Collect those page elements that are critical to the telling of the tale. Move them around until order and harmony emerge. Then ask yourself what-if questions: What if the main image were larger? Would it help the design and the telling of the story? What if the main image were smaller? What if the title were red rather than black? What if I set the journaling in a different type font? (See Figure 4-3.) Be open to reordering your images through the entire design process. Don't be satisfied until they tell the story you want them to tell.

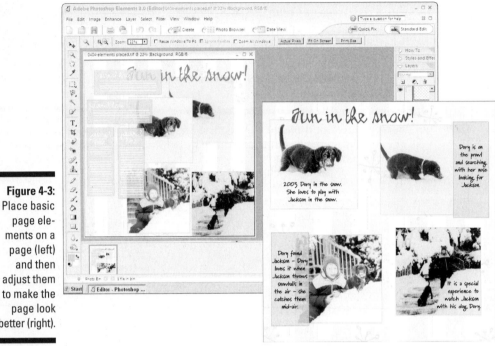

Courtesy of Adobe Photoshop Elements 3.0 and Scrapbook Retailer magazine (Designed by Michelle Guymon)

**Figure 4-3:**
Place basic
page ele-
ments on a
page (left)
and then
adjust them
to make the
page look
better (right).

Proportion and harmony are considerations in the art of page design. Size, proportion, and placement can make or break a page. Using the simple tic-tac-toe scrapbooking grid to position key items on your scrapbook page (see Chapter 7 for detailed instructions) can help you create a balanced layout.

Let your page rest or cure for a while — especially if you're having trouble with it. After a day or two, the page may look entirely different to you. If there's too much material, you'll know it, and you'll know, too, if there's something missing. If you return to the page and it doesn't speak to you, try one or more of the following tricks to improve the design.

### Sizing and resizing images to achieve special effects

Experiment with enlarging and reducing your images and see how this affects your page design. Many artists do this — superimposing an enlarged and prominent anchor onto a small image of an ocean liner, for example.

Images were once enlarged or reduced to appear approximately the same scale as their neighbors. If you placed an elephant and a boy on the same page, you made sure the elephant was sized in proper proportion with the boy. In contemporary design trends, realistic size relationships aren't as important. In fact, designers like to make statements by creating "unrealistic" image sizes.

### Varying the shapes of your page elements

Your scrapbook pages will look better if you have a variety of image sizes and shapes. Long rectangular photos next to square images next to normal rectangular pictures can make for a visually exciting design. You can even cut your images into strange shapes and then wrap text around them.

### Clustering images

You can create interesting effects by *clustering* or grouping images of different quality on the same page. Suppose you're working on a page about your sister. You choose an image that shows her clearly — but you can create "references" to her life history by also including some aged or fading images. The less-than-perfect images of your sister doing things that define her life shouldn't be the central focus of the page, but centralizing the clear image and framing it with these blurred or faded images gives you a nice effect (see Figure 4-4).

You can also cluster images of equal or comparable quality that are variable in other ways. Suppose, for example, you want to do a scrapbook page about your friend scrapbooking. Use a general shot to show her in the process of scrapbooking, take some close-ups of her hands as she works, and then take a shot of her finishing her project (see Figure 4-5).

**Figure 4-4:** Though some images on this page are blurry or unclear, they still convey a sense of this person's life.

*Courtesy of* Scrapbook Retailer *magazine (Designed by Michelle Guymon)*

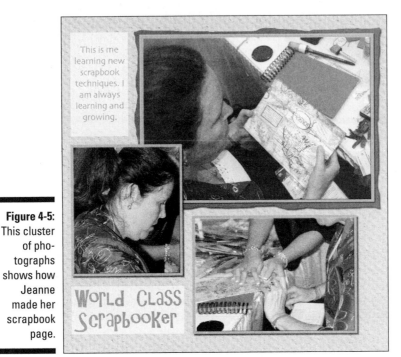

**Figure 4-5:**
This cluster of photographs shows how Jeanne made her scrapbook page.

*Courtesy of* Scrapbook Retailer *magazine (Designed by Michelle Guymon)*

# Keeping Your Computer Happy: Discarding or Relocating Leftover Files

When you're working with digital scrapbooks, you don't have to deal with the waste and mess that traditional scrapbooking inevitably creates. With digital design, there are no paper pages jamming the wastebasket. No glue disasters. No bad crops that can't be immediately fixed. You don't have to put away tools or gather and restore materials. In all of these ways, digital scrapbooking is as neat as a new pin. Nevertheless, because your files take up valuable hard drive memory, you will have to adjust, streamline, and clean up after you complete a digital scrapbook.

Scrapbooking uses tons of computer space. When you build scrapbooks digitally, you usually save versions of your designs as you go along. If you happen to create a fabulous design on a page, you can save it and reuse certain parts of its basic elements on other pages in the scrapbook. And if you ruin a page design in some way, you don't have to start over. You can just go back to your last version and continue working from there. Digital scrapbooking makes it easy to duplicate the good things that happen, but this constant saving process can create a jampacked computer hard drive.

In addition, many people don't just save their files in one format, resolution, or size. Multiple versions of the same material take up hard drive space and can easily overload a computer over time. Here are some of the different ways a scrapbooker may save just one image:

- ✔ In different design versions of their original form
- ✔ In the unique file format of the program they're using
- ✔ In either TIF or JPEG format so the files are faster to print
- ✔ In various resolutions for use in different sharing modes (72, 100, and 200 dpi for example), and in different sizes
- ✔ In PDF format because PDF files are so easy to share (See Chapter 18 for more information about sharing your digital scrapbooks.)

If you notice your computer is taking a super long time to perform tasks it used to do in the blink of an eye, you're overdue for a clean up.

Here are some ways to trim the excess fat off your hard drive:

- ✔ **Delete unused or obsolete images.** This simple step creates a lot of storage space on your computer.
- ✔ **Save the original, but get rid of the outdated versions.** Inevitably, when you work with the originals to fit them into your project design scheme, you create altered versions of the original — many of which you'll never use again. Keep *one* safe copy of the original image you use in a project.
- ✔ **Find out how your scrapbooking program uses images:**
  - **Some programs put each image into the scrapbook page file.** If you have such a program, you don't need to keep the original photo file in your project file. If you can discard the copied images you don't need, you save yourself even more file space.
  - **Some programs link their scrapbook files to the image files in your project folder.** They do this so the scrapbook file doesn't become unmanageable as a result of including all the image files. In this case, you need to keep the proper image files because the program needs them in order to display these images.
- ✔ **Review your image files and optimize their sizes.** Let's say your original images are all 5 x 7 inches and 300 ppi. As you review your images, you find that many of them have been reduced to about 2 x 3 inches on your scrapbook pages. Reducing the physical size of the original image to the proper size for your document can save you large amounts of memory.

✔ **Adjust the points per inch (ppi) of an image to match the quality level of your printer.** Many printers can't take advantage of the quality in a 300 ppi image. If your printer can only use 150 to 170 ppi, why include all the extra resolution?

The argument for keeping the extra resolution would center around the possibility of someday printing the scrapbook with a new printer, or having the file printed at a photographic store.

✔ **Save your project files on CD or DVD disks.** Even if you want to keep one version of the scrapbook on your computer to view or print out, you will still *save space by placing any other file versions on disk*. Of course, you'll want your digital scrapbooks on disk anyway as a backup in case your computer crashes. See Chapter 1 for more information about archiving your finished projects on CD or DVD.

# Chapter 5

# Exploring Popular Digital Scrapbook Styles

- - - - - - - - - - - - - - - - - - - - - - - - - - - - - - - - - - - - - - - - - - - - - - - -

### In This Chapter

▶ Digitizing the main scrapbooking styles

▶ Imagining some other style types

- - - - - - - - - - - - - - - - - - - - - - - - - - - - - - - - - - - - - - - - - - - - - - - -

*M*ost scrapbookers choose to create their scrapbooks using a certain *style* (a genre or type of design), partly because doing so helps unify and give cohesiveness to the scrapbook, and partly because scrapbooking manufacturers have developed materials that work with the conventions particular to these different styles. Both traditional and digital scrapbookers gravitate toward the major scrapbooking styles that are most extensively supported by the industry (see *Scrapbooking For Dummies* for more on scrapbooking styles).

The most popular scrapbook style categories include: heritage, pop, crafty, shabby chic, classic, modern, and artist. In this chapter, we show you how you can use digital tools and techniques to create these styles in your digital scrapbooks. We start by briefly describing the most used style categories and also suggest some other specific categories to encourage you to forge innovative style types of your own.

If you want to get an idea of what it takes to create a complete digital album in one style, you can check out Chapters 14, 15, and 16 — where we take you through the process of creating albums in the classic, heritage, and pop styles, respectively. We also cover how to create fun theme pages in Chapter 17.

## Looking at the Major Scrapbooking Styles

To give you an idea of how scrapbooking styles can affect the scrapbooking process, we show you what works and what to look for when you're designing digital layouts in a specific style. Remember that we're talking about style *categories* — and that within these general categories scrapbookers experiment with a wide range of variations. One person's heritage-style scrapbook may look very different from another's. Both scrapbooks might feature old or aged images, but one may look Victorian and the other may have a Western look.

In most cases, your personal tastes and aesthetic values dictate your decisions about style. If you decorate your home in shabby chic, chances are you'll use the shabby chic scrapbook style to create some of your scrapbook albums.

The photos you decide to scrapbook may also suggest certain styles. Usually, one style per album is plenty (you can create lots of variety and contrast within that one style type). Of course, you can mix styles in an album (you can do anything you want in scrapbooking), but the mix would have to be very carefully thought out and executed.

## Getting a digital handle on the heritage style

The heritage style has traditionally featured aged or worn-looking imagery to tell stories about the past. This look has become so popular that many scrapbookers now use it to commemorate even contemporary events, especially weddings. If this style appeals to you, look at the following tips (and check out Chapter 15, where we show you how to use digital tools to create a family heritage album).

Heritage books often contain more explanation and description than other scrapbook album types. Digital scrapbookers have a big advantage when it comes to journaling in this style because it's so easy to create pages of biographical and other info with the word processor and to cut and paste text as needed.

Here are a few tips for creating a heritage-style album using some high-tech digital tricks:

- ✔ **Use your photo-editing program tools to repair and restore old photographs.** Badly damaged original heritage photos can be cleaned up and improved with your digital tools (see Chapter 10 for a detailed walk-through of this process). Because you're working in a heritage style, you don't want to make the pictures look brand new. A little aging is desirable. You repair and restore just so that the imperfections of the old photos won't interfere with seeing the images clearly.

- ✔ **Give contemporary photos the heritage look by "aging" them.** Stain *copies* of the originals with coffee or tea to make them look old. Tear part of a copied photo on purpose to give it that worn look. Add sepia tones with your photo-editor's filters. Then print it out, age or tear it, scan it back into the computer, and paste it in place (as shown in Figure 5-1).

✔ **Search for old-fashioned type fonts.** Look through your photo-editor's font selection or buy commercial collections that have the heritage-style fonts you want.

✔ **Find period quotes and phrases.** Use a search engine to pull up quotations from the Elizabethan, Victorian, and other historical periods. You can cut and paste these into your heritage pages, and change the font sizes and colors to go along with your designs.

✔ **Scan in or take digital photos of heritage-style backgrounds.** When looking for heritage-style backgrounds, try to find material that "matches" the era of the photos and other items you've chosen for your foreground images (very old Encyclopedias and other old publications are possible sources for heritage background materials). Use the Sizing tool to adjust their sizes in the computer so they're perfect for your page design. (Memorabilia and embellishments can also be sized and manipulated to fit.)

**Figure 5-1:**
Photos can
be easily
aged using
the tools
found in
your digital
editor.

*Courtesy of Microsoft Digital Image Pro 10 and Jeanne Wines-Reed (Designed by John Stratton)*

## Using digital tools to concentrate on the crafty style

Crafty, easily the most popular of all the scrapbook styles, focuses on the homemade, cute, and folksy. It can also showcase special craft talents such as needlework, beading, tole painting, and quilting. Hand-drawn letters with geometric embellishments are the norm for craft style journaling.

You can use digital tools to mimic the handmade elements of the crafty style (*and* produce the effects you want in a lot less time than it would take to create them by hand) or you can scan the "real" items and use the images in your craft-style albums.

Try some of the following techniques to create a crafty layout or two:

- ✔ **Create crafty patterns.** Place one handmade (scanned) or computer drawn crafty design element onto your digital page; a piece of cross-stitching or a small tole painted flower, for example. Copy and paste it to get two identical elements (two stitched pieces, two flowers). Then copy and paste again and you'll have four — again and you'll have eight, and so on. In a matter of a very few minutes, you can create a complete and beautiful border of a hundred or more little stitches or flowers. Or you can use your crafty creations to make frames around photos.

- ✔ **Scan hand-drawn letters into your computer.** Encourage your flair for the crafty by making your own original handmade letters. Scan them and then cut away the background from around the letters (see Figure 5-2 and refer to Chapter 10 for instructions on how to complete this process).

- ✔ **Use your color tools to recolor elements so that they match and/or complement your other page elements.** The crafty scrapper can find all kinds of clip art designed for the crafty style — in clip art books, on the Internet, and other places. You can color in outlined clip art with your digital color tools. Use the Eyedropper tool found in most photo-editing programs to help you select colors from one page element so you can color or tint other items on the page that exact same color (see Chapter 11 for directions on colorizing images).

- ✔ **Use your digital camera to create crafty backgrounds.** As scrapbookers build crafty-style pages, they collect pictures, embellishments, and other elements appropriate for this style. If you can't find a background to suit your needs, use your digital camera to set up some patterns or objects to create digital backgrounds that will complement your crafty design scheme.

- ✔ **Create different craft-style albums in different page sizes.** This style lends itself to many different size formats, which can be used for a variety of purposes — such as sending small thank you books to wedding shower or birthday party guests (see Figure 5-3). A little tip: Alter your crafty style in these specialized scrapbooks to meet the requirements of specific social situations.

*Courtesy of Microsoft Digital Image Pro 10 and* Scrapbook Retailer *magazine (Designed by John Stratton)*

**Figure 5-2:**
Get rid of the background around your hand-made letters before pasting them onto your scrapbook page.

**Figure 5-3:**
Small digital scrapbooks make wonderful thank you gifts for your party guests.

*Courtesy of* Scrapbook Retailer *magazine (Designed by Michelle Guymon)*

TECHNICAL STUFF

---

## Studying pop trends

Study the color palettes, shapes, and textures used by successful pop artists and use their ideas when you design your pop pages with the Color, Line, and Filter tools in your editing program. Remember that pop art fads come and go. The '60s were alive with bright primary colors and the shapes often came from (or were) everyday objects — like Andy Warhol's Campbell's Soup can. Later, there was an interesting contrast between bright acid colors and simple folk art colors, shapes, and textures. Sometimes pop style splits into several factions. In the '80s, cows became popular with one group (black and white) and computer graphics with another (flat strong colors).

---

## *Putting some pop into your digital layouts*

Pop (short for popular) style is current, topical, temporary, and volatile — and probably tells more about contemporary society than any other scrapbook style (see Figure 5-4). A thousand years from now, a scrapbook that includes pop iconography would be as interesting to an archaeologist as a stash of some boy's transformers with their weird little moving parts.

Pop is a natural style for digital scrapbookers because they can push the digital tools (especially the filters) to their limits without overstepping the bounds of the style's conventions. And they can express their creativity with very few restrictions. When you work with pop, anything (well almost anything) goes! (See Chapter 16 for a walk-through of how to create an entire family reunion digital album in the pop style.)

The pop-style conventions and elements change as the fashions of the day change. It's great for kids and people who like up-to-date trends and cutting-edge developments. If that describes you, read on. With the pop style, there are no special digital techniques or embellishments that give you the "look" you're after. You have to know what you want and find a digital way to make it happen.

Pop images, slogans, music, art, and so forth bombard us daily. You find them in advertising campaigns, politics, publications, comic strips, movies, and on the Internet. It's okay to use some of this material, but not all of it. Digital scrapbookers should be aware that even though it takes no more than a right mouse click to save and copy an Internet image into a scrapbook, it's still someone else's creative work (see Chapter 8 for info on copyright laws).

You can find sites that offer free pop (and other) images (take a look at the appendix for some sites we recommend). Or, you can trace the source of an image you like and ask permission to use it in your scrapbook.

*Courtesy of* Scrapbook Retailer *magazine (Designed by John Stratton)*

**Figure 5-4:**
Pop-style
designers
often use a
variety of
geometric
shapes on
their pages.

Here are some tips for creating a pop scrapbook album:

- ✔ Make a list of things *you* think are good examples of "pop." Use items from this list as embellishments to spice up your pop-style scrapbook pages.

- ✔ Apply different filters to an image (from the Filters menu in your photo-manipulation program). Which special effect filters best match your "pop" design ideas?

  Filters that work well on one image might not work as well on another.

- ✔ Notice which colors are popular in your "pop" world and incorporate them into your scrapbook pages. Use your digital tools to apply these colors to elements on your pop scrapbook page. (See Chapters 8 and 11 for information about using digital coloring tools.)

✔ Figure out some new and wild way to display your pop scrapbook pages (explore some of your sharing options in Chapter 18). Some people are putting scrapbook pages on the inside and outside of boxes instead of putting them into book form.

## Finding ways to digitize shabby chic

Can the rumpled elegance and mismatched opulence of shabby chic find happiness with cutting edge digital tools and techniques? We say yes, it can — even though shabby chic is perhaps the most difficult style to do well digitally because much of its allure is about flaking paint and the texture of rust. The shabby chic style lends itself to the type of digital scrapbook page you could print, add to, mount in a shadowbox, and hang on the wall.

That said, there *are* interesting digital possibilities in this style — including the following:

✔ **Combine real embellishments with digital ones.** Print out a digital scrapbook page for a shabby chic album and then adhere traditional embellishments to it, such as tags, eyelets, beads, wire, and buttons. The real shabby chic type embellishments provide a great contrast to the virtual or digital elements on your shabby chic page. If you want to "redigitize" the page, scan the whole thing so you can share it digitally.

✔ **Get down with your photo-editing program.** Shabby chic is a highly tactile style and to imitate the necessary looks and textures digitally, you have to focus on boosting your colors and contrast, *and* depend heavily on the color filters in your photo-editing program.

✔ **Emboss your page.** Shabby chic stylists like to use embossing because it suggests an "old-fashioned" look. Fortunately, many photo-editing programs offer an Embossing feature. When you *emboss* page elements, they appear as though they've been pushed into or out from the page. Most of the programs that offer this feature allow you to frame an area with embossing, but a few programs let you select and emboss specific page elements, such as a page title or an embellishment.

✔ **Age your images.** As with the heritage-style scrapbook, shabby chic material is often aged or tattered looking. If you have a pristine photograph, you may choose to digitally age the image so that it matches the shabby chic style of your scrapbook.

✔ **Get plenty of pictures.** Shabby chic scrapbookers take and collect photos of shabby chic objects found in museums, antique stores, and other places. A small digital camera (plus a couple of memory cards) is perfect for capturing these images — or for getting pictures of gardens and garden settings, which also fit right in with the homey shabby chic style (see Figure 5-5).

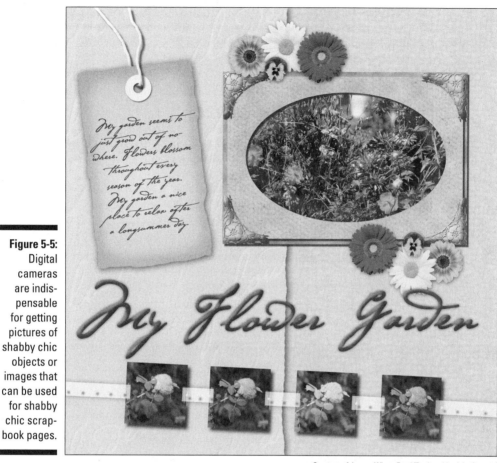

**Figure 5-5:**
Digital
cameras
are indis-
pensable
for getting
pictures of
shabby chic
objects or
images that
can be used
for shabby
chic scrap-
book pages.

*Courtesy of Jeanne Wines-Reed (Designed by John Stratton)*

## Using digital tools that help you achieve the exacting standards of a classic style

The carefully crafted classic style takes the best designs from the past and combines them into a unified style that can be described as understated and timeless (in Chapter 14, we show you how to create a classic-style, digital wedding album). This style is characterized by perfectly balanced composition, exact proportion, posed photos, and minimalist principles (no extra page items should detract from the purity of the composition and the high quality of the images.)

Although most digital tools (including the following) can be used in one way or another to make scrapbook pages in any style, the tools we identify in this section are the ones used most often by the classic stylists to meet the highly prescribed demands of classic-style conventions:

- ✔ **Turn on your ruler option when opening a new document.** This feature provides rulers to help you see where page items are placed. Then you can accurately apply temporary guide lines to your page (see Figure 5-6) — an important consideration in classic compositions. Placing the cursor on the top or side ruler and left clicking your mouse will bring a green (usually green) horizontal or vertical guide line onto your page. (Some programs make you find another command somewhere in your Menu bar to move the guide line.) Note that the ruler option is different from the Snap to Grid function and the tic-tac-toe grid — both of which are also useful for the classic stylist (see Chapter 7 for more info on these).

- ✔ **The Sizing tool lets you resize most page elements to meet the needs of your page design.** (See Chapter 6 for specific instructions about how to use this tool.) Classic stylists equalize elements with the Sizing tool to achieve the balance that's so important in this style.

  The one limitation of the Sizing tool is that in most programs, no history of its use is provided. What can happen is that you enlarge a photo, reduce it, enlarge it some more, reduce it a bit, and finally enlarge it for the last time. The question you find yourself asking is, "How much past 100 percent have I enlarged this image?" This is important because it affects how well your image prints. If you find yourself in this situation, measure the final size of your image, import the image again, and enlarge it to the size of your first image. You'll see the percentage of enlargement in the Image Size dialog box (depending on the program you have chosen) and you can decide whether you've enlarged too much.

- ✔ **Use your arrow keys rather than the mouse to nudge a picture or other page elements into position on your layout.** Classic elements have to be positioned "just so." After selecting an element with the Move tool, you can move the object up, down, right, or left with your arrow keys. The arrow keys move the image in very small increments, so you get a more exact placement than you do if you use your mouse.

- ✔ **Use your printer to proof pages.** What looks good on the computer monitor doesn't always look good printed out. Colors are especially deceptive. The reason is that computer screens and printers operate under the auspices of two different theories about color. Screen colors are usually lighter and brighter than printed colors. Colors are important in any style scrapbook, but they can be particularly tricky in classic-style work — where colors are typically subtle and muted. You need to print your design out in color to check whether the colors work as you expect them to. Check the placement of page elements too. They may look different on the printed page and have to be adjusted.

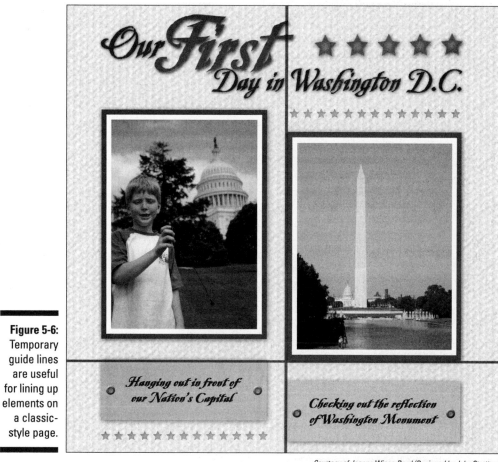

**Figure 5-6:** Temporary guide lines are useful for lining up elements on a classic-style page.

If you're going to print hard copies of your digital pages to make a bound, printed-out scrapbook album, make sure to use the same printer that you used to proof your pages. Otherwise, the vagaries of different printers might bring you some unpleasant surprises.

## Making digital pages in the modern style

The modern style adapts well to the digital format. Visit a modern art exhibit at a museum to get a feel for this style. Look for its common characteristics and emulate the ones you like as you plan your modern-style designs. The lines and shapes that signal the clean modern style (think Danish modern furniture and accessories) can be easily created with your digital tools.

Think of the modern style as a contrast and a response to the classic style. The modern style is sleek, bold, and fun rather than rich, subtle, and perfectly balanced. It's the type of scrapbook a businessman (or woman) would take to a professional presentation (*if* people used scrapbooks for professional presentations!).

Here are some digital tips for making a scrapbook in the modern style:

- ✔ **Make geometrical shapes with your line tools and use them to design borders and photo frames.** Click the elliptical, round, oval, square, and rectangle icons to make various geometric shapes that can be used to organize and design your pages in the modern style.

- ✔ **Use clean-lined text fonts that mimic or complement the structural lines and shapes of your layout elements.** The emphasis should be on readability and clarity. Remove any font that smacks of "cute" or nostalgic. Keep your fonts clean, but warm.

- ✔ **Combine photographic images with graphics you create with your digital drawing tools.** If you have made your page design appropriately modern, you can loosen up a bit with the photographs. Look for photographs that are warm and real in their portrayal of the subject matter. Let your images illustrate the best in human nature.

## Analyzing the digital artist style

Those who use the artist style in their albums may be said to see themselves as artists who scrapbook rather than scrapbook artists. They express themselves originally. This is the style for the free spirit. If that's you, and if self-expression and self-satisfaction are important to you, read on.

Digital tips for working in the artist style include the following:

- ✔ **Apply artistic filters to your images.** You can, for example, do a whole scrapbook making the images look like watercolors using the Watercolor feature in your filters menu. The digital tools available in your photo-editing program make it relatively easy to work with different media styles.

- ✔ **Use really fancy fonts.** In some scrapbook styles, the really fancy fonts don't work well, but in the artist style you can have fun with them.

- ✔ **When taking photographs, try getting some extreme close-ups.** It's kind of a cheap trick, but taking close-ups and then tilting them a little often gives an "artsy" look to your images.

- ✔ **Repeat some images.** Repeat a particularly nice image or embellishment, placing the series in a line on one side of the page. Choosing the right image or embellishment and sizing it properly can make your page look *quite* stylish.

# Surveying Other Scrapbooking Styles

In a perfect world, a "scrapbook style" would specify a formally defined design system, and a "theme" would refer to a given topic for a scrapbook. But no matter how much sense this makes, the boundaries of this convenient definition begin to blur the second someone tries to categorize the different ways that scrapbookers choose to approach their work.

Whether you see a design concept as a "style" or as a "theme" really doesn't matter, but having a concept to think and create with gives you the framework you need to build and expand your story. That structure ensures that you'll keep viewers interested and cover all of the important material in the stories you want to preserve.

"Themed" scrapbook pages and albums are very popular, and as scrappers have worked with them over the years, they've developed techniques and "looks" that have become integrally associated with specific themes (sorry, but some of the most frequently used *themes* have such identifiable conventions that they're often referred to as *styles*). Here are a few examples.

## Styles for baby

Baby scrapbooks often include cute clip art images that surround slightly blurred or soft looking images of babies in cuddly poses. Bright primary colors may also run rampant — as do plenty of bunnies, teddy bears, and little zoo animals.

Here are a few tips for creating digital baby scrapbooks:

- ✔ **Use or create digital fonts that go with the style you choose and change their colors to match your page elements.** Favorite fonts imitate alphabet blocks or crayon letters.
- ✔ **Use clip art to make frames for the baby's photos.**
- ✔ **You may want to include page embellishments that match the design elements of the nursery to document the baby's first years.**

## Designing with favorite fantasies

People who really enjoy their fantasies appreciate scrapbooks designed around their favorite fantasy styles. Any old fantasy will do — either one of yours or some favorite of the person you're making an album for. One fantasy style might use fairy tale characters or child-oriented characters such as those found on Sesame Street or at Disneyland. Or you can use characters from literary fantasies such as *Winnie the Pooh* or *Harry Potter*. Another fantasy style might include the *Star Wars* characters or a *Lord of the Rings* motif.

Here are a few tips for creating digital fantasy scrapbooks:

- ✔ **Paste images of yourself (or someone else) in illustrations that include your fantasy characters**. This is easy to do using your image-editing program.

- ✔ **Find fonts that give your pages the "feel" of the fantasy.** Old English, Arabic, or Teutonic fonts work well, but sometimes they're so ornate, they become hard to read. Use an ornate font on the first letter of each text block and a more readable font for the rest of the body copy.

- ✔ **Enlarge the first letter so it really stands out.** This is called a *drop cap*. You may need to put the first letter in one text box and the body copy in another text box to make the text work properly. (For more on drop caps, see Chapter 12.)

## Experimenting with the eclectic style

What makes an eclectic scrapbook page so charming is its totally unpretentious attitude — no snob appeal, no status issues. Just someone's memories presented in the way that person wants to present them. Because it has no rules and few standards, the eclectic style album can be aesthetically stunning or totally trite. Emerging and taking its shape from what's at hand, what mood you're in, and how it looks in a particular context, its focus is on having fun and collecting the images, embellishments, and materials you really like.

Here are a few tips for creating digital eclectic scrapbooks:

- ✔ **Don't plan anything.** Too much thought will kill the spontaneity. Work freely, and experiment with digital effects (filters) that you haven't used before.

- ✔ **Print out your eclectic scrapbook and put it away.** Put your eclectic book away for a few months before you edit. Then you can see more clearly what needs to be changed. Your digital tools make it easy to throw out what you don't like and incorporate more of what you do.

## Tying in to specific time periods

Focusing your design around a particular time period is especially valuable when doing historic scrapbooks of your relatives. That's because the historical context offers a wider perspective on their lifestyles and the realities that governed their lives.

Here are some tips for creating digital time period scrapbooks:

- ✔ **Use your Internet search engines to do some research and collect material.** Copyright issues are less critical here because many of the online images from days gone by are in public domain and free for anyone to use.

- ✔ **You can also scan images from old encyclopedias and other sources.** Opaque them with your digital tools so you can use them as backgrounds for your album.

- ✔ **Imagine yourself in a different time period.** Make your scrapbook like the people in that era would have made theirs.

When recreating a time period, be especially careful to show life as it really was rather than how you see it or want to see it. For example, many scrapbookers use muted colors and stereotypical images when recreating the past. This is great when putting together a heritage-style scrapbook, but real life in the past wasn't so monochromatic. True, the people of yesteryear didn't have the color possibilities we enjoy today, but the faded colors we see on old worn-out antiques were vibrant when these items were new. So include color.

Take your color palette from some artifact of the period (think of the possibilities in the art deco era!). Use your digital tools to split a page in half. Let one side show colors as you normally see them in heritage-style pages and the other side show vibrant colors as they might have appeared in times past.

## Fooling around with fashion

For some people, fashion is an obsession. A scrapbook without fashion references can't truly represent such a person. If you're scrapping for a fashion-plate, infuse the particular fashion style of your subject into every element of every page.

Here are a few digital techniques to help you along:

- ✔ **Use your digital drawing tools.** This style of scrapbook is especially suited for people who can draw fashion-style illustrations (cartoon renditions of fashion illustrations are even more fun).

  Those who don't draw can trace a fashion photograph to make a line drawing. It doesn't matter whether the tracing is good or not — the funkier the better. Scan in this tracing and use it as an embellishment for your scrapbook page. If you make certain to enclose all your lines, you can convert your image from grayscale (black and white) to RGB (color) and then fill the shapes with whatever color(s) you choose (see Chapter 11 for procedure details).

✔ **Place various fashion accessories on your scanner and scan them into your computer.** Belts, earrings, buttons, buckles, or assorted pieces of jewelry can all be used to dress up your fashion page.

✔ **Run a fashion shoot with your digital camera.** Sometimes you can get your family or friends to pose for you when you have an idea for an image you need for your page. This can be especially fun for scrapping teenage birthday parties. Make all the kids look like fashion models — and *even they* will think the resulting scrapbook is cool.

## Focusing on vocation

Vocation is highly important to most individuals, and the extra effort you take to work with a vocation design pays off. It shows that you really appreciate and understand the person you made the scrapbook for.

After you establish a vocational style, you can then create themes that utilize this style. Here are a few tips for creating digital vocational scrapbooks:

✔ **Include key images for the profession.** The scrapbook page or album you make for someone in the home construction industry may include blueprint images and scanned images of sticks of wood, tools, bricks, and so forth.

✔ **Use metaphors that apply to the profession.** For example, you may be doing a scrapbook for an accountant. The style would be a reflection of balance sheets, tax forms, numbers, profits, expenses accounts, bank statements, and so on. One theme might be "When life doesn't add up!" You could include photos of the time the car had a flat tire, the night you spilled coffee on your husband's tie, or the day the kids fixed lunch and destroyed the kitchen.

✔ **Style your pages after something people use every day in their jobs.** Scrapbooks for veterinarians can use fonts that resemble the fonts used by drug companies and the page layouts may resemble veterinarian journals.

## Designing for sports lovers

For some, sports are a passion. Because the sports fan is such a common character in our society, there are many sources for sports material you can use in your scrapbook designs — such as from a sports team's public relations or advertising department.

Even the team lawyers who spend so much time protecting their logos, images, and corporate image wink at the use of copyrighted material in personal scrapbooks. Just don't try to resell or distribute your material. These people catch on pretty quickly because they have a whole army of loyal fans who are ready, able, and willing to rat you out.

Here are a few tips for creating digital sports scrapbooks:

- **Pay attention to the details!** The guy who wears two different colored socks at the same time will pick up on the slightest variation of his favorite team's colors. Make the colors as exact a match as possible. Logos, mascots, and players' numbers require the same attention to accuracy and detail.

- **Find ways to include the game-time food and the game-time antics.** Document the pregame preparations and the silly rituals. Include the goodtime buddies and the archrivals. A sports-oriented scrapbook should have room for everyone and everything.

- **Don't forget to include the shenanigans of the "sports challenged" members of the family.** A lot of "outlaw shopping" goes on during an important four-hour game!

- **Make a special-edition scrapbook if your sports fan's team gets to the playoffs.** Newspaper clippings, magazine photos, playoff ticket stubs, and promotional team items all make perfect sense as scanned elements in a playoff scrapbook.

- **Pay special attention to buzzwords and game highlights each year.** You'll find at least a half dozen really great moments. Make certain you recognize these and include them in your book. Journal a little about how people reacted to the events, and whether there were changes in the sport because of them. This information can elevate your scrapbook from a record of your hobby into a documentary for posterity to read and enjoy.

## Adding historical value to your sports pages

Teams change their look every year as sports styles and new ad campaigns are implemented. Keep up with these changes and your scrapbooks will take on added credibility and value.

In this sense, sports are a reflection of the society that they attempt to serve. The style of the sport will often reflect the idealized image of what fans want to see in themselves.

## Even more scrapbooking style ideas

Keep your eyes open for other ideas that will provide focus for your scrapbook layout designs. We list a few possibilities here to get your imagination in gear, but you'll soon start thinking up innovative style concepts of your own.

- ✔ **The Western style:** Lately, there's been a movement to return to an understanding of the pre-Hollywood Western style — a style characterized as natural, clean, and nature-oriented. Symbols of the old Western style include old guns, mining tools, hunting trips, cowboys, and run-down homesteads.

- ✔ **An important event:** Historical scrapbooks attempt to accurately record the facts of selected events, but *your perception of the events* is equally important. In deciding to do a historical style scrapbook, recording a personal event is probably of more value than choosing to chronicle a national event. After all, there will be many people compiling records concerning the national events, but how many will be writing a single word about the very human experiences we all deal with on a daily basis?

- ✔ **Ethnic history:** Scrapbooking is the perfect medium for the study and preservation of our heritages. Who influenced your speech patterns and where did your values come from? How did your family change when they moved into a new culture and did they stay in contact with people or relatives in the old country? How is the next generation changing and do you think these changes are for the best?

  Try to get some real family stories to include in your scrapbook. Don't rely on just one source for these stories — you may pick a tall-tale-teller.

- ✔ **Geography:** How about a stylistic focus on geography, one that would reflect the environment and the styles of this country's diverse areas? We like the geographical style perspective because geography speaks to human basics. It undercuts borders, social classes, politics, and all the arbitrary (but mostly wonderful) systems and structures humans have created. Incorporate a few identifying characteristics from some of these areas into the designs of your scrapbooks. (You could also, of course, scrapbook in styles that depict different countries as well.)

# Part II
# Brushing Up on the Basics

The 5th Wave — By Rich Tennant

"If I'm not gaining weight, then why does this digital image take up 3 MB more memory than a comparable one taken six months ago?"

## In this part . . .

One great thing about digital scrapbooking is that you can create impressive scrapbook pages *as* you practice and master "the basics." Here's what the basics include: using specific tools and techniques for digitizing and manipulating photos; designing digital pages, layouts, and albums; finding, digitizing, sizing, and incorporating all kinds of neat graphics; and using digital text in innovative, appealing ways. In the following chapters, we show you how you can master these basics and finish lots of fantastic, fantabulous digital layouts at the same time.

# Chapter 6

# Mastering Basic Digital Photo Processing

*In This Chapter*

▶ Using your equipment and software processing tools

▶ Preparing scanned images

▶ Making the most of stock photo collections

▶ Downloading images from the Internet

*I*n this chapter, we give you tips on how to get great digital photos. Then we tell you how to take full advantage of your camera's features, so you can spend less time adjusting your images and more time on your scrapbooks. We also cover some of the important aspects of processing digital photos — not just the ones taken with your digital camera, but also the photos and images you scan, the ones on CD and DVD collections, and the many images you can download from the Internet.

We give you tips on how to work with your equipment and software (cameras, scanners, and editing programs) to achieve first-rate digital photo processing results: selecting the images you want to keep, using standard digital manipulation features and techniques, and working repair and restoration miracles on damaged digital photos. All of this might sound difficult, but it's not. It's just basic digital photo processing (you can find the advanced techniques in Chapter 10).

# First Things First: Taking Great Digital Photos

Digital cameras give you instant results; no waiting for film to be developed! You can see your photos right away on a digital screen, or print them on a home printer. If you don't like the way an image looks, you can erase it seconds after you shoot it and take another shot — or manipulate its little pixels until the image looks like you want it to look.

To get the most out of your digital camera and to get great shots, keep these basics in mind:

- ✔ **Note how the available light is affecting your subject(s).** Well-lit subjects make good pictures. If there's not enough light or too few or too many shadows, your picture won't be all that it can be. The automatic flash won't compensate for poor light. Most automatic flashes only work on subjects that are less than 10 or 12 feet away. Often, the flash creates a "hot spot" in the picture where the color appears washed out. Sometimes, you can correct this problem by backing up and retaking the shot, and sometimes, just moving the hot spot will help.

- ✔ **Stabilize the camera.** If you can't use a tripod, lean against a wall or some other stationary object, plant your feet firmly on the ground, and hold your breath as you take the picture. Many people like to look at the screen on the back of their cameras when they take digital shots (a technique that can help you properly frame your shot), but without a stabilized camera, you're likely to get blurry images (especially in low-light conditions).

- ✔ **Take plenty of extra shots.** You're not paying for film development, so snap away and discard the images you don't need. You'll never regret taking those extra "insurance" shots (the second or third shots often turn out better than the first).

Most digital cameras are easy to use, and the photo quality is great, but taking wonderful digital photos requires being familiar with the camera. So read up on your camera's features to get the very best images you can with it.

## Shooting at maximum resolution

The *resolution* of a digital image tells you how many pixels (or dots) it has per inch — the higher the resolution, the more pixels per inch (ppi) and the sharper the image. A low-resolution (low-res) image might have 72 to 100 ppi and a high-resolution (hi-res) image 300 or more ppi.

Some digital cameras designate hi-res settings with *words* rather than numbers — using terms like "best" or "fine," or "superfine." If your digital camera does this, you can determine the exact resolution (ppi) of the images it takes by importing a photo into your editing program.

As a general rule, you want to use your camera's highest resolution setting. The high-res settings make larger image files (more pixels per inch), but you want your original images to be high-res because they're sharper and clearer than low-res images. You reduce the size of these files later when you import them into your editing program. When you size the original images from your camera in your photo editing program to prepare them for your scrapbook, remember this little shorthand rule: Increasing the resolution is "bad" (will exaggerate the flaws in the original image) and lowering the resolution is "good" (will result in a sharper image).

## Creating your own interesting photos

Yep, you can take shot after shot with your digital camera, delete the duds, and keep the gems. *However* . . . if you use the tried-and-true tips we provide in the following sections, you'll get many more gems and lots fewer duds.

### The basics of setting up shots

The advice of professional photographers never varies: pay attention to lighting, close in on your subject(s), put people in your shots, and use your equipment (tripod, lenses, and so forth) to its best advantage.

Remember too that you have to read about your camera's capabilities to get quality shots — it's important, for example, to find out how your camera's lenses work in order to make the best adjustments for each situation.

Photo opportunities can present themselves when people aren't resorting to the "picture faces" that often mask personality and emotions. Newspaper photographers call these pictures *candid* shots. Many scrapbookers work to get as many candid shots as possible for their albums (though, as we show in Chapter 14, posed formal shots also have a place in scrapbooking).

For more detailed information and instruction about setting up your shots, see our *Scrapbooking For Dummies* and the very helpful *Digital Photography For Dummies* (Wiley).

### Finding some new angles

Try experimenting with strange angles and crazy candid shots. Most will need to be thrown out, but once in a while, you may end up with a winner.

To get highly creative photos, take some shots from the side, some from above, and some looking up from the ground. Find different ways and new angles that tell you something different about your subject.

Photographing your subject in parts is especially effective with inanimate objects. Take a look at the hood ornament from grandfather's old Pontiac (see Figure 6-1). Look for unique details like this when you photograph something; sometimes these details are more interesting than the whole object. Look for telling detail in people subject photos, too. A photo of your subject's hands, for example, can convey (or at least suggest) volumes.

*Courtesy of istockphoto.com*

**Figure 6-1:**
A detail shot of the unique hood orna-ment on this old Pontiac represents the design quality of the whole car.

## Planning your photographic time table

Commercial photographers usually figure they have to take 40 or 50 shots to get one usable image. With digital cameras, you can afford to do this too. But it still takes *a lot* of time to shoot images, evaluate them, and then either save them or shoot some more images.

You can save yourself some time by using the following suggestions:

- ✔ **Estimate how long it takes to shoot 40 pictures and then multiply that time (one hour?) by the number of pictures there will be in your scrapbook.** Happily, you probably don't have to take 40 shots for every picture you'll use, but some shots may need even more work (especially when you take photos of kids or animals).

- ✔ **Schedule the time and the resources for taking the images you need for embellishments.** How much time will you spend going to and from the places where you get your embellishments?

- ✔ **Get some ideas for background shots.** How long will it take you to find the textures, objects, or landscapes you need for those perfect backgrounds?

The creation of some of your backgrounds may require special digital techniques. Do you have the necessary programs and skills for this, or will you need to schedule in more time to get some help?

✔ **Factor in time for "clean-up" and adjustment.** After you start your scrapbook, you may need to take additional shots to fill in or correct some images you took previously. Will you have the time and the resources to do this? If not, can you change your design without hurting your story?

Even if you don't want to do such elaborate planning for every scrapbook you make, this approach pays off in big dividends. You may be taking photos of a birthday party so you can "just make a little scrapbook" of the event. If you take 20 shots and think you have enough images, take an extra 10 for good measure. You may be amazed by how much you value those extra images after you start putting your scrapbook together. Sometimes that strange photo of the dishes from the party piled up by the sink or the family room filled with torn paper and empty chairs will be the perfect ending for your scrapbook — along with that shot of your daughter asleep with her new doll.

# Taking Advantage of Your Digital Equipment's Built-In Processing Features

By mastering the built-in processing features of your digital equipment, you can produce better quality and easier-to-use images for your scrapbook work. Make it a habit to routinely use the processing features of your digital camera and scanner hardware and software features. Your aim is to come as close as possible to duplicating the photo processing results you want. Then you only need to use your photo-editing program to fine-tune the photo and add special digital effects.

## Looking into your digital camera's picture viewing program

Using your digital camera's viewing program can streamline the process of loading your images into your computer. These programs, often called *album programs,* display and file your digital images. Some of the viewing programs that come with digital cameras are easier to use than others (this may be a factor you want to consider when you're buying a digital camera). It's great to know that these improvements are rapidly incorporated into the newer digital cameras.

Here are some tips about viewing programs:

- Good photo-viewing or album programs that let you see several images at once make it easy for you to choose the images you want to keep by eliminating some of the guesswork and the tedious one-image-at-a-time viewing process.

  These types of viewing programs also make it easier to choose the best images from a series of similar shots. You're much more likely to pick out the best of the images when you can see them at the same time.

- Many album programs allow you to print out your images at the exact sizes you need for your layouts. This is reason enough to get in the habit of using your camera's viewing program. That's because photo sizes are so important in scrapbook page design; important whether you're going to stay totally digital or you plan to use printed versions of your photos in hard-copy scrapbooks. Either way, getting exact sizing at the shooting stage means less time spent on processing.

- If your camera's album program isn't doing the job, you can simply close it and use the camera as if it were another hard drive — by going to Start and clicking on My Computer. You can then drag and drop your images into a folder (either a folder you create on your desktop or one you make for your scrapbooking projects).

## Cultivating the camera cropping habit

Sometimes it's obvious that you need to cut excess from your digital shot (*way* too much sky!). Check to see whether your digital camera has a Cropping (or trimming) feature that you can use when you haven't set up your shot as well as you might have. You can save yourself time by using this function because you won't have to crop so much later when you build your pages.

Two warnings here though:

- **Be sure not to crop out background you'll want later.** The details of a setting (like natural scenery or the architecture of a place) are often very important to your scrapbook story, and you may capture some of those great details as you photograph the "people subjects" in that story. If you cut out the "setting details" in order to focus in on a person or other subject, you may be sorry later when you're putting together your scrapbook at home — a few thousand miles away from that gorgeous winter vacation spot. Your vacation story will lose a little something if it's missing those inspiring scenic details.

✔ **Don't crop too close to the central image in your photo.** You may later want to cut the whole photo into a shape that will go with a particular shape theme in your design layout, and you want to make sure you have plenty of room around your focal point image. If, for example, you want to cut the photo into a square shape to match a square-themed layout, you need some space between the image and the edge of the photo. Without that space, your image will look cramped.

# Enlisting the help of your scanner's hardware and software settings

When you scan images not taken with a digital camera, you *digitize* them, transforming them into pixels. You can use the scanner's hardware settings for sizing and cropping (see Chapter 7 for info about scanning oversized images). These scanner features are, however, primarily designed to keep an image from degrading as it's scanned, so except for large and obvious crops, it's usually easier and more productive to use your scanning software program for adjustments. Plus, you should *always save a scan of your original* before you start manipulating it.

In this section, we go over some of the scanner basics and scanner software settings that will be useful in helping you get the best possible finalized images. Even though, at first, all these settings may seem daunting, using them properly will give you a lot more control from the start.

### Improving your scanning setting savvy

One of the keys to good scanning is buying good equipment (and good equipment doesn't necessarily mean expensive equipment — it means good hardware combined with good software). But another essential key is *you*. Your faithful attention to the following details can help improve the looks of all of your scanned images:

✔ **Clean your scanner.** Keep that scanner clean! Fingerprints, dust, or smudges on the glass scanning surface affect the quality of your scans.

✔ **Figure out how to use the settings in your scanning program.** Mastering the settings in your scanning program pays off. Many scanned images are ruined because the pixels per inch (ppi) has been set too low, or the color setting is not correct. Sometimes, the descreen function is set for scanning a newspaper clipping and then never adjusted back for photographs.

### Changing the default setting in your scanner software

The default settings are usually set for basic color scanning. Convert the default setting in your scanning software from Quick Scan Mode to Professional Scan Mode or Advanced Scan Mode.

### Working with the dots or pixels per inch settings

Set the dpi (dots per inch) or ppi (pixels per inch) setting to 300. (We generally use ppi in this book, but sometimes scanners and printers use the two terms interchangeably.) This is print quality resolution and it's adequate for printing your images. Some people (and some scanner instructions) would have you scan at 600 or even 1200 ppi. If you do this, you create huge files that can hang up your programs or crash your computer if you try to use them. In a few instances, these super-high resolutions may be useful, but for most projects, 300 ppi is more than adequate.

Scan the same image in 200, 225, 250, 275, and 300 ppi resolution. Print all the versions out on your printer and see which image gives you a good picture with the least resolution (lowest resolution number will translate into smallest possible file, that is, it will take up less memory room). When doing this test, use the best paper you have. The paper makes a great deal of difference in displaying resolution on a photograph.

After you determine the lowest resolution you can use in your printer, avoid scanning at a higher resolution. Doing so will only force you into working with larger files. One exception, though! If you're going to have your images printed by a commercial printing service, you may choose to keep scanning at 300 ppi so you can get better prints (on the commercial printer that will be able to handle the higher resolution). And if you get your prints at a photography store rather than a discount store, resolutions higher than 300 ppi may be needed. Check with the store printing experts to see what resolution(s) they can handle.

## Utilizing Editing Programs to Improve Your Digital Images

Whatever its origin, after an image is in digital form (shot with a digital camera, scanned, or imported), you can further process and/or adjust it by using a photo-editing program. (We recommend various programs for every experience level in Chapter 3.)

Photo-editing programs can improve and enhance a digital photo by altering the characteristics of its pixels (see the color insert section to check out examples of photo-manipulation techniques). Some of the more basic photo-editing functions scrapbookers use to process digital images parallel the functions available on their digital cameras and scanners. These procedures include changing size, adjusting resolution, and cropping.

When you call up an original digital image in a photo-editing program, you save it with its original name and rename it as you work on it. You may end up with several versions of the same image after you complete your work on it (with files of different names or version numbers). If you don't rename the changed version(s), you overwrite and lose the original image — so you'll have to rescan the original or, if it was an image in your camera that you've since deleted, you can lose the image entirely. So always *save your original* and do your work on your renamed copy.

One issue that's rarely discussed is *generational loss* — the loss of quality every succeeding time an image is duplicated. This loss takes place even if you use a very expensive scanner. One big reason for using photo-editing programs is that they make it possible to adjust the image using tools that help reduce the generational loss factor.

## Adjusting size and resolution

Digital images, whether created by cameras or scanning, often need to have their resolutions adjusted for use in different applications. In most editing programs, a pop-up task box shows you the size of your digital photo and its resolution (ppi). (Figure 6-2 shows a task box in Jasc Paint Shop Pro, but most photo sizing screens look similar.)

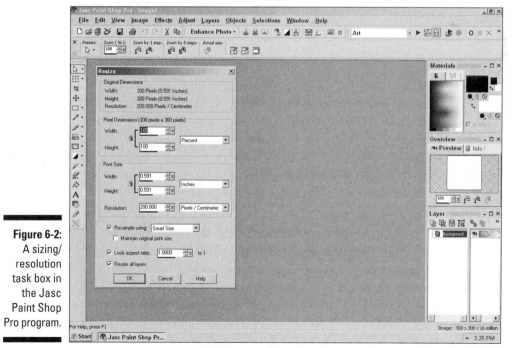

**Figure 6-2:**
A sizing/
resolution
task box in
the Jasc
Paint Shop
Pro program.

*Courtesy of Jasc Paint Shop Pro*

Size and resolution are two different measurements: *Size* measures the physical size of the image (for example, 6 x 4 inches). The *resolution* measures how many pixels per inch (ppi) the image is set at. An image of 300 ppi has 300 pixels per inch. Such an image is obviously *denser* (packed with more pixels per inch) than a 72 ppi image. And in the world of imagery, denser generally means an image is clearer and has more detail.

The size/resolution task box in most good photo editors includes the size of the new photo file as well as the size of the original file. Comparing the new file size with the original can tell you something about how your image is going to look.

Whenever possible, you want the new image file to be the same size *or smaller* than the original image file. If your image size information tells you that the original image size was 1864K and the new image is 984K, you're fine, because you're not adding more pixels to your image. If your original image size is 650K and your new image is 2460K, you have resolution problems. These numbers mean that your original image only had 650K of information, but the new image you're creating has significantly more (2460K in this instance). Again, increasing the resolution, adding more pixels is "bad" (will exaggerate the flaws in the original image) and lowering the resolution is "good."

Computers don't do a very good job of creating new information to meet the pixel requirements of an enlarged image — except when they have a built-in *interpolation component,* which is a mini-program designed to add pixels for an image. An interpolation program can do a pretty good job of making up visual information, but even these programs have their limitations.

### Reducing the size of your image

A photo you take with a digital camera is often saved as a very large-size image (many inches wide by many inches high), even when it's saved in the camera's usual low default resolution of 72 ppi (see "Shooting at maximum resolution" earlier in this chapter). You often need to reduce the overall size of the image and increase the ppi to match the resolution requirements of your printer.

An image taken with a digital camera might measure 8 x 10 inches. Obviously, you want to change this size to fit your scrapbook (to a 3-x-5-inch image, for example).

Here's a step-by-step description of how to use a photo-editor's sizing process to reduce the size of an image:

1. **Find the Image section on your program's Menu bar and select the Image Size feature.**

2. **Adjust the image size of the photo to match the desired size for your photo.**

   Keeping the Constrain Proportions option checked will keep your image proportionate to the original and prevent it from getting distorted. If you make a mistake, just exit the size/resolution box *without saving* and start again.

3. **After you change the numbers in the task box to size your photo to its desired dimensions, stay put!**

   Don't click the OK button to leave the task box. Size and resolution are intricately linked, so there's more you have to do. When you resize, you need to check and adjust the resolution of the image.

4. **Adjust the ppi to match the resolution requirements of your printer.**

   See the "Working with the dots or pixels per inch settings" section earlier in this chapter for tips on establishing this setting.

## Increasing the size of your image

Reducing the image isn't usually a problem (especially if your original image has been taken at a high resolution), but enlarging the image too much may cause it to appear *pixelated* (blocky).

How much enlargement is too much generally depends on the resolution of the original photo *and* how you intend to reproduce it. Most images can be enlarged 10 to 15 percent without much change. If you enlarge the image by twice or three times, however, you need to reduce the resolution (ppi) to make the total size of the new image similar to the total size of its original. This will keep the new image from looking pixelated, but it may look grainy when it's printed.

Here's a step-by-step description of how to use a photo-editor's sizing process to increase the size of an image:

1. **Find the Image section on your program's Menu bar and select the Image Size feature.**

2. **Adjust the image size of the photo to match the desired size for your photo.**

   Keeping the Constrain Proportions option checked keeps your image proportionate to the original and prevents it from getting distorted. If you make a mistake, just exit the size/resolution box *without saving* and start again.

3. **After you change the numbers in the task box to size your photo to its desired dimensions, stay put!**

   Don't click the OK button to leave the task box. Size and resolution are intricately linked, so there's more you have to do. When you resize, you need to check and adjust the resolution of the image.

4. **Reduce the resolution (ppi) until the total size of the new image is similar to the total size of its original (when you adjust resolution, the image size will change automatically).**

   Doing this will keep the new image from looking pixelated, but it may look grainy when it's printed.

5. **If you're going to print your image, you may need to further adjust the ppi to match the resolution requirements of your printer.**

   See the "Working with the dots or pixels per inch settings" section earlier in the chapter.

### Figuring out file formats

Know what file format you're using to save an image. TIFF (`.tif`) files provide the most accurate images, but most digital cameras save in a JPEG format. A JPEG (`.jpg`) is a compression-style file format that sacrifices quality for small file size. Recent scrapbooking programs have built in provisions that make JPEG files almost as good as TIFF files, though. If an image is originally taken in a JPEG format (as most digital camera images are), converting the image to a TIFF file format won't improve it. Scrapbookers want to save their images in the file formats that will work best with their particular scrapbook programs. As a general rule, most scrapbookers want a program that handles both TIFF and JPEG files.

# Cropping

Veteran scrapbookers know a lot about cropping. They often gather at cropping parties where they use many different types of scissors to *crop* (or trim) around images in their photos. (See *Scrapbooking For Dummies* [Wiley] for more on traditional cropping).

Cropping with scissors can be fun, but it can also be tedious and time consuming, especially when you're doing detail cropping — cutting around curves and into tight corners. It's *much* easier to crop digitally. You can crop the parts of an image you don't need with a few clicks of that handy little computer mouse.

In most editing programs, cropping is a two step-process:

1. **Use the Select tool to make a box around the section of the photo you want to save.**

   The icon for selecting the crop area looks like a square made of a broken line. (That broken line will stay on the image until you press the Deselect feature found under the Selection area on the Menu Bar in most programs.)

2. **Select Crop, and the program will automatically cut out the section of the photo you selected and throw the rest away.**

   Look for the Crop tool in the Menu bar. It's usually found under Image or Edit. (see Figure 6-3).

If you make a mistake, just select Edit from the Menu bar. Your program will probably allow you to Undo your last operation.

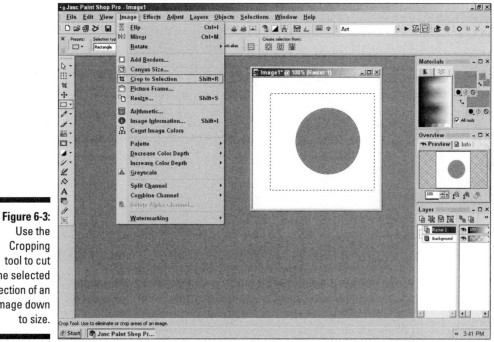

**Figure 6-3:**
Use the Cropping tool to cut the selected section of an image down to size.

*Courtesy of Jasc Paint Shop Pro*

## Changing your photo's position with the Rotate tool

Scrapbookers use Rotate to straighten an image that looks crooked because it hasn't been scanned in just right. For design purposes, you may also want to use the Rotate function to set a straight photo at an angle.

You can find the Rotate feature under Edit or Image on the Menu bar in most programs. When you select this tool, a box appears that allows you to turn an image clockwise or counterclockwise in numeric increments.

Some full-featured programs also allow you to rotate an image manually. If your program has this tool, it will probably be located on the side toolbar. To use it, select the image you want to rotate, and then choose Rotate. A special box should appear around the image (sometimes with a bar sticking out on one side). Grab the box or the bar with your cursor and rotate your image to the desired angle.

## Finding the Flipper

Suppose you decide you want the people in your two-photo layout to look like they're facing each other on the page. Trouble is — they're both looking to the left in these photos. With your editor's Flipping feature, you can flip one of the images so that its subject is facing right. Additionally, several full-featured programs allow you to flip an image both horizontally and vertically. Usually, their default flip setting will apply horizontally (sending the image from right to left and vice versa).

In some programs, the term *flipping* refers to reversing an image from top to bottom, while the term *mirror image* means reversing an image from left to right or vice versa.

Although most photo-editing programs can easily flip an image, finding the Flip feature can be difficult. Often, the Flipping tool appears on the side toolbar and is indicated by two arrows pointing in opposite directions. But sometimes it's found in the Menu bar under Image. Some programs even hide it under a subtitle such as Attributes or Transform. Keep looking — you'll find it. When you do, just select the Flip tool, and flip your photo.

## *Selecting brightness and contrast*

The Brightness and Contrast tools in your photo-editing program can improve most photographs by adjusting the lightness or darkness of an image and/or by increasing its contrast (see the color insert section). Most images need to be slightly brightened and their contrast increased for optimum picture quality. *Contrast* makes individual items in the picture easier to see. This procedure can improve the images to a startling degree.

Look for these features under Edit, Image, or Adjust on the Menu bar. Select Contrast and a dialog task box will appear with a slider and a numeric box for Brightness and another slider and numeric box for Contrast (see Figure 6-4). Move the sliders and you can see how those movements change your image.

**Figure 6-4:**
It's easy to adjust for brightness and contrast with this dialog task box.

*Courtesy of Jasc Paint Shop Pro and Jeanne Wines-Reed*

## *Reducing red-eye*

We love this red-eye removal feature and so will you. Although the red-eye retouch element isn't available in all photo-editing programs, it's quickly becoming a standard because of its usefulness and its popularity. You can use it on color photos when the pupils of your photo's subjects are red as a result of the camera flash. Newer photo-editing programs give you a choice between human and animal red-eye fixes.

The Red-Eye feature seems to be in a different location in almost every program. (Figure 6-5 shows Jasc Paint Shop Pro's Red-Eye feature under Adjust on the Menu bar.) The procedure for a red-eye fix varies slightly from program to program, but basically it goes like this: You select the eyes, then choose and click the Red-Eye tool. The results are automatic and usually wonderful: Zap! Those demon eyes are gone.

**Figure 6-5:**
Get rid
of red-eye
with this
special tool.

*Courtesy of Jasc Paint Shop Pro and Jeanne Wines-Reed*

## Sharpening your photo images

Digital scrapbookers often use a Sharpening tool to bring more focus to fuzzy photos. Most photo-editing programs have a Sharpening feature that will help correct this problem.

Look under Filter or Adjust on the Menu bar to find the Sharpen tool (see Figure 6-6). The program's Sharpen tool can sharpen your image automatically. And if the image still isn't sharp enough, select the Sharpen feature again or try the Sharpen More feature. If you overdo it and the photo becomes too grainy, go to the Edit area on the Menu bar and Undo the last operation.

**Figure 6-6:**
Use the Sharpen Filter dialog box to get those fuzzy photos into focus.

*Courtesy of Jasc Paint Shop Pro and Jeanne Wines-Reed*

# Repairing Scanned Photos

Your older photos may have been through moves or transfers of ownership, or they may have spent significant downtime in the attic or garage. The evidence shows up in rips, tears, water spots, holes, and folds. After you scan these photos, you can repair the damage in a variety of ways (see an example of a repaired image overlaid with a faint tint in the color insert section). Scrapbookers use the Clone tool for most photo-damage problems and in other instances when they want to duplicate parts of an image; a technique we discuss in Chapter 10.

Here are basic instructions for fixing a damaged photo:

1. **Scan your photo.**

2. **Open the scanned image into your photo-editing program and adjust for brightness and contrast.**

3. **Rotate the image to make it as straight as you possibly can and crop the photo if you need to eliminate unneeded background.**

4. **Use the Cloning tool or Healing tool to repair tears in your photograph or to eliminate dust spots, scratches, or folds.**

   See Chapter 10 for more on the Healing tool.

5. **Use the Enlargement tool (the magnifying glass icon on the side toolbar) to enlarge the image so you can see your work clearly.**

6. **With the Eyedropper, choose a gray color to touch up parts of the photo if you're working with a black-and-white photo or to pick the colors you need from the image if you're working with a color photo.**

   The Pencil tool works beautifully to change the shading of individual pixels, while the Paintbrush tool is the best one to use for drawing in lines. (See Chapter 10 for instructions for how to use the Pencil and Paintbrush tools.)

# Chapter 7

# Exploring Layout and Design Options

*In This Chapter*

▶ Reviewing basic design principles

▶ Applying design principles to scrapbook layouts

▶ Designing with digital tools and techniques

*W*hether you're making an all-digital, part digital/part traditional, or an all-handmade scrapbook, this chapter will help you with the following: understanding and using tried-and-true design principles; working more knowledgeably, confidently, and efficiently; *and* discovering some interesting techniques for showcasing those oh-so-important images in your designs.

The same design principles scrapbookers use to make traditional scrapbooks apply when you work on digital scrapbook projects (see our *Scrapbooking For Dummies* published by Wiley, to discover more about traditional scrapbook layout and design conventions). So if you have experience creating traditional scrapbooks, consider this chapter a quick refresher.

# Brushing Up on Visual Design Principles

Experimenting with the latest design schemes doesn't necessarily guarantee the best-looking pages. Instead of always copying the designs and layouts others have created, you can find out what makes design tick — and begin to understand it on a nuts-and-bolts level. Then you apply basic design principles the way *you* want to apply them, creating innovative, original pages (while practicing and advancing your design skills at the same time). Before you know it, people will be copying you!

In this section, we go over the basic elements that scrapbookers typically apply to scrapbook design: balance, harmony, unity, rhythm, and working with positive and negative space.

## Balance

In scrapbook design, *balance* refers to the equal distribution of visual weight on a layout. The term *layout* can apply to a one- or two-page spread, though sometimes scrapbookers use extenders to create larger layouts. You can find out more about extenders for traditional scrapbooks in Wiley's *Scrapbooking For Dummies*. But know too that some digital scrapbooking programs also have functions that allow digital scrappers to produce extended pages.

In a balanced layout, the page elements are evenly weighted: the same degree of lightness or heaviness on the top as on the bottom — the same on the right as on the left. Size and color components help determine an item's weight: larger, darker elements are heavier than smaller, lighter ones.

As is the case in other venues, balance on a scrapbook layout can be achieved either by placing page elements symmetrically or by placing them asymmetrically:

✔ **A symmetrical design** is based on parallels — such as parallel objects or parallel positions. You see symmetrical design in classical and neo-classical art and architecture: for instance, two matching urns on either side of a garden path, or perfectly spaced identical columns at the entrance of a public building. Some people find symmetrical design too predictable to be interesting, and will go to great lengths to avoid matching page items or balancing them too symmetrically.

✔ **An asymmetrical design** relies on color, texture, shape, and size to *create an illusion of balance* rather than balancing identical or similar objects on the right and left, or top and bottom of a page. Similarities and suggested similarities in position and other relationships are juxtaposed to create balance.

You can use your good sense and aesthetic intuition to test your pages for balance. After you create a page or a spread, print it out, set it on a table, and walk away from it. Don't look at it at all for at least an hour. When you go back, just *glance* at it — quickly. You want a fast first impression, not a studied critique. Does the page *feel* more visually heavy on one side than on the other? If so, you'll want to "even out" the weight to get better balance by rearranging the elements on your page until you get the balance right. Trust your instincts. They know all about balance, and they'll let you know whether or not you've achieved it!

# Harmony

A painting, a singing group, an orchestra — each of these can be said to be harmonious when all of its separate elements work well *together*. You can create harmony by connecting visual elements according to their similarities: similarities in size, shape, color (matched or coordinated), line, shape, texture, and so on. Many of the scrapbook industry's manufacturers produce packaged layout elements that have been carefully harmonized: plain and patterned papers, stickers, and so forth.

# Unity

You achieve *unity* on your page when all of its elements look as though they belong together. Unity is about more than harmony. It's about the page elements *needing* each other. You can't take away any of the elements of a unified page without impairing the visual effect of the whole. Every item works with the others to tell the same story.

Remember that consistency helps create unity. Digital tools and techniques make it easy to apply minor but important adjustments that help unify a design with a few clicks of your computer keys. You can quickly scale a photo to a slightly larger or smaller size or alter the color of a design element to make a better (more consistent) match with other items on your page or throughout your album.

After everything is in place, you can turn the layers of your page on and off to help you determine whether you've chosen and placed items well enough to create the harmony and unity you're after (see Chapter 4 for more info about layers and layering).

# Rhythm

Rhythm, another concept developed as a visual design principle, has to do with the way in which the eye moves over a scrapbook page: How fast does it move? How often does it stop? How long does it linger?

Page design incorporates rhythms in many areas, including placement, item relationships, and repetitions of color, shape, and size. What you do about all of these choices plays a part in determining the particular rhythms your pages elicit.

To test rhythm effects on a page, try imagining your eye as a ball. Let it travel around your page. Does it roll smoothly, or does it ricochet from one object to another like a pinball? Does it get hung up in one place or does it continue to move smoothly, taking in all the items on the page? Trying this exercise on your pages (and adjusting page elements accordingly) will translate into a significant improvement in your design skills.

## Positive and negative space

In scrapbooking, *positive* space is occupied space — space taken up or filled in by items, images, and other design elements. *Negative* space can refer either to the page background or to any empty space on the page. The ways you decide to use positive and negative space on your scrapbook page will help determine its mood.

Ask yourself this question — and answer it truthfully: If there's an empty space on a page, do I feel compelled to put something in it? Like many others who scrapbook, your way of dealing with negative space may be working hard not to have any. That's okay, of course. But you want to guard against a result that makes your page look confusing or too busy.

By making a few design adjustments, you can turn a cluttered layout into a well-designed layout. Try reducing the color intensity levels of your page items, for example. Muting the items that support your focal elements reduces their intrusiveness and allows the primary page elements to regain their rightful prominence. The clutter then becomes part of a subtle but interesting background pattern that remains intriguing on the second, third, and even on successive viewings.

An artist usually *wants* to draw the viewer's eye to positive space, but a design that's too chaotic or busy may work against that aim. The creator of a scrapbook page does well to give the eye a limited number of space resting points — an especially interesting photo or graphic or two. The viewer's eye appreciates being able to linger before moving on to other page elements.

Perhaps surprisingly, paying attention to how you use negative space (sometimes called *white space*) on your layouts is an extremely important design consideration as well. The improper use of negative space can make a page look unfinished. When you start becoming aware of negative space, you find many instances where awkward-looking applications of negative space are just as distracting as poorly designed positive shapes.

Some of the best ways of working with negative space include the following:

✔ Slowing down the eye to set a comfortable tempo for viewing your scrapbook page.

✔ Drawing attention to a featured design element — surrounding that element with a significant quantity of negative space intensifies the importance of that focal item.

✔ Balancing design elements by consciously contrasting them with the negative space on the page. If the page elements are dark, the negative space should be a light color. If the page elements are light in color, the negative space should be dark. This simple positive/negative color concept will *always* improve the balance of your scrapbook pages.

When you think your page is finished, look specifically and carefully at the negative space and see what shapes emerge from it. This exercise can take a little practice, but keep at it — you'll soon begin to understand and use negative space in ways that will impact other elements in your designs.

## Color

Selecting colors that go together has often been a difficult challenge — not only for scrapbookers, but for professional graphic designers as well. The fact that design schools teach a variety of color theories and that there's more than one type of color wheel used by artists who mix and match colors supports this view. (See Chapter 4 for more detailed information about how to use color in scrapbook design.)

Here are two easy-to-remember suggestions for the digital scrapbooker about color:

✔ Your choice of style (see Chapter 5) will help you find your colors for a particular project — a pop style for instance, can handle clashing colors, but a classic-style scrapbook should use complementary colors.

✔ Start collecting examples of color combinations in the magazine page designs you find especially appealing. When you plan a new scrapbook album, look at these samples and copy the color combinations. As you study the examples, you get a feel for color and for what looks good together. Before too long, you'll be able to create your own great color combinations.

# Applying Design Principles to Your Digital Scrapbook Pages

As you begin to recognize and understand basic design principles, you also discover how to apply them in your own work. In this section, we give you pointers on how scrapbookers have used design principles to develop techniques. These techniques use lines and shapes to help ensure balance, clarify focal points, and create structure, depth, dimension, and emphasis.

## Marking out a grid

Experienced artists and designers relate each design technique they use to a basic proportional plan. They use grids as layout templates to help them decide where to place items. You too can make better choices about positioning design elements if you first mark out a grid (or grids) for your page.

### Using the scrapbooker's tic-tac-toe grid

Traditional scrapbookers superimpose a tic-tac-toe grid over a scrapbook page or layout; they create the nine-cell configuration by dividing it both vertically and horizontally into thirds. Some just imagine such an invisible grid; others lay a tic-tac-toe scrapbook template on the page and mark the intersecting line points. The following section explains how to place a grid on your digital pages.

Your page's most important elements should be placed where the grid lines intersect because the eye sees these intersections as the most active and most interesting spots on the page.

### Using the digital Guide Line tool

When you work digitally, you can create grid lines with the functions in your photo-editing programs. In some programs, you have to turn on your Rulers to get these guide lines to show up on your monitor (your program instruction book can tell you how). You pull the guide lines from the top or side of your working area and use them to create your tic-tac-toe grid by dividing the page into thirds (see Figure 7-1).

The Guide Line tool also lets you identify center points: the center point of the whole layout, the center for a photo, the center of a photo frame. By finding the center point on a page, a carefully placed guide line can also assist you in centering photographs or other page elements.

*Courtesy of Adobe Photoshop Elements 3.0 and Jeanne Wines-Reed (Designed by Sarah Johnson)*

**Figure 7-1:** Placing important page elements at the intersecting lines of a tic-tac-toe grid helps you create a balanced composition.

Select a percentage of enlargement to view the guide line in relation to the page elements you're aligning and stick to it. If you use various percentages, your alignments won't be consistent.

After you set up the Guide Line grid for the purpose of placing your page items (positioning focal items on the grid intersections, for example), you get rid of them. They will have served your purposes and helped you create a well-designed page. Of course, you need to keep working with and adjusting your design elements, but the grid has provided you with a solid, and necessary, starting point. (Snap to Grid, another positioning adjustment tool that will automatically snap a selected page element to a grid line, is discussed in Chapter 14.)

## Creating balance

The purpose of making a scrapbook page is to document a life experience: some event, moment, or memory that you think is worth preserving and that you'd like to share with others. You don't want any part of your story to be overpowered by the page design and layout.

Your understanding of balance as an important design principle plays a big part in helping you create a page where the design elements work together to support and communicate the experience you want to preserve.

Clearly, items that carry more visual weight than others will dominate the design. The "weight" of an item can be determined by its shape, size, color, texture, and placement on the page, as in the following examples:

- ✔ Solid, dark, vibrant, or intense color makes objects appear heavy.
- ✔ Detailed illustrations (patterns), multiple angles or edges, and non-traditional shapes can also project more visual weight.
- ✔ Simply placing an object close to the bottom of the page can increase its visual weight.
- ✔ Objects that are simple in shape, lighter in color, lacking in decorative elements (patterns), or placed high on the page seem visually lighter.

Create a balanced layout by positioning differently weighted elements so that they work with each other instead of against each other. Make certain one area of the page isn't too heavily weighed down. Spread the decorative elements around until the page feels complete and balanced.

## Finding your focal point

In scrapbooking, focal points can refer to main items on each of your scrapbook pages — or to the whole scrapbook. Generally, each scrapbook album has a specific focal point of its own, and all of the pages in the album relate to that focal point in some fashion: supporting it, enhancing it, and playing interesting variations on the stated theme.

Even as the design of an individual scrapbook page supports the focal theme and overall design of the album, that page design still has to establish its own particular focal point to hold the viewer's interest — and that focal point is usually an image (or images). The story unfolds from the photograph. Let your journaling, for example, elaborate on the photograph, teasing out its details and adding background information that relates to the photo.

Every design element on that page should relate to and support the focal point of the page as well as the focal point of the album as a whole so that a viewer can easily understand what it is you want to communicate. Take a look at Figure 7-2 to see a scrapbook page with a clear focal point.

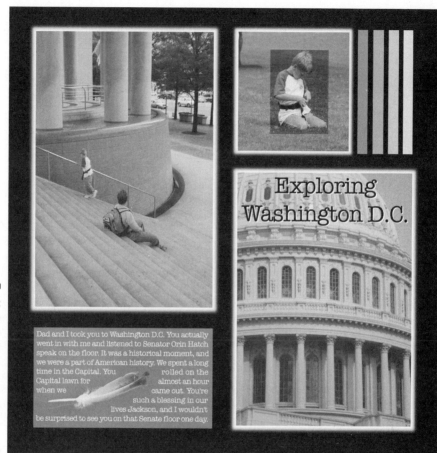

**Figure 7-2:**
The page title (Exploring Washington D.C.) is the clear focal point of this scrapbook page.

Dad and I took you to Washington D.C. You actually went in with me and listened to Senator Orin Hatch speak on the floor. It was a historical moment, and we were a part of American history. We spent a long time in the Capital. You rolled on the Capital lawn for almost an hour when we came out. You're such a blessing in our lives Jackson, and I wouldn't be surprised to see you on that Senate floor one day.

*Courtesy of Jeanne Wines-Reed (Designed by John Stratton)*

## *Using lines and shapes to create structure, depth, and dimension*

Like the real world, the little worlds you create on your scrapbook pages are made of lines and shapes — so your pages don't need to be flat or boring. You can use lines and shapes to give your pages bones, jazz them up, and to construct some "real world" depth and dimension.

Both lines and shapes tell the scrapbook story visually. They guide the eye to look in this or that place or direction and to follow a particular order. And by introducing movement and dimension, they make the story you want to tell on your page more interesting.

### Thinking about lines

Lines exert tremendous influence on the eye, and they can have a significant effect on the mood a scrapbook page conveys. Being aware of how lines impact the viewing process can influence the various ways you use lines in your designs.

Any straight line directs the eye to and from objects. Vertical lines are active and draw the eyes upward toward selected page elements. Horizontal lines are relaxing and coax the eyes from one side to the other.

Curved and wavy lines can add motion and rhythm to a page. They exude personality — expressed in the number of curves they have and/or the magnitude of their arches. Thicker lines have more weight and presence; thinner lines can inject a subtle or dainty touch into your page design.

Lines can quickly draw the eye off the page (and that's not where you want it to go). Take special care that your lines point *toward* page elements rather than *away* from them.

Lines are used to good advantage by scrapbook designers to create a structural context for page items. They often use lines to make borders for and frames around the outside edges of scrapbook pages. They also use lines to create different sizes and styles of frames for images and other page elements. (See *Scrapbooking For Dummies* [Wiley] for an extensive discussion about using lines in scrapbook design.)

Making a grid is one of the all-time best uses of "invisible" lines in design, and using the invisible tic-tac-toe line grid is a big success story in the history of scrapbook design (see "Marking out a grid" in this chapter).

### Seeing shapes

If you think of scrapbook page design as an exercise in organizing different shapes, you may have an easier time designing your layouts. After you place the elements on a page, see what shapes naturally suggest themselves: a triangular shape, an oval, a square, or a circle? The eye flows over curves easily, so rounded shapes tend to produce a calming effect. Angles and corners, on the other hand, add tension to a page design.

Using the tools in your computer program, overlay an "invisible" shape or series of lines on your page, making sure this overlay matches or complements the shapes you think reveal themselves in the elements you're using. Line up your page items along the invisible lines of these naturally occurring shapes or tangents. Many a page design has been dramatically improved when a scrapbooker makes the simple change of lining up all the photos on the page along a shape's or a line's edge.

Shapes can also be used to draw attention to certain points on the page. You can add dimension to a page by overlapping shapes. Try it. You'll find it's an especially effective technique for creating depth and dimension and for introducing a hierarchy of importance in your page elements.

Notice how graphic artists are using lines and shapes in magazines to position the page elements. Try to determine why your favorite pages are better than the ones you're not so crazy about. You can do this by deciding what design principles are being used and how the artist is applying those principles.

## Creating emphasis

When you're designing a scrapbook page, decide what you want to be noticed first. Choose an image that highlights the page's purpose (and relates to the scrapbook's overall focus), such as a person, an occasion, a place, or time. You can, of course, create emphasis with color, size, contrast, and texture by directing lines or shapes toward the focal element or by surrounding it with white space. A big, bright red element with arrows pointing to it is going to be noticed!

One of the most important design considerations for creating emphasis is expressed in that old cliché often used by realtors: location, location, location:

- ✔ Generally speaking, centered page elements are boring. Items placed smack dab in the middle of your page can look isolated and lonely. This arrangement certainly draws attention to an element, but use the centering convention very sparingly — only when you're focusing on an item that's interesting enough to stand on its own. If it's not a *wow* item, you can move it and add other elements, or you can rely on lines and shapes to add more design interest and balance to the page.

- ✔ Most often, the best design solution is to place a single important element off center over one of the tic-tac-toe intersections (the natural point of interest for the page) and support it with lines and shapes. Putting the elements you want to emphasize on the intersections of the tic-tac-toe grid will draw the eye right to them (see "Marking out a grid" in this chapter).

# Enhancing Your Design Strategies with Digital Operations

There are a few digital operations that are very popular, very basic, and used very consistently by digital scrapbookers. Some of these processes are explained in detail in other sections of the book, but since they tie in so closely with page design, we want to mention some of them here too.

## Using scanners and cameras to prepare unusual design elements

Remember: You have to digitize any design element you want to put into a digital scrapbook. You can scan most regular-sized photos plus other images, materials, and all kinds of objects with your scanner. This is one of the quickest ways to get these things into your computer and onto your digital scrapbook page. Sometimes enlisting the help of your digital camera can also help match your digital design elements to the requirements of your layout.

There's more to scanning than the simple procedure we sometimes associate it with. Today's scanners are much more complex than copy machines — and their capabilities have far-reaching implications for design. With a little bit of knowledge, you can use the scanner and scanning operations to significantly enhance your scrapbook designs.

Here are some suggestions relative to the mechanics of scanning:

✔ **Incorporating large flat items into your layout designs:** What happens if the photograph or document you need to scan is too large for the scanner? You can scan it in pieces and stitch the pieces together in your digital-editing program. Or, if this doesn't work, you can take a photo of the oversized piece with your digital camera and then size the image to fit your needs. (The "Solutions for scanning problematic images" sidebar discusses these options in more detail.)

✔ **Digitizing 3-D design elements:** You can scan many of the 3-D objects you want to incorporate into your designs, but you may want to use a camera to capture the image instead. If you do, you may choose to use a colored background so that you get some colored reflections on your object. The project will usually be more successful if you shoot outdoors because your photograph will turn out either greenish or yellowish when you shoot in your home. Depending on the kind of indoor lights you have, you'll get a yellow cast (from incandescent lighting) or a greenish color (from florescent lights).

If you want to (or have to) shoot indoors when you use your camera as a scanner, you can solve the greenish/yellowish tinge problem by purchasing photo white light bulbs from a photography store. These bulbs fit in normal light sockets. If you put them into small lamps, you can adjust the position of the lamps to give you the lighting you need. Most people find they need at least two sources of light for this kind of photography.

One of the most important things to be aware of when you scan unusually shaped or textured embellishments (especially those with rough surfaces or edges) is that you need to protect your scanner bed. Any mark or dust will affect the final image. If you scratch the glass, that scratch will also affect every scan you make from that time forward.

## Descreening printed photos

Scrapbookers can buy photographs, post cards, programs, travel information, and other items to use as design elements in their scrapbooks. A true photograph (one that's reproduced on photographic paper rather than printed) can be easily scanned and used in practically any application, but printed photographs often create problems.

Because a printed photograph is produced with an almost invisible dot pattern, scanning it can produce a *moiré* look (a rosetta or patterned texture all over the photo). Sometimes, you can turn an image a little and reduce the moiré pattern (but not always). This same issue arises when using pictures from books and magazines. Some (but not all) scanning programs have a Descreen feature you can activate to help remedy this situation.

## Solutions for scanning problematic images

You can scan an oversized photograph or document in sections on a scanner and then stitch the sections together in a photo-editing program. To do this, you have to open one image and then adjust your canvas size so you can bring in another scan and line it up with the first scan. The problem with this method is that the edges of the images don't usually line up correctly because the scanner's lens is curved and images distort slightly at the extreme edge of the scanning table. You don't usually notice this unless you try to stitch images together.

To solve this problem, just take your big image outside on a bright day and place it on a white background (white paper usually works better than white cloth because it's flatter). Put your digital camera on a tripod and shoot your large image. For extra-large images, you may have to hang the paper and the image on a wall so you can get the camera far enough away from the image to include the whole thing. After loading the digital photo into your computer and your image editing software, you can cut the white background away from the image if you need to.

Here's how to descreen an image:

1. **Place the item to be descreened in your scanner bed as you usually do.**

2. **Access your scanner by opening the scanner program.**

   You may want to set your scanner up so you can control it through a photo-manipulation program such as Photoshop Elements (see Figure 7-3).

3. **Select the Professional or Advanced version of the operations screen.**

4. **You'll see three options for descreening**.

   The options are expressed in lines per inch (lpi): newspaper (85 lpi), magazine (133 lpi first), or fine prints (175 lpi).

5. **Select one of these options (try the magazine option at 133 lpi) and then scan your image.**

6. **If the scanned image looks good at 100 percent, then you've done it.**

   If the scanned image has patterns all over it, try a different descreening option.

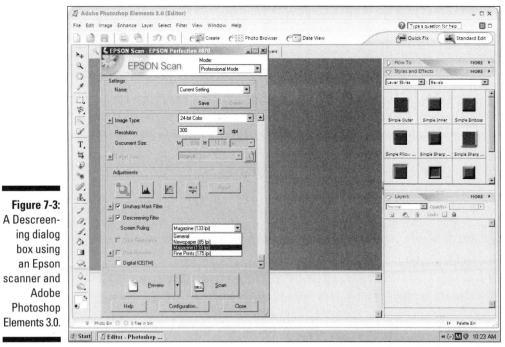

**Figure 7-3:**
A Descreening dialog box using an Epson scanner and Adobe Photoshop Elements 3.0.

*Courtesy of Adobe Photoshop Elements 3.0 and Epson America, Inc.*

Occasionally, the pattern persists no matter which descreening option you try. Open the scanner lid and turn the image slightly. Then follow the listed steps again. Quite often, this fixes the problem.

## *Making your photo a background*

Digital tools make it easy to use a photo as a background that complements your overall page design. (We tell you how to turn your photos into background pages in Chapter 11.)

Background photographs are different from other photos. The best background photos don't compete with the other elements in your page design. The background photo can and should support the theme of the page and the album, but that support should be subtle.

Suppose, for example, you're doing a scrapbook page highlighting some of your grandmother's recipes. You have an old photograph of your grandmother and three of her handwritten recipes to use for the page. You could use a photo of her kitchen wallpaper and clean kitchen table for a background photo. Properly lightened to avoid conflict with the foreground images, the photo could make a wonderful background for the page.

Personalized background photographs can be used with great effect in concert with conventional (commercial) background scrapbook paper. Try using just a section of a photograph as an image "strip" with regular background paper on either side. This is especially useful when the photograph you want to use as a background is too detailed. The partial photograph helps set the mood and the scrapbook paper provides a less detailed background — one that won't compete with the words and images you place on it.

Of course, not all photographs work well as background images. To find the right photograph, look for one that has some interest, but isn't *too* dynamic. Remember — you don't want the background image to dominate or even compete with the other elements that have to go on the page. Chapter 11 provides more advice about choosing photos that make interesting backgrounds.

Some (maybe much) of a background image will be covered. Decide what should show and what can be obscured. If you choose a photo of a group of people, for instance, make certain that your page embellishments don't cover any of their faces. The people are important or you wouldn't be using that photo — and even though you dim the background photo, you don't want to suggest that you're obliterating the people in it. Place your foreground page elements over other, less detailed sections of the background.

## *Tiling your images and photos*

*Tiling* is a simple digital design effect that refers to the process of repeating an image or photo so that it tiles your whole screen or page with identical pictures (see Figure 7-4). Many editing programs have a feature that allows you to automatically tile an image. With other programs, you must copy and manually paste the image in place.

Tiling gives your page rhythm through repetition. The story of the experience you want to convey on your page is emphasized and can take on more personality when you repeat its central image.

**Figure 7-4:**
Notice how
the photos
and the
stars are
tiled.

*Courtesy of Jeanne Wines-Reed (Designed by Sarah Johnson)*

After you have your photos tiled on the page, you can add some photo effects to give the images diversity. For example, you can progressively fade the images from left to right. Or you can change the color of some of the photos. You can even apply various filters to the images (see Chapter 11 for more on how filter functions can enhance your design elements).

## Texturing your photos

A photo editor's texture filters can be applied to digital photographs to give them a wide variety of special looks (see the details in Chapter 11). These texture effects do their magic by picking up on the colors or contrasts of the photo to determine how to apply the texture. Because each photograph is different, the textures will be applied differently, too. This is why there's an adjustment button on many of the filter effects. The adjustment button lets you control (to some degree) how the filter will be applied. You definitely want to use it when you display a series of photographs that all show the same texture effect.

Texturing your photos usually works better as a background effect than it does on your primary photographs. But then, every rule has its exception(s). Sometimes, adding texture to a photo can change a low resolution disaster into something really attractive.

## Collaging or montaging your images and photos

If you like making *collages* (montages), the good news is that photo-editing programs are perfect for this type of project. Using your computer to make digital collages could become a habit!

The Layering feature in photo-editing programs keeps each image separate and allows perfect control for overlapping (see Chapter 4 for more on layering). You can enlarge or reduce images, and you can recolor them or adjust their relative brightness and contrast. You can erase parts you don't like and you can combine images to appear as though they were photographed together. You're not limited by the composition in your photograph. You can add other items: different photos, papers, embellishments, or whatever you think will make your scrapbook page more interesting. For instructions on making a collage (montage), see Chapter 11. For a look at a some lovely collages, see the color insert.

# Chapter 8

# Enhancing Your Pages with Digital Graphic Elements

· · · · · · · · · · · · · · · · · · · · · · · · · · · · · · · · · · · · · · · · · · · · · · · · · · · · ·

## In This Chapter

▶ Going over the basics

▶ Working with clip art

▶ Dealing with drawings

▶ Using photos from outside sources

· · · · · · · · · · · · · · · · · · · · · · · · · · · · · · · · · · · · · · · · · · · · · · · · · · · · ·

*I*n traditional scrapbooking, people collect graphic elements — stickers, stamps, cutouts, clip art, hand drawings, and numerous other materials — to complement their own photos and decorate or embellish their pages. Digital scrapbookers use these elements too, but they, of course, have to get the graphic elements into digital form first.

In this chapter, we give you the lowdown on some digitized graphic elements that will add interest to your digital scrapbook pages and tell you how you can download or order free (or cheap) graphic elements from the Internet (check out the appendix for a list of reputable Web sites loaded with graphic resources).

## First, a Few Technicalities

Digital graphics can include digitized photos shot with digital cameras, graphics downloaded from the Internet, and/or images taken from photo CDs. Other graphics may have been digitized by scanning. (Scrapbookers who scan and use 3-D embellishments, photographs taken by others, and other digitized materials need to always remember to adhere to copyright rules.)

In this chapter, we only touch the surface of all there is to say about digital graphics — but we do give you enough of an overview so that you can feel comfortable integrating graphics into your digital albums from a variety of resources.

## Understanding digital graphics types

There are two basic types of digital graphics: bitmapped graphics (also called raster graphics) and vector-based graphics. High-end editing programs will read these and other kinds of file formats so that you can use the different formats for your projects.

A bitmapped or vector image can be saved in WMF format (a special windows file format). The WMF file format's flexibility has made it increasingly popular. Newer programs such as Photoshop Elements 3.0 can import WMF files — though the older version of the program, Photoshop Elements 2.0, couldn't import them. For more on vector graphics, including how they're different from pixeled images, see *Photoshop Album For Dummies* by Barbara Obermeier (Wiley).

### Bitmapped art

Suppose you want to save a drawing as a *bitmapped* image (a flat image composed of pixels — sometimes referred to as a *pixeled map*). You can do this by digitizing it with a scanner and saving it in a file format such as GIF, TIFF, JPEG, or BMP. You can alter or change a bitmapped image (your digital camera produces bitmapped images by the way) in a photo-editing program such as Photoshop Elements or Digital Image Suite 10. Just remember that if you enlarge a bitmapped image too much, its pixels eventually become blocky looking (as shown in the drawing on the left in Figure 8-1).

### Vector graphics

The advantage of a vector graphic is that, unlike a bitmapped image, it can be enlarged or reduced and the points will remain at the same ratios. That means you can enlarge or reduce vector images without distorting or blurring them.

You create a vector image by placing points on the screen with a computer-drawing program. Your drawing program automatically stretches lines between the points. If the lines are attached to the entire string of points, they create a shape, and you can "fill" this area with color or other elements.

Scrapbooking programs that use vector graphics include Paint Shop Pro and CorelDraw Essentials, and the editing programs that use vector images include Paint Shop Pro, Illustrator, CorelDraw, and Freehand.

**Figure 8-1:**
The flower on the left is an enlarged bitmapped image; note how it's pixilated. The flower on the right is an enlarged but clear vector image.

Full-featured photo-editing programs can work with a great number of different extensions, and a good photo-editor program will read some of these various vector file formats so that you can use the images. If you're not familiar with working with vector files, try importing a file into one of the aforementioned drawing programs to see whether the vector controls work.

If an image is vector-based, it has a proprietary file format from a drawing program: CDR (Corel Draw), AI (Adobe Illustrator), PSP (Paint Shop Pro), and so forth. When you see these file extensions, the vector aspect of the image is usually still active and the image can be manipulated.

## Reviewing the importance of resolution for digital graphics

In working with digital graphics, remember that the number of pixels per inch (ppi) in a digital image makes a difference in how the image will look on your monitor and on a printed page. Many people claim that 150 ppi is a good enough resolution for printing out images or scrapbook pages on a home printer. This is true for some printers, but the new crop of photo-grade print-ers can utilize a full 300 ppi — which will give you a better printout.

An image resolution of 72 ppi is adequate for those projects created strictly for the Web (because they will only be viewed on a computer screen). That means you can make use of many of the low-resolution (or low-res) graphics available on the Web for digital pages that you're not going to print out. (Refer to Chapters 2 and 6 for a more detailed rundown on resolution and printing issues.)

## A word about copyrighting

The Internet is a bottomless well from which scrapbookers can draw count-less images. Digital scrapbookers select and save images they like and use them later in their scrapbook pages. You can capture many of your favorite Internet graphics with a simple right click of your mouse.

But many of the Web images people download are copyright protected. Some of these have been lifted from copyright protected material. The chance of being prosecuted for using such material is low, but that's not the point. No one should use these materials without first contacting the copyright owners to get permission.

Some people think that it's okay to just credit an author for material they use, provided they don't sell the material. Technically, this ain't so! Credits should be listed as per instructions from the owner of the copyright material. You need written permission from the copyright holder, and you must follow his or her instructions regarding proper crediting procedures. These same gen-eral guidelines apply to trademark and patent related items.

Photographers, writers, artists, publishers, musicians, and other creative people copyright their work in order to profit from it. The copyright protects the work, so that others can't publish it — at least not without permission.

If you cut out a page from a book you've purchased and insert it into your scrapbook, you're not violating copyright law. The people who made the book have profited from their efforts and have no claim against you. If, how-ever, you purchase the same book, and make a copy of a page to put in your scrapbook, you're in violation! The publishers can claim you robbed them of an opportunity to sell another book — a book you would have had to buy for the purpose of cutting out material for your scrapbooking projects. (Most probably, a publisher would only bring suit if you copied a page from his book, reproduced it, and then sold copies to other people. In such a case, you'd clearly be profiting from the use of his material.)

## A cautionary tale about the Internet

Digital scrapbooking is coming into its own, and digital graphic resources are beginning to proliferate on the Internet like proverbial wildfires.

Reputable businesses routinely ask for information about age, sex, hobbies, general income, and geographic location. If this information is asked for and given in general terms, it's good for you and good for the businesses. A few precautionary measures are in order, however, including the following:

 ✔ **Personal information:** When looking for free digital scrapbooking material, be cautious about giving out too much detailed personal information. Giving away your address, phone number, or special identification information such as social security number, mother's name, or driver's license number can lead to identity theft or other problems.

 ✔ **E-mail address:** Be discriminate about giving out your e-mail address — unless you want a lot of e-mails and want to risk having your address sold to other companies who will send you even more e-mail. Many people set up an extra e-mail account to handle Internet junk mail.

You also need to watch out for *spyware,* programs that can be installed on your computer without your knowledge to track your Web usage. Spyware gets installed when you visit certain Web sites. Every time you visit the Internet, this spyware sends messages back to its owners telling them which Web sites you visit. New forms of spyware have been developed that can locate more sensitive information, such as bank account numbers or other personal data stored on your computer.

Check into spyware protection software (some of which you can get for free off the Internet). This software either stops the spyware from getting on your computer or cripples it so that it can't send your information back to unscrupulous Internet predators.

# Manipulating Clip Art

*Clip art* is a generic term for ready-made drawings or illustrations. Traditional scrapbookers differentiate among clip art, templates, background papers, and embellishments. In the computer world, though, all of these elements are used in the same manner: digitally. When you learn how to use one type of digital graphic element, you know how to use them all.

## Looking for printed clip art

When clip art books first came out, people literally cut (clipped) the images out of the book and glued them onto a page of paper. Now they can copy and paste digital clip art images (see Figure 8-2). Some scrapbookers still use the old-style clip art books and scan the images into their computers. When these images are colored, they take on a whole new look. It's also simple to enlarge them because they don't usually have dot patterns.

Printed clip art books can be found in hobby or stationary stores. They're quite inexpensive and as a rule, don't have any use restrictions (this is because the images in most of these booklets *are made* to be cut out and used in publications). The clip art is usually organized according to themes, such as patriotism, holidays, working men, frames and borders, and so forth. You may find the booklets contain just the kind of embellishments or illustrations you need.

**Figure 8-2:** Notice the clip art owl being placed on a scrapbook page using the Jasc Paint Shop Pro program.

*Courtesy of Jasc Paint Shop Pro*

A good place to begin your search for clip art books is at www.clippix.com. They're priced from about $5 and up and relate to all sorts of topics. Also look on www.amazon.com for a large selection of clip art books and CDs that feature many old-style drawings and prints (especially useful for heritage scrapbook pages). This listing is redundant, so limit your searches by asking for specific kinds of clip art material. For additional clip art resources, refer to the appendix at the end of this book.

## Gathering clip art from the Internet

One of the most popular fee-based clip art sites is www.clipart.com. Most of the clip art you find on this and other Internet sites is made for use on the Web. It's very small (usually less than 3 inches) and it has a low resolution (72 to 100 ppi). The small file size allows the images to be transferred quickly over the Internet. Although this type of clip art works great for a Web scrapbook or e-mail graphic, it doesn't enlarge without distorting and won't work well for a printed scrapbook.

## Using clip art

Finding an appropriate clip art image for a particular design scheme amid all the images in a clip art library is often a challenge. Some clip art collections come with a reference book; others have a search function that helps you find what you're looking for. Before buying a collection of clip art, read the instructions and talk to salespeople to find out whether you can easily access the images.

Many types of clip art can't be enlarged very much without badly distorting the images. It's true that clip art created with vector graphics can be enlarged or reduced without sacrificing quality, but your program has to be able to handle vector graphics saved in the format offered by the clip art company. For details about vector graphics, including how they're different from pixeled images, see the section "Understanding digital graphics types" earlier in the chapter.

Here's how to insert a clip art image:

1. **Make sure you've saved the clip art you want for your scrapbook page somewhere on your desktop or your hard drive.**

2. **From the Edit section on the Menu bar, select either Open or Import.**

   Which of these you choose will depend on the type of clip art and the photo-editing program you're using.

3. **Use the Browse function to find the clip art image you want, and then select it.**

   The clip art image will open itself in a new (or second) document.

4. **Select that image by going to the Select section of the Menu bar and choosing the Select All feature.**

   You then see a broken line around the new clip art image.

5. **Go to the Edit section of the Menu bar and use either the Copy or Cut feature to get the image from the new document.**

6. **Now select your original document (probably your scrapbook page) and go again to the Edit section of the Menu bar.**

7. **Choose Paste to place the clip art image onto your page.**

8. **Reselect the new (or second) clip art image document and close it without saving.**

9. **The clip art image you pasted onto your original document or onto one of its layers can now be adjusted or placed just like any other element on your page.**

   See Chapter 10 for further editing suggestions.

# Incorporating Illustrations and Drawings

Many scrapbookers want to use high-quality illustrations or drawings for their scrapbook pages. They want these images to be reasonably large and they want the detail to be clear when their pages are printed out. What's more, most scrapbookers want to use this material for free.

You may have a hard time finding free high-res illustrations and drawings online. Most of the better sites offering illustrations or drawings (either on CDs or by subscription) charge for their images. However, if you look long enough, you *can* find some free illustrations and drawings that work for print applications.

Check out www.freebyte.com. This site is dedicated to finding the best free sites on the Internet. If you click on the link for clip art, images, and photos, you'll find some good links to investigate.

Two good sites for illustrations and drawings are www.barrysclipart.com and www.gif.com. Both offer the same clip art collection, but it's a good collection and the images can be used in large sizes (most are about 3 x 4 inches at 200 ppi).

One reason many people like using photo-manipulation programs such as Photoshop Elements and Paint Shop Pro is that illustrations and drawings can be colorized (and otherwise manipulated) very easily (see Figure 8-3). The coloring procedure is worth looking into because it can very quickly convert a plain illustration into an eye catcher. (Try sizing and coloring your hand drawings after you've scanned them — you'll be amazed at the great results.)

Though the following stepped-out technique works best for black and white illustrations and drawings, it can be adapted to color images. Here's how you do it:

1. **To open the line drawing into your photo-editing program, choose File and then Open from the Menu bar.**

2. **Then choose Browse — this will take you through your computer files until you find the image file you want.**

3. **Select the image file.**

**Figure 8-3:** This fish outline has been improved by coloring in its middle stripe and the sea-weed using Jasc Paint Shop Pro.

*Courtesy of Jasc Paint Shop Pro*

4. **Go to the Image section of your Menu bar and choose the Mode feature.**

   If the illustration or the drawing is listed as grayscale, change it to RGB (red, green, and blue; designates the computer's color selection system) so that you can add color.

5. **Now open the Contrast/Brightness feature in the Enhance or Adjust section on the Menu bar.**

6. **Make the image as bright as possible and the lines as dark as possible.**

   You do this because many outlines have been *anti-aliased* (the center of the line is black while the outer pixels are grayed so you don't see the jaggy edge of a pixel formed line). By increasing the brightness and contrast of the image, you have made the gray edges of the lines as dark and sharp as possible.

7. **Select a color from the color picker and use the Color Fill feature (paint bucket) from the side toolbar to fill in an enclosed area with color.**

8. **If the color flows outside the enclosed area, select Edit on the Menu bar and Undo the color fill.**

   The enclosed area is evidently not totally closed. If your color doesn't flow outside the colored area, continue to Step 10.

9. **Use your Magnifying tool (on the side toolbar) to find where the outline is broken and then close the opening with the Pencil tool.**

   Try filling the enclosed area again. If all the breaks are closed, the fill will work properly.

10. **Continue to fill areas of the illustration or drawing with various colors until the image is properly colored.**

If you don't like how a color looks, undo the color and then refill with a new color. Putting one color over another often affects the outline as well as the area you want to fill. This is due to the fill control, which is in reality filling an area based on the value difference between the white fill area and the black outline. If you fill in the white area with green, for example, and then try to refill the area with red, there won't be enough value difference between the green fill and the black outline for the program to discern a contrast. You can adjust the tolerance and complete the operation, but it will be a trial-and-error process.

You can scan your child's illustrations and drawings into the computer too — not to recolor them but for the purpose of controlling the size of the drawings so you can neatly incorporate them into your scrapbook page designs (as shown in Figure 8-4). See Chapter 11 for more information about making hand drawings to use as embellishments.

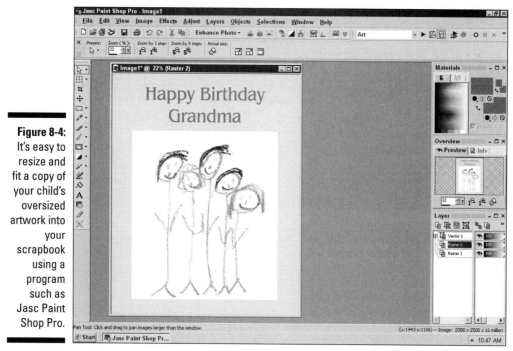

**Figure 8-4:**
It's easy to resize and fit a copy of your child's oversized artwork into your scrapbook using a program such as Jasc Paint Shop Pro.

Courtesy of Jasc Paint Shop Pro and Shay Cornia

# Using Photos from the Internet

You can access some reasonably high-res images for free on the Internet, but you have to download them to see what kind of quality you're getting. Most scrapbooking sites have a gallery that gives instructions about how to use their materials.

Surprisingly, you may have a fairly easy time obtaining high-quality photographs off the Web. Naturally, you can find many low-res photographic images, but we know of several good sources for historic images and a handful of good sites for getting contemporary color photos for personal use (not commercial use) as well — see the appendix. If you visit enough of these sites, you should eventually gather a collection of extremely useful free material.

## Downloading issues

You may have to experiment a little to download the image you need. Each site works just a little differently. Usually, you have to click your mouse on the image and then a larger image appears. Sometimes, you download by right clicking on the image and saving it to your desktop. Other times, you click a download button to get the proper image for your download.

In some cases, special download arrangements have been provided so that the user can download a high-res version of the image. Sometimes, an image is so important to you that you want to use it no matter what its size. If you can't locate a high-res download or it's impossible to grab the image from the Web, you can still get most of these images just by e-mailing the Web master and requesting the image. Make sure to describe how you plan to use it. Many Web masters or site owners will e-mail you a usable copy of the image with no strings attached.

Some of these images will take forever to download if you only have a dial-up Internet connection. One solution is to download images such as this when you go to bed. Then, even if the download takes up to 8 hours, you won't mind at all.

If you find yourself downloading many large images, you may decide that it's worth the extra cost to get a faster Internet connection. However, be sure to ask plenty of questions about the new connection — because in some locations, certain "fast" connections aren't that much faster than a dial-up connection.

## Stocking up on stock images

As is the case with clip art, stock images can be found in a variety of different places — including the Internet and stock CDs and DVDs that you can purchase. Stock photos are useful: they're professional quality images; and, they often come in themed packages that work well with many scrapbook projects.

Stock images don't usually include people because the hairstyles and clothing date the images so quickly. If you want people in your photos, you have to take your own people photos or purchase them from a commercial stock photo service such as www.istockphoto.com.

Once again, look at www.freebyte.com and www.morguefile.com and refer to the clipart, images, and photos. Various stock photographers place their images at sites like this so they can get their names out to designers across the country. Scrapbookers can use these images without having to pay for them because regular scrapbooks aren't commercial items. By the way, if you're working on a commercial project, you'll have to pay to use these images. (Images on this site come in different resolutions — the resolution or image size is listed on the tag under each photograph.)

## Tapping into state archival sources

Unlike some of the images in the national photo archives, state photo archives don't usually allow you to use their images for free. One nice thing is that you can often find what images they have on the Internet and then arrange to have prints made for a reasonable cost. After you have the print, there's not usually a copyright that would stop you from using the image in your scrapbook. Sometimes, by asking the right questions, you can find photo archives run by university or historical groups that have already scanned their images and will allow you to download these images for free or for a minimal cost (especially if you furnish your own CDs).

Stock photo CD or DVD collections are usually divided into popular categories, including vacation spots, holiday activities, sports, animals, and so forth. The collections are pricey, but they often offer exceptionally high-quality photographic images that are easy to use and simple to manipulate. They look (and often are) professional, although like clip art images, some of these stock digital photos are used by so many others that they become ho-hum.

Check to find out whether you have to abide by specific attribution rules before you can use one of these collections.

# Chapter 9

# Making a Statement with Basic Text

## In This Chapter

▶ What's up with printing, type, and fonts?

▶ Avoiding font problems

▶ Coordinating text with album design

*I*deally, a scrapbook album's photos, memorabilia, accessories, and embellishments all work together to convey its story. In this chapter, we show you how basic type fonts, headlines, handwritten text, and various decorative typographic elements can also help tell your stories.

How long text will last, how it's used, and how to design with text are all important issues for the scrapbooker. But clearly, the words in an album are hardly an end unto themselves. Scrapbookers make the best use of typography when words and letters support rather than dominate the whole album design. Here, we familiarize you with what typography consists of, give you tips on avoiding type problems, and show you how to use, manipulate, and incorporate text into your digital scrapbook designs. (For more advanced text techniques, see Chapter 12.)

## Translating Text Terms

We think it's important to review the following terms before you begin working with text in your digital scrapbook:

✔ **Point size:** *Point size* refers to how large the type is. Most people size body text type at 11 or 12 points for easy reading, and use larger sizes for titles and headings — anywhere from 18 to over 100 points!

✔ **Ascenders and descenders:** These terms refer to the parts of a letter that go up and down (like branches and roots) from the letter's trunk. A small case "h" has a tall ascender coming up from the trunk of the letter. A small case "p" has a descender coming down from the main part of that letter. Being mindful of ascenders and descenders is important when you select fonts. Fonts that don't have pronounced ascenders and descenders are difficult for some people to read — they may not, for example, be able to tell the difference between an "h" and an "n."

✔ **Alignment:** Note how the text on this page has an even left margin. The first letter of each sentence of a paragraph is lined up with all the first letters of the other sentences in the paragraph. The right margin, however, is jagged. All scrapbooking programs will allow you to set your type ragged right, justified, or centered. If you chose Ragged Right (flush left), your text will align like the text in this paragraph you're reading. If you chose Justified, the text will line up on both the left and the right margins. Sometimes, you may want your lines of text Centered on a page, in which case each line of text will be centered according to the length of the words in the line.

✔ **Line spacing or leading:** Even though most scrapbook programs use *auto-leading* (automatic spacing between lines of text), you can change that spacing, or leading, if you want to. Trying these two procedures will give you the hang of how you can manually control line spacing:

• **To space your lines closer together or farther apart:** Just put each line of text in a different text box (we discuss typing in text boxes later in the "Keying text into your digital layout" section); then use the arrow keys to nudge the text boxes closer to or farther away from each other. This trick is great for adjusting titles and small blocks of text.

• **To make sure all your text lines are an (exactly) equal distance from each other:** Draw a box that identifies the space between the first and second lines of your text, making sure that the box clears the bottom of the letters on the first line and the tops of the letters on the second line. Use that box as a "spacer" between all the rest of your text lines — placing the top of the box under one line and moving the next line up until it touches the bottom of the box. Using this "measurement box" technique ensures that all your lines are evenly spaced (leaded).

If you want to use a program for your scrapbooking that has sophisticated leading adjustment features, we recommend CorelDraw Essentials 2. At $70 to $80, it's the only program we know about under $350 that has these features. If you decide you want a high-end program for text manipulation and other scrapbooking tasks, we suggest you look at Adobe Illustrator CS2 ($350 to $400).

✔ **Kerning:** *Kerning* refers to the amount of space between two adjacent letters or two adjacent words on a line. You may want to expand the kerning so the text is easier to read or tighten it to fit more words on one line. Most programs use a default kerning setting, but you can adjust the kerning manually by putting letters in different text boxes — so you can move them closer together or farther apart from each other without distorting the letters of the text (see the "Keying text into your digital layout" section later for more information about text boxes). Naturally, this isn't something you want to do very often.

Some high-end programs include a *Tracking* feature, which allows you to easily adjust the kerning (CorelDraw Essentials 2 is the only program priced under $100 that offers a Tracking feature). People use this feature mostly for titles, although they sometimes adjust the space between letters to make a word look better.

# Working with Fonts

Although fonts can play an important role in text design, they often present a real challenge to the beginning digital scrapbooker. For one thing, font terminology seems strange (and it is). For another, different programs seem to have different versions of the same or similar fonts (and they do!).

In this section, we tell you what fonts are, explain the two important types of font (body and display), fill you in on how your computer uses the fonts, and finally, tell you where you can find some fabulous fonts to use in your scrapbooks.

## The origins of printed texts and the fonts that made them

In the mid-15th century, Johannes Gutenberg fashioned some reversed wooden letters, set them on a table, and locked them in place. Then he inked the tops of the letters and covered them with a piece of paper, pressing the paper onto the letters. Thus it was that Gutenberg created the first *printing press.*

Wooden letters proved to be less than satisfactory as the demand for printed texts grew, and it wasn't long before someone began making letter molds and casting them in metal. This process was named after the French word for casting *(fonte)*. Most foundries made only one letter style, often naming the style for the foundry itself (or for the city where it was located). Foundries who made the most popular font(e) styles were also the most prosperous.

## Going over some font basics

Different font styles are used to give variety and character to the printed page, and the digital scrapbooker needs to consider whether different fonts are appropriate for specific projects. Some fonts are fancy, some are plain. Some are easy to read, but other, more decorative fonts, may not be (see Figure 9-1).

Most body font characteristics can be manipulated to fit into your overall design. It's easier to read a font when its letters have a variety of thicknesses. Fonts with *serifs* (tails) are usually easier to read because the serif helps your eye follow the line of text. Of course, the boldness of a font also helps the reader see the letter properly, although sometimes too much bold text can be a deterrent to easy reading.

Some of the more popular fonts include Times, Garamond, Souvenir, Helvetica, Futura, and Arial. Actually, these are examples of font "families." A font, on the other hand, is a *single style* of lettering — so that a regular weight Times is considered to be one single font while the italic version of Times (the same type family) is also considered as a totally separate font. The bold, bold italic, condensed, or condensed italic are also separate fonts — even though they all belong to the Times font family.

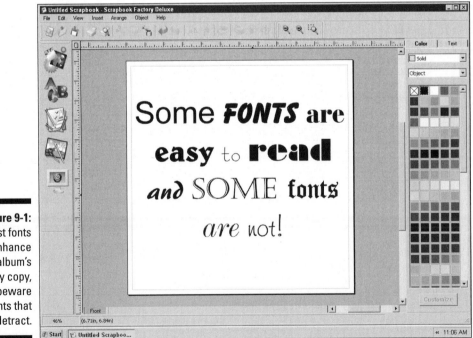

**Figure 9-1:**
Most fonts enhance your album's body copy, but beware of fonts that detract.

*Courtesy of Art Explosion Scrapbook Factory Deluxe*

---

## Upper and lower cases

When the early printers bought a set of letters, they kept them in specially designed drawers (or cases, as they were called). Letters that were used often (like "e") were allotted bigger sections than those that weren't used much (like "q"). Capital letters were grouped in one drawer (or case) and regular letters were grouped in another drawer (case). Printers usually put the capital letters in the top case and the regular letters in a lower case. This is where we get the terms *upper case* and *lower case* letters.

---

There are two parts to each font: the screen font and the printer font. The *screen font* is often represented by a suitcase icon with the name of the font family as the file name — such as Garamond. The printer fonts, usually represented by a big letter icon, include the font name and its particular single styles — such as *Garamond Bold Italic* and *Garamond Roman*.

When you copy font files from one location to another, you need to include both the screen and the printer fonts (if you don't, you create a *broken* or incomplete font). When you include *only* a screen font, you can see the font on your computer, but the printout looks rough and jagged. If you only save your printer fonts, you won't be able to see the font in your program.

## *Exploiting the design possibilities of body and display fonts*

When selecting fonts for your text, divide your selections into two categories: body fonts and display fonts. Use the body fonts (which have to be easy to read), for large blocks of body copy. Use the more decorative display fonts to support a style for the scrapbook page — especially for headlines or subheads. Even though some of these fonts are hard to read, that doesn't matter too much when they're used so sparingly.

The realm of display type is a wonderland for digital scrapbookers — who use them to support design scheme and to add character and flair to their texts. You've seen fonts that look Western, German, or Old English, and others that are reminiscent of the Roaring Twenties or some other historical period. These display fonts can give your page character and style, and as a scrapbooker, you'll probably want as many of these as you can find.

## Understanding how your computer stores and copies fonts

Initially, people envisioned the computer more as a typewriter than a printing press — so the first computer fonts looked like typewriter fonts. Eventually, different font styles were incorporated into the programs and manufacturers created new fonts to get people to buy their new programs.

Most programs use the fonts that have been installed in your computer's system folder. And when you buy a program that comes with new fonts, these new fonts are automatically installed in your system folder when you install the program. Any other programs on your computer can also use these system fonts. So when you use a font with your word processor, you can copy the text into your scrapbook program and the same font will appear on your screen.

Font storage slows down your computer start-up time, so you don't want to store too many fonts in your system folder. Given the fact that start ups generally have progressively gotten slower with each new program release, you won't want to slow down your computer even more by loading too many fonts.

## Forestalling font problems

Fonts may become problematic when you try to share your scrapbook pages. Even when you and your friend have identical scrapbook programs, the special fonts on the pages you send your friend will look different on her monitor if those fonts aren't on her system.

The best general solution for font problems is to save your scrapbook page in a format that doesn't need to access fonts to show them — and that would be the PDF format. The fonts in a PDF file are embedded as you create them — they're actual graphics that don't change. (We need to mention that there *are* a few fonts that can't be embedded because of the way they're made. When you send or share your PDF files, check to make sure the receiver isn't experiencing any font problems.)

The advantages of sharing a page in the PDF file format: anyone can view your page, it looks the same on any computer, and it can be printed out. (The only thing you can't do with a PDF file is make corrections or changes to the page elements.)

## Sending copies of your fonts

When scrapbookers share pages with friends, they sometimes include copies of the fonts they used on the pages along with their scrapbook files. This solves the font problem for the receiver, *but it is illegal* to give other people copyright-protected fonts. Commercial printers get around this copyright problem by claiming to throw away the fonts after they finish printing your project. In this way, they get to use the font for the person who evidently has a right to use it, but neither the font owner nor the printer can be accused of stealing or giving away fonts.

Here are a few other pointers to help you avoid potential font problems:

- ✔ **Because fonts are opened and used so often, they're especially susceptible to corruption.** A corrupt font is difficult to identify and often impossible to fix. The cheaper fonts tend to go bad more quickly than the name-brand fonts, so it's wise to use only name-brand fonts on your system.

- ✔ **Fonts can crash your programs.** One corrupt lower case *e* in a large document made a program crash every time the computer operator scrolled past the page it was on. It took hours to find the single corrupt letter that affected the integrity of an entire document.

- ✔ **It's easy for a hacker to stick a virus onto a font but hard for you to get rid of it.** If you like to download fonts off the Internet, always check them for computer viruses by using a virus detection program.

## *Finding fantastic fonts*

Today, you can buy CDs from companies that specialize in publishing and creating fonts; download expensive, inexpensive, or free fonts from the Internet (see the appendix); or even make your own fonts (see Chapter 12). Many fonts are well crafted, but some aren't. Be picky about which ones you choose to put on your system.

Selling fonts is big business — you have to be careful not to "borrow" copyrighted fonts. And be sure to select a font that will work with your computer (PC or Mac). Reputable font sellers will always indicate whether their fonts are made for PCs or Macs.

You may find a Mac font you want to use on your PC (or vice versa). Font conversion programs will sometimes work, but not always. There are at least four major types of computer font systems — and many, many subcategories, versions, and brands. Getting everything to match up properly with converted fonts is quite difficult. People who really know fonts don't usually use converted fonts unless they absolutely have to.

### Purchasing font collections

Fonts often come in themed packages (scary fonts, kids' fonts, calligraphic fonts, scripts, you name it!). You can even find fonts that highlight characteristics of different cultures, languages, events, holidays, or time periods.

Here are a few font-shopping guidelines:

- Fonts can be expensive if you buy from well-established font-making companies such as Adobe or Berthold, and they can be less expensive if you deal with small, independent artists, companies, or office supply stores.

- The more reputable the font company, the less trouble you're likely to have with the fonts. However, you can often get more creative fonts from the smaller, independent companies.

- The size of the type should be adequate so the reader doesn't have to squint or use a finger to follow along when reading. Look for a reasonably heavy font with both thick and thin parts to the letters.

- Serif fonts (those with "tails" on the ends of the letters) are usually easier to read than texts without tails. This is because the tails help the eye follow along from word to word.

### Downloading fonts

Good online sources for fonts include: www.1001freefonts.com, www.acidfonts.com, www.fontfreak.com, www.bertholdtypes.com, www.twopeasinabucket.com/freefonts.asp, and www.adobe.com.

When downloading fonts from the Internet, be careful to download only from reputable sites. It's easy to get a virus or a bunch of unwanted e-mail when you download from some locations.

## Incorporating Text into Your Scrapbook

The *journaling* (the hand written or computer-typed story) for a scrapbook album takes some planning and organizing. If you include a brief outline of your album's whole story in a sketch or mock-up book, you may find it easier to position your photos and journaling text (see Chapter 4). Which photos you use and where you decide to place them always gives you ideas about how large each of your text sections need to be. See Chapter 12 for advice on formatting long sections of text (or journaling) in digital scrapbooks.

Notice what graphic artists do with type: how they give it personality and character. You may want to start saving interesting type examples in a file so you can try to duplicate the effects you like on your scrapbook pages.

## Keying text into your digital layout

Scrapbooking programs use two methods for inserting text into a design. In the first, you click to open a text window where you type the text into a text box and then apply the text onto the design. If you need to alter the text, you have to open the text box again to work on the text. The second method allows you to set your type directly onto the design in a text box that is just a dashed line. Naturally, the second method is easier to use.

Although you can type directly onto your pages, many digital scrapbookers prefer to use a word processing program. A good word processing program can help you with the writing basics: spelling, sentence construction, and even punctuation. And it's easy to create a word text document, manipulate it to fit into your design scheme, and then copy and paste it onto your scrapbooking program. You can make quite a few design moves on text in most basic word processing programs, including the following:

- ✔ **Indicate your margin justification preference.** Flush left, justified (flush right), or centered.

- ✔ **Change the color of the text (see Figure 9-2).** Use the Insert Text/Color selections or look for an uppercase A on the Menu bar that lets you change the color of highlighted letters or words. When you click on the A (or the little arrow on the side of the A), a dropdown palette of colors appears. If you see only a limited number of colors on this menu, look for an option that says More Colors. Select this option and you can find just about any color you need.

- ✔ **Select a font and adjust its size.** When you select a font, it will appear on your screen in either a default size (usually 12 point) or in the size of the text you were last working with. Adjust the size of the font to support your immediate purposes. Headlines should be the largest, subheads a medium size, and body copy and captions the smallest.

- ✔ **Use the pseudo font controls on the Menu bar.** You'll see a **Bold** and *Italic* and sometimes an <u>Underline</u> icon. You give your text added impact when you use (*not* overuse) these controls. You can even make a bold font bolder by also adding the pseudo bold to it.

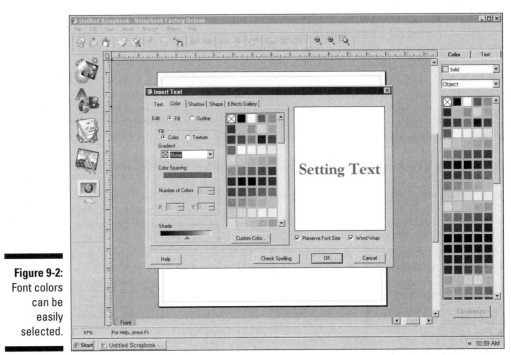

*Courtesy of Art Explosion Scrapbook Factory Deluxe*

**Figure 9-2:**
Font colors
can be
easily
selected.

A *pseudo font* is a computer-generated alteration of a font. When pseudo fonts are printed out, they often look different than they do on the screen. This is because they need to be interpreted by the printer. In most cases, it's best to use the actual fonts rather than the pseudo fonts, but the pseudo fonts can be helpful in certain circumstances. For example, some fonts don't have a bold font available. The only way you can get a bold font is to use the pseudo font. You can also apply pseudo fonts when you need a bolder-than-bold font. If you select the actual bold font from the font menu and then apply the pseudo bold on top of that, you get the extra-bold you want.

## Using handwritten text in digital scrapbooks

If you plan to print and then write in your digital albums, find out how different writing instruments will affect the appearance of your text. Fountain pens have a look all their own, and calligraphic pens can turn a simple handwriting style into something quite elegant. Practice a little with the special nylon-tipped calligraphic pens that have become so popular in recent years. They're easy to use because you don't have to worry about recharging your pen with ink.

Also, be mindful of the type of paper you use for printing your digital pages (Chapter 2 includes additional advice about paper quality). If you plan to write on the pages, print them on a lightweight parchment-colored paper and write with inkwell-dipped pens — the text looks great! Or use a slick coated paper and write on it with metallic colored ink. The coated paper will make the metallic ink look spectacular. As a rule, matte paper gives ink a flatter appearance, and coated or shiny paper makes ink look brighter. Be careful when putting ink on shiny paper — ink often takes longer to dry on this type of paper.

You may want to handwrite and then digitize your handwriting by scanning it for your digital scrapbook. If you do this, increasing the contrast of the document will make it easier to read. Include a few flourishes and you can create some interesting handwritten embellishments. Many of the antique-oriented clip art collections include old-fashioned swirls, designs, and flourishes you can copy to incorporate into your handwriting efforts.

But no matter how good the penmanship, a handwritten text can't compete with a good body copy font for easy reading and for quick integration into a digital design scheme. What you can do, if you're keen on using your own handwriting in your digital albums, is to have your handwriting made into fonts so you can "type" in your own handwriting (see Chapter 12 for more information about designing your own fonts).

# Part III
# Taking Your Digital Scrapbook to the Next Level

The 5th Wave                    By Rich Tennant

"I love the way you've montaged Grandpa's WANTED poster with cousin Doug's arrest record."

## In this part . . .

If you think that an elite design group carefully guards advanced design tips and secrets, think again! *You* can upgrade the quality of your scrapbook pages as easily as the next guy: by improving the look of your photos, making extraordinary backgrounds and foregrounds, incorporating cutting-edge text designs, and even venturing into the audio/visual scene. These advanced digital techniques (and the tools you need to do them) require some study and practice, but the stunning, professional-looking results are well worth your effort.

# Chapter 10

# Tackling Advanced Photo Correction

## In This Chapter

▶ Checking your photo-editing software

▶ Getting to know cloning and healing

▶ Mastering color correction

▶ Retouching tools

▶ Removing extras

*P*hotographs play a starring role in scrapbooking, which is one reason digital scrapbooking has become such a hot item. Scrapbookers love the fact that after you digitize (or scan) a photograph, you can do practically anything with it — even alter its basic characteristics. You can stretch it, change its color, size, or shading, and use filters on it to get painterly effects. You can even draw and paint on it — whatever suits your fancy.

Sometimes, you want to use advanced photo manipulation on your photographs just to play around with design. Other times, you may have more practical reasons for using your program to manipulate images — such as repairing a photo damaged by water, fire, mold, or other deteriorating processes. *Or,* you may just want to remove a few things: an old boyfriend, some extra pounds, a couple of laugh lines, or a double chin.

Using advanced photo manipulation on your original digital (or scanned-in hard-copy photographs) isn't that difficult — after you understand how the various tools work and how to manage the processes.

In Chapter 6, we provide basic photo processing tips. In this chapter, we tell you about some more advanced photo correction tools and techniques, explain what they're best suited for, and let you know about the results you can expect. We also walk you step-by-step through a few advanced photo manipulation procedures.

# Making Sure Your Photo-Editing Software Is Up to the Challenge

You will probably choose the program or programs you use to edit your digital photos based on your budget, your skill level, and the tools you need to build the kind of scrapbook pages or albums you want.

If you want to keep things simple, you can process your images with the photo-editing software that came with your scanner or with any of the beginner software options suggested in Chapter 1, which allow you to resize your photos, adjust resolution, crop, eliminate red eye, and the like. Flip to Chapter 6 for more information about these basic photo-editing techniques.

But if you're ready to try out more advanced techniques, you may need to invest in more advanced photo-editing software we suggest in Chapter 3 (Adobe Photoshop Elements, CorelDraw Essentials 2, and Paint Shop Pro 9 are the most feature-rich in terms of making scrapbook pages). You may also opt to purchase a computer drawing program — especially if you like to draw and create images and other scrapbook design elements from scratch. Adobe Illustrator or Macromedia Freehand are two very popular drawing programs.

You can download several low cost or even free photo-editing programs off the Internet. Some of these are surprisingly good and include many of the same photo-editing tools found in the higher priced photo-editing programs. If you're not planning to dive too deeply into digital scrapbooking right now, downloading one of these programs allows you to test the waters. To explore this option, go to www.tucows.com and type *photo editing* in the search window. Be sure to select the proper type of editing program because the search engine often gives you all sorts of related programs. Look for a good freeware photo-editing program. The rating system will aid you in selecting a one.

If you plan to buy a commercial product, download a trial version of the software if they offer one. For example, on the Microsoft Web site (www.microsoft.com) you can find their Digital Images Suite 10 or the Picture it! Premium 10 program. You can download these programs and try them and even compare them with other programs, before you actually purchase one.

You can even experiment with using more than one program to design your pages. Many skilled professional graphic artists achieve special page effects by using Adobe Photoshop, Adobe Illustrator, and Quark or Adobe InDesign on the same project — because one program can do things the others can't. Some scrapbook artists are pushing the digital scrapbook design envelope by using multiple programs to get stunning effects.

Working in several programs can be costly — not just in terms of the *very* high price of software tools, but also in terms of the time it takes to master them.

# Introducing Cloning and Healing

We've already briefly touched on cloning in Chapter 6, explaining how to select a piece of a photo and use it to fill in a damaged area. Here we cluster the Cloning tool with the Healing tool, which performs similar operations with slightly different effects.

## Attack of the Cloning tool

To *clone* is to duplicate. The Cloning tool selects color and texture from one area of a photograph or graphic and duplicates it — transferring that selection to another area of the image. You brush this piece onto the desired area using the Cloning tool or Cloning stamp — usually found on an editing program's side toolbar.

The Cloning tool can restore photos by fixing dust spots, scratches, or tears or it can remove unwanted elements in a photo by covering them over with the color or texture that you choose — because you don't want to create "holes" in your image. For example, say you do want to get rid of an old boyfriend in that photo where *you* look gorgeous. You can use the Clone tool to clone appropriate sections of the photo and superimpose them on your ex until he disappears. For additional ways to remove unwanted objects see the "Cutting Out Unwanted Objects" section later in the chapter.

You can also use the Cloning tool to add elements. With a little practice, you can even draw in the toe of a shoe or some other item in the photo that may not have ever been there. Or, you can take specific elements from the photograph and duplicate them in other areas. For example, if you have a picture of a tree without many leaves on it and you want the tree to have more leaves, you can clone the leaves from one area to another and fill your tree with leaves. Here's how:

1. **Click on the Clone tool and place the cursor over the area (piece) you want to duplicate.**

2. **Click the Alt key and then click the left mouse button.**

   You have now selected the color/texture piece.

3. **Click the left mouse button again over the location on the photo you need to overlay.**

**4. Without releasing the mouse button, brush the color/texture from your selected location onto the new area.**

You can adjust the size of the Clone tool brush to match the requirements of the job you're doing. With Cloning, you can choose Brush Size and Brush Characteristics (hard, scratchy, or soft edge). Some programs allow you to manipulate and control the opacity of your Clone tool, so that you can make images more or less opaque — that is, you can let more or less light into the images (a *translucent* image has a lot of light, an *opaque* image doesn't).

## Healing damaged images

Not long ago, Adobe Photoshop came out with a new tool called a Healing tool. It was so popular it soon found its way into Photoshop Elements 3.0. It works like the Cloning tool found in most good photo-editing programs, but often does a better job of blending color and retaining texture as it heals imperfections.

Even though this very "smart" tool can blend color and texture so well you won't see where the tool was applied, you still need the regular Cloning tool. That's because the hard edge of the Healing tool doesn't let you draw in missing parts as easily as does the Clone edge when doing photo repair. But the Healing tool does do a better blending job — in some instances, even better than an Airbrush tool can do.

The Healing tool is one of those tools you have to use to see if it works for the situation you want to correct, but remember that many programs don't have this feature, so you don't want to spend all day looking for it.

If you want to use it, try the Healing tool for the following:

- ✔ Photo repairs on a face — it doesn't produce the splotchy look that can result from using the regular Cloning tool.

- ✔ Repairs to areas where the colors or textures are complicated.

- ✔ Beautifying your subjects by brushing out folds, wrinkles, and blemishes — you can make anyone look like a fashion model!

## Adjusting Color

You can use your scanner software to change a color image to a black-and-white image — but not vice versa (see this technique in action in the color section of this book). To change the color image to black and white, scan it using the 256 grayscale setting.

If you scan a black and white image with the color (RGB) setting, it will remain black and white — but you can use your photo-editing software to add color by using the Paint Brush, Airbrush, or Paint Bucket to fill in different areas of the black-and-white image with selected colors.

With most photo editors, you can alter the color of an image with several different tools. The Hue, Saturation, and Lightness features are the easiest to understand (see Figure 10-1 for a visual of these features). These are global controls (they affect all of the image[s] on the layer you're working with) and can be found within the Adjust or Enhance areas on the Menu bar. You control the color (hue), the strength of the displayed color (saturation), and the contrast (lightness) of the image by sliding this feature's control bars (to lower or higher saturation levels) or by entering in a numeric value.

The *Hue* control bar alters the color of the image. This feature works really well for *monochromatic* (single color) images — it can change the color from a red to a blue, for example. The Hue control doesn't usually work as well with multicolored images or an image that contains many objects, because it shifts *all* the colors an equal amount. Your primary object may look good, but other objects can end up with strange color combinations. In some images, this strange combination works, but only in *some*.

**Figure 10-1:**
The Hue,
Saturation,
and
Lightness
dialog box.

*Courtesy of Adobe Photoshop Elements 3.0 and Jeanne Wines-Reed*

The *Saturation* control bar is often used to enhance background photos. Taking the color saturation down in a photo mutes and softens its colors — perfect for background images because you want them to retain their color without competing with the primary images in your design. Digital scrapbookers also use the Saturation tool to give their embellishments a boost by moving the bar to a higher saturation level to make colors extremely intense.

The *Lightness* control bar is used for burning out an image. It gives you control over how washed out you want an image to appear. This is especially useful when you want an image to look ghostlike. Used in connection with one or more of the filter effects, moving the lightness bar can help you create some very interesting images.

# Retouching with Digital "Painterly" Tools

Tools such as the Dodging and Burning, Paintbrush, Pencil, Pen, and Airbrush tools mainly derive from Photoshop's origins as a sophisticated color photo-retouching program for work destined for print. Most scrapbookers use these tools to do photo correction work or just to produce great effects on their imported digital images. We go over the uses of these tools in the following sections. You can also use them to *create* images rather than just applying them to digital images imported from your camera and other sources.

## Dodging and Burning tools

These two tools are related because they're used in the same way — though to get opposite effects. Suppose one section of a photo is lighter than the rest of it. By selecting the Burn tool and specifying an appropriately sized brush (from the Brush Selection feature box), you can brush the area to make it darker. (See a color photo featuring the dodging and burning techniques in the color section.)

You may find areas that are very dark in relation to the rest of a photo — especially if it's an old photograph. *Dodging* is one way to make these dark areas match the rest of the photo. Dodging is also used to lighten some of the background so that a chosen element will appear more subdued. With careful application, you can wash out the background without destroying the detail.

These tools can also be used to age photos by burning cracks into the image or dodging (darkening) areas such as those you see in old damaged photographs.

Both the Dodge and the Burn tools are usually found on the side toolbar.

## Playing with the "brush" tools

Scrapbookers have found the Selection Brush feature on the side toolbar in Photoshop Elements to be very handy for cutting out and smoothing the edges of images.

Every tool listed as a brush isn't necessarily used like a traditional brush (there's only one *real* Paintbrush tool on most tool bars). So even though it's a commonly used term, the word *brush* is definitely one to look up when you get a new program. Sometimes, it's used to refer to processes not normally associated with brushing techniques. The Red-Eye brush tool is an example, and so is Photoshop Elements' Selection Brush tool. You use it to select part of an image for whatever purposes you have in mind (the Cut, Copy, and Paste commands work with this feature as they do with any other selection-type tool). The regular Photoshop program doesn't have the Selection Brush tool. It *does* have a box you use to choose (select) brush sizes, and it does have a Paintbrush tool you can use for coloring.

You can choose the Selection Brush tool in Photoshop Elements and then choose your brush size to do all of the following:

✔ **Adjust the edge quality of the brush so you can get either a sharp edge or a soft edge to an area you want to cut out.** A soft edge helps the item blend in when you paste it into a new photograph.

✔ **"Color" out sections (with different sized brushes) by choosing the unneeded section with the selection brush.** By selecting the tool, you can also select a large brush size (to quickly brush out large portions of the picture) or a small brush (to get into those tight areas). Because the Selection Brush continually adds to the area to be selected, you can change brush sizes and continue to select various areas of your image.

✔ **Adjust the hardness level for your brush and you can automatically create a *feather* (a fuzzing or "fringing") around the edges of your selection.** The hardness level is located on the Menu bar when the selection brush is chosen.

## Breezing through airbrushing

The airbrush is the magazine editor's secret weapon. Most cover model pictures are highly airbrushed. Skin blemishes, wrinkles, tummy folds, body hair, and cellulite are carefully airbrushed away. Even those slick cars you see in the ads have been heavily touched up with an airbrush — unwanted reflections smoothed away and highlights enhanced.

The Airbrush tool is like a can of spray paint. You can control how fast the spray of color comes out with the opacity adjustment. (Figure 10-2 shows an Airbrush tool at work.) It's equally as useful on a black-and-white image as it is on a color photo.

**Figure 10-2:**
This baby looks even happier after we used an Airbrush tool to remove the blotchiness from her face.

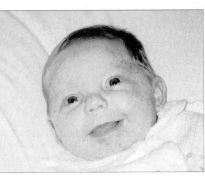 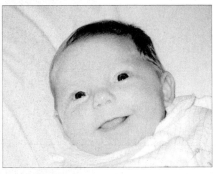

*Courtesy of* Scrapbook Retailer *magazine (Designed by John Stratton)*

When using the Airbrush tool, you can also select a brush size and sometimes (depending on the program) a brush shape. As a general rule, you use a larger brush for an Airbrush than you would normally use for drawing or painting. This allows you to lay down a more even color or tone. Selecting an Opacity of 15 to 20 percent allows you to easily feather the edges of your work; blending the image's edges with the area that surrounds it. Unless you're writing words with the Airbrush, reduce the Airbrush Opacity so you can "sneak up" on the color or tone you need.

Different programs hide this wonder tool in different locations, but the name's generally the same *and* it's a tool that's well worth looking for. (In some programs, you have to select your regular Paintbrush tool to get to your Airbrush tool!) Take a look at some of the airbrush procedures you may want to try:

✔ By using the Color Selection tool in conjunction with the Airbrush tool, you can pick out any color from your photo or any color from the color selection palette. On a black-and-white image, you can select any tone from the picture, or you can go to the color selection box and select a tone from there. Then just point the cursor and airbrush on your color.

✔ You can also use the Airbrush to draw out letters and make words, make shadows for items that need them, or fill in areas with gradient color.

✔ If your program doesn't have a Healing tool, you can use the Airbrush tool to smooth over imperfections in your photos. It's great for feathering out harsh transitions in the photograph and for inserting shadows.

✔ This tool also works especially well in conjunction with layers (see Chapter 4). For example, if you want to add a shadow to some object, select a layer behind the object as the active layer. Then you can airbrush right over the object without affecting it in the least. The shadow will appear under or to the side of the object you airbrush.

One advantage to airbrushing in a shadow rather than using the Automatic Shadow tool available in many programs is that you can better control the shadow color. Most people think that shadows are gray, but they're really a grayed color of the object on which they're cast. For example, if your shadow is falling on a light blue wall, the color of the shadow is a medium gray-blue. Understanding this painter's trick can help you create more natural looking shadows.

## Pushing the Pencil tool

The Pencil and Paintbrush tools are very similar in that you can draw a freehand line in whatever color you choose with either of them. The primary difference between the two is that the Pencil tool has a harder edge than the Paintbrush tool. The Pencil tool is useful, in tandem with the Eyedropper tool, for making picky little edits of individual pixels when you're really zoomed in. For example, if you have an image with a dust spot or a few off-colored pixels:

1. **Select a single pixel brush size for your Pencil tool.**

2. **Zoom in and select an appropriate color from a nearby pixel.**

3. **Then use your Pencil tool to draw or change the color of the errant pixel.**

## Practicing with the Pen tool

Many programs have a Pen tool, and some have a Pen tool *section*. A Pen tool is usually (but not always) associated with drawing a vector line (see Chapter 8 for an explanation of vector — as contrasted to bitmapped — graphics). In this type of drawing, you begin by clicking the left button of the mouse and placing a node (a dot) onto the screen. Additional clicks add more nodes with lines extending between the nodes. You have to make sure your last click is on top of the first node. Then you've created an enclosed shape that can be filled (by using a cut or copy and paste procedure) with color, patterns, and even with images and photographs.

# Cutting Out Unwanted Objects

You may also want to cut out an image and paste it in front of a background, in front of another image, or in a different photograph. For example, you take a photograph of a flower and want to cut it out of that photo and put it in another photo. You can do this in several different ways. The method you choose will depend on how you want to use the image. In this section, we show you how to use the Eraser tool and the Magic Wand to complete this procedure.

## Eraser tool

The most straightforward way to cut an object away from the background and paste it elsewhere is to *drop out* (get rid of or erase) the background in a picture (see Figure 10-3). Here's how:

1. **Select the Eraser tool.**

2. **Position it over the area you want to erase.**

3. **Left-click as you move the cursor around the outside edges of the flower.**

4. **Select the flower with the Rectangular Marquee tool.**

5. **Paste it into the new photo.**

The disadvantage of this method is that the flower's edges appear harsh and unnatural when the image is placed in the new photo. Selecting a soft edge for your Eraser tool helps make the image look more natural, but it usually still looks too harsh.

Even with the bad edges problem, the Eraser tool is bound to be one of your favorites. The Eraser tool also allows you to clean up holes, tears, or writing on scans of documents written on a white page.

**Figure 10-3:** Using the Eraser tool to get rid of the background around the flower.

# Magic Wand

Another method for cutting out images is to use the Magic Wand tool. You can activate the Magic Wand to either select the image to be cut out or to select the background you want cut away. (In Figure 10-4, you see the magical Magic Wand at work.)

Here are some tips:

- ✔ If you select a piece to cut it out, feather its edge so it will have a soft, natural looking transition. To do this in Photoshop Elements 3.0, check the anti-alias box and perhaps adjust the tolerance for the Magic Wand tool so it will properly fuzz (or feather) the edge of the image.

- ✔ If your image shows a flower growing up through the grass and you want to eliminate the dark sky in the background, select the sky background with the Magic Wand and then cut out that part of the background. Repeat until you have all the background eliminated.

✔ A variation on this technique is to select the background and then Inverse or Invert the selection so that it's the main image that's cut out. You can then paste it into another photo, or keep the image and maybe fill the old background area with new background material. (The Invert or Inverse command is under the Selection or Select area on the Menu bar.) Often, this technique eliminates most, but not all, of the background. But even if you only remove part of the background with this method, you can cut down on the amount of erasing you end up doing.

The Magic Wand tool can compensate for the Eraser's rough edges by specifying that the edges of the image need to be feathered. (In Photoshop Elements, the Feathering tool is under the Select area on the Menu bar. In Paint Shop Pro, the Feather option appears when the Magic Wand is selected from the side toolbar.)

If you select something with the Magic Wand and then change your mind, go to the Select or Selection area on the Menu bar and hit either the Deselect or the Select None feature to turn off the selection lines. To select more than one item, hold down the shift key and select each subsequent item.

**Figure 10-4:** Notice the dotted line made by the Magic Wand tool. It surrounds the area that can be deleted.

*Courtesy of Adobe Photoshop Elements 3.0 and Jeanne Wines-Reed*

# Chapter 11

# Getting Creative with Advanced Effects

· · · · · · · · · · · · · · · · · · · · · · · · · · · · · · · · · · · · · · · · · · · · · · · · ·

### In This Chapter

▶ Creating montages and panoramas

▶ Modifying color

▶ Using filters and plug-ins

▶ Building embellishments

▶ Designing backgrounds

· · · · · · · · · · · · · · · · · · · · · · · · · · · · · · · · · · · · · · · · · · · · · · · · ·

*W*hen people understand digital scrapbooking basics, they invariably begin exploring more sophisticated graphic techniques that glamorize their designs and turn ordinary pages into showstoppers. In this chapter, we explain how to create montages and panoramas, give you some tips on working with color and filters, and show you how to make embellishments and backgrounds. Give a tip (or two) a try!

Upgrading your page elements may require equipment or program updates. Review the info in Chapters 2, 3, and 10 to determine whether you've got enough hardware and software power to try the techniques we describe in this chapter.

## Enhancing Your Page Design

Montage and panoramic designs are easy to create with digital tools. And, you can make especially impressive montages and panoramas by using the Size and Opacity features found in many scrapbooking programs.

## Scaling montage elements down (or up) to size

Digital montages have changed as computer graphics programs have improved. Instead of being limited to choosing images of similar size, you can now pick any image and size it to scale with digital tools. You can montage a picture of a surfer riding a big wave with images of a nurse, a banker, and a pig scaled to size so that everyone rides the surfboard together.

## *Making the most of montage*

A *montage* is an image made from two or more separate images (see the color section for an example). Say, for example, you have old pictures of two friends who didn't know each other in 1960. You can montage them so it looks like they posed together in that long ago year — and then add a background that ties in with your story.

You can also use montage to create surreal images — pictures of things that could never happen in real life. Take a picture of your children sitting in the curve of a new moon or . . . imagine what you will — and create it!

### *Montaging backgrounds*

In scrapbooking, montages are most often used for backgrounds. For a heritage album about your grandmother, you may want to use a montage of her belongings as a background. Here's the step-by-step process:

1. **Decide whether you want your montage to appear flat or dimensional.**

   If you want a flat montage, you either have to avoid using 3-D objects entirely, or you need to flatten them.

2. **Flatten 3-D objects by digitally superimposing them on old deckle-edged photographs (photos with thick, white, wavy edges).**

   They'll look like they were taken with an old camera and printed on 30-year-old print paper.

3. **Enlarge a photo of an old newspaper so it appears in relative scale to the photographs.**

   Place the newspaper image on an angle under the "old" photos and put some shadows behind the photographs so they look like they're sitting on the newspaper.

4. **Overlay an antique-looking color on the entire background and adjust the opacity of the color so that the background shows through faintly.**

5. **Add your title and journaling.**

   If the journaling is difficult to read, drop a colored box behind the text so that the text stands out from the background and reads easily. Then adjust the opacity of the colored box until you can both read the text and see the background images showing through the text box.

### Montaging foreground elements

You can also montage foreground images and other page elements. Find pictures of your grandfather and grandmother when they were children, for instance, add other page elements, and montage the whole set into one image. Another example: Take a photo of someone holding up a small fish and replace the small fry with a huge fish. Here's how:

1. **Open two images in your photo manipulation program: the fisherman holding his catch photo and a separate image of a huge fish.**

2. **Cut out the image of the big fish by selecting the fish and using the Magic Wand tool to cut it out of the original photo.**

3. **Paste it in a new file.**

4. **Close the new huge fish file and open the fisherman photo.**

5. **Now paste the image of the huge fish into the fisherman photo.**

   The program will place the fish image on a new layer (*never* exactly where you want it!).

6. **Use your digital tools to rotate, size, and place the huge fish so it looks like the fisherman caught it.**

   See Chapter 6 to review these tools.

## Creating a panorama layout

A *panoramic* photo shows an extra-wide view. Some cameras offer a panoramic setting, but often the best panorama shots are made by combining several carefully taken shots and digitally combining them to form the wide image (see a beautiful example in the color section).

When taking pictures you intend to make into a panorama, always use a tripod to keep your photographs properly lined up (or indexed) with each other. If you hold your camera by hand, the camera (hence the shot) will tilt slightly every time you shoot and you'll have to rotate your images in your editing program to make them line up with the other shots. When the shots don't line up perfectly, you have to crop the image to make it square. Overlapping the images gives you some room so you can easily "stitch" the images together, making it possible to put your ideal shot on one side or the other of the center fold in your scrapbook (see "Creating your panoramic layout" later in this chapter).

### Taking a panoramic series of photos

To take a panoramic series, you must take an overlapping series of photos. Here's how:

1. **Adjust the legs of your tripod to create a level photo platform.**

2. **Mount your camera onto the tripod.**

3. **Look through your camera lens or on the LED display on the back of the camera and decide on the best view.**

   Note where the edge of the shot is located on both sides.

4. **Take the ideal shot and then swivel the camera to the right to take the next shot. Make certain you overlap *a little* of the first shot in your second shot.**

   The overlap in the photos insures that you won't have a gap between one picture and the next.

5. **Rotate to the right again and take another shot, remembering to overlap a little.**

   Return to the original shot and repeat the process going left. Take one extra picture — on either the right or the left side.

   Take at least six shots for your panorama picture.

### Creating your panoramic layout

When you have your photos in hand, you need to stitch them together to create one photo. Here's how:

1. **Transfer the shots to your computer, call up your photo-editing program, and open your best shot (the one with the best view).**

2. **Decide how big you want your image to be.**

   If you want a full-page view of your image, you won't be using your entire panorama (unless you make multiple-page fold outs). You can also reduce the size of the panorama so that the whole image fits on your page(s) from side to side, but then the image won't be very tall.

3. **Enlarge your canvas so you can paste in the other shots on both sides of your best view.**

4. **Call up the next shot (going to the right or the left) and then position the pictures to get rid of the overlap you gave yourself when you were photographing.**

   Because the shots were lined up vertically when you used the tripod to take your shots, you only need to concern yourself with positioning the images horizontally. If you take all your shots at the same time and with the same camera, you won't have color matching or brightness level issues either (see Figure 11-1).

**5. When all the photographs are in proper position, flatten the image (see Chapter 1) and save your panorama shot.**

If you want to brighten your image or give it more contrast, this is the time (if you adjust the individual images before you flatten, they won't match each other). For information on adjusting brightness and contrast, see Chapter 6.

## Using a vertical panoramic perspective

Panoramas can be vertical as well as horizontal. Just lock your tripod so that it rotates vertically rather than horizontally. You might use a vertical panorama for images of a giant redwood or a tall building, monument, or ship. (These panorama shots are good candidates for framing and hanging on your walls.)

Test the rotation of your camera on the tripod. For some reason, it's harder to rotate your camera properly in a vertical shot than it is in a horizontal shot.

You can combine both vertical and horizontal panorama images into one image. Shooting and printing the panorama involves the same steps described earlier, but laying out the panorama would take a little extra care. The finished panorama would be displayed as a cross with the horizontal and vertical shots intersecting somewhere in the middle.

**Figure 11-1:**
If photos have been taken properly, all you need to do is slide each image into place.

*Courtesy of Adobe Photoshop Elements 3.0 and istockphoto.com*

# Trying Out Some Commonly Used Color Variations

Graphic artists do a lot of experimenting with color because variations in color have significant implications for the "look" of their work. Although most of them would agree that using a pure white canvas for a base is a must (any hint of color in the white will affect colors in your other layers), they approach color in a wide variety of different ways. The following are just some examples of how you can use coloring tricks in your own designs.

## Converting color images to grayscale images

Converting a color to a black-and-white image (RGB to grayscale) is easy — though each photo manipulation program seems to locate this feature differently. Look in the manual or in the image section on your Menu bar for the Grayscale feature. Sometimes you have to go through a Mode menu.

After your image has been converted to grayscale, you may wish to increase the brightness and/or contrast of the image (see Chapter 6 for instructions). The color section includes a nifty example of a color photo converted to black and white.

## Saturating and desaturating images

*Saturating* an image intensifies its color and *desaturating* it washes out the color (makes it less intense). There are several ways to saturate and desaturate, and each technique affects the image in a slightly different way.

To saturate your image, you can copy and put layers of the exact same image on top of each other or you can use the color correction tools and the Saturation feature (see Chapter 10). To desaturate, you can use the Brightness/Contrast feature (see Chapter 6) or reduce the opacity of an image if your program has the Opacity Adjustment feature (see Chapter 10).

## Tinting an image

The term tinting is sometimes used to refer to converting an image to duotone. We show you the instructions for making a duotone from Photoshop

Elements as an example. Though this program has one of the more complicated processes for making a duotone, it also offers the most control in getting just the right shade and combination of colors (check your instruction manual to see how your photo-editing program makes duotones).

1. **Change a black-and-white photo back into a color image by selecting the Mode feature and choosing RGB color.**

   RGB color is preferable for scrapbooking because it creates a smaller finished file.

2. **Select the Hue/Saturation/Light feature and check the Colorized button.**

3. **Then slide the hue button until you get your color.**

   In some programs you must change the image to a 24-bit image before you can complete this operation.

4. **Once finished, bring the color level back down to save file space.**

Tinting means different things to different folks, however. Here are some other examples:

- ✔ You can put a box of color over a graphic image and then reduce its opacity until the graphic shows through. This will make the image look desaturated, but it's not really. Many people refer to this instead as a tinting process.

- ✔ You can tint or color specific elements of a picture. Say you want to give the tree leaves on a black-and-white image a green tint. Select the Airbrush tool and airbrush the green you want over the leaves. Then adjust the opacity so that the color doesn't overpower the black-and-white detail in the picture.

- ✔ To some people, tinting an image means filling in a black-and-white line drawing with flat color (see Chapter 8 for the how-to on doing this).

# Creating Special Effects with Filters and Plug-Ins

Filters can turn flat, boring photographs or other everyday page elements into original masterpieces by making them look like hand-created works of art — one of the reasons why applying photo-editing filters to digital images gets most scrapbookers pretty excited. Without having to master the techniques, they can make images look as though they've been painted or drawn in various artistic styles — including watercolor, colored pencil, dry brush, palette knife, and fresco. Look at the color section for examples of how filters can enhance images.

A *filter* is an effect that alters images in a certain way. A specific filter can make an image look like it's being blown by the wind, created as a stained glass, made out of neon lights, and other awesome, quirky, or even horrible (if you use them too heavy-handedly or too often) things. These filter effects, designed to manipulate image pixels in strange and wonderful ways, can be applied to a selected piece of an image, to just one layer, or globally.

*Plug-ins* (separate programs that you can install on your computer), are popular for people who like to use and experiment with filters. When you install a filter plug-in, it will interface with your main program so you can access and use the plug-in's functions.

You can get additional filter plug-ins for Adobe Photoshop Elements and Paint Shop Pro, but the best of them are expensive — sometimes more expensive than the original program. Check first to see whether or not the plug-ins work with your program. If you love filter effects (we do), you may want to look into purchasing a full copy of Photoshop. It's expensive, but it gives you several more features than Photoshop Elements — and if you're already familiar with Photoshop Elements, the learning curve is easy. You can also download Adobe packaged filters from the Internet (some are free, some aren't).

Some programs have easy-to-use filters, while others have filters with several controls for adjusting the way the filter is applied. To actually apply a filter isn't that hard, but getting the "proper" look can sometimes be a hit-and-miss process.

## Working with filters

To understand filters, just start playing with them! Open a photograph in your photo-editing program and run through the filters to see how each one affects the photo (see the filters list in Figure 11-2). In Paint Shop Pro, the filters are in both the Effects and Adjust menus on the Menu bar.

After each application of a filter, select Edit on the Menu bar and undo the filter change. Then you can use the same photo to see what the next filter will do to the photo. For further discussion on these particular tools, please refer to the *For Dummies* book written about your particular photo-editing program.

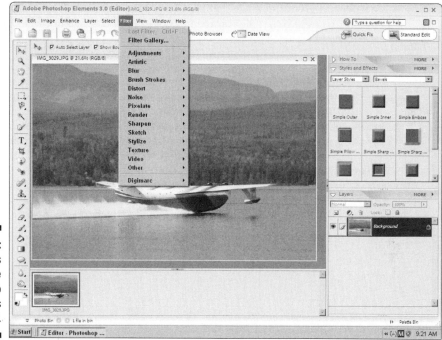

**Figure 11-2:**
The Filters list in Adobe Photoshop Elements 3.0.

*Courtesy of Adobe Photoshop Elements 3.0 and Jeanne Wines-Reed*

Here are some tips for applying painterly and other filter types to your pages:

- ✔ Add shadows and highlights to give flat, one-dimensional images and objects a three-dimensional look and to give your composition a more interactive and dramatic feel.

- ✔ Change the color in a photograph to create a personalized drawing or painting.

- ✔ Artistic, Brush Strokes, Sketch, and Texture filters are the most frequently used on scrapbook photos.

- ✔ To emulate a drawing, try Colored Pencils, Fresco, Crosshatch, Chalk, Charcoal, and Graphic Pens.

- ✔ Filters that work well with the painting concept include the following: Airbrush, Palette Knife, Rough Pastels, Sponge, Watercolor, Craquelure, Mosaic Tiles, and Texturizer.

Filter effects can be wonderful when used properly — but not so wonderful if they're applied indiscriminately or carelessly. The time and personal attention you spend working with the filters will show through on the final product. You can seldom get away with just applying a filter haphazardly, because every photograph is different and responds differently to filter applications.

Because each photo reacts differently to different filters, you need to use the adjustments to make the photos in your scrapbook layout or album all look similarly textured. This is a trial-and-error process, so be patient. If you apply a filter and don't like the result, just undo the filter effect (the Undo option is usually under the Edit section on the Menu bar).

In Chapter 6, we explain how scrapbookers use the popular Sharpen filter to improve the overall look of a fuzzy image. Here's a quick list of some other examples that will give you a good idea of how filters work. Have fun experimenting!

✔ Although the texture tools may be found in your program's filter section, many programs locate them elsewhere. This is because texture relates to artistic styles or other listed filter effects. Using the tools in this group of filters can add dimension to your photographs.

✔ Blurring filter tools are often used to blur out a background to make one item or section of a photograph stand out. Say you have a picture of a flower. Select the flower with your Magic Wand, and then inverse the selection (choose Inverse under the Select section of the Menu bar) to apply a slight blur to everything but the flower — giving the flower center stage in the photograph (see Figure 11-3). See the step-by-step project on applying a Gaussian blur in the following section.

**Figure 11-3:** The blurred background highlights the flower in this photo.

*Courtesy of Adobe Photoshop Elements 3.0 and Jeanne-Wines Reed*

✔ Get creative by applying combinations of different filters to the various layers you use as you build your scrapbook pages. Apply some filter effects on your background layers to give your page depth and texture (try art media, artistic style, and texture effects); then use lighting filters on your upper layers to give your images more dimension and impact.

Working with several filters often means experimenting before you get just what you want. But your patience pays off. Fortuitous accidents happen fairly consistently when you work with filters. Be prepared to save your "good mistakes." If they're not quite right for the project at hand, you can use them later in other projects.

✔ If you want a background photograph to look like a drawing or painting, apply filters — and then use a copy of the actual photograph on the same scrapbook page. The viewer will draw upon the similarities and the interest created by repetition and common details.

## Applying a Gaussian blur

Some programs offer several levels of "blurriness." The Gaussian blur, a heavy (and popular) type of blur is the answer to a question frequently asked by prospective digital scrapbookers: "How do I blur the backgrounds of my photos to bring the subjects into sharper focus?" Here's how to do this using a Gaussian blur:

1. **Select a digital photograph that has a subject you'd like to make more prominent.**

2. **Load the photograph into your photo-editing program.**

3. **Use the Magic Wand or the Selection brush to select the photo's subject.**

   A broken line will outline the subject. If the tool hasn't outlined the entire subject, hold down the shift key and select the area of the subject not outlined. (If there's not enough contrast between the subject and the background, you may find it difficult to get the outline.)

4. **Inverse the selection so that everything but the subject is selected.**

5. **Apply a Gaussian Blur filter to that selected area (background).**

   The subject of the photo should now appear sharper and more prominent because all the rest of the photo will be slightly out of focus. To further enhance this effect, select the Brightness and Contrast feature and lighten the selected background area.

---

### Using filters to balance a layout's foreground and background

No matter how much you mute a background, it may still clash too much with the foreground elements on your page. Use filters to get the contrast you need between your background and your foreground. You can easily apply a drawing or painting filter to the background so that it will complement rather than compete with the foreground images.

---

# *Making Exciting Embellishments*

Embellishments "dress up" the basic elements on scrapbook pages (see *Scrapbooking For Dummies* [Wiley] for more on embellishments). Creating *digital* embellishments may present a challenge for traditional scrapbookers — who are accustomed to using ribbons, metal brads, and other "touch me, feel me" embellishments on their handmade pages. But not to worry. Because we list Web sites in the appendix that are so good at doing digital ribbons, brads, tags, and other embellishments, it seems counterproductive to spend space on showing you how to create them yourself. Instead we focus this section on showing you how to incorporate hand drawings, interesting photo objects, and scanned 3-D objects.

## *Making hand drawings to use as embellishments*

It's often easier to draw with an actual pencil, pen, or paintbrush than it is with a computer mouse — and you can create some very nice pages using hand-drawn embellishments (see the color section for scrapbook pages featuring hand-drawn embellishments).

After you complete a hand drawing you want to use in your digital scrapbook, place it on the scanner and scan it two to four times larger than the size it will finally be on your scrapbook page. Then you can clean up the image and make it look exceptionally sharp when you reduce it back to its page version size.

Determine the image scale of an embellishment on the basis of how large an image it will produce. Images that are too large may crash your computer or slow it down. Keep images smaller than 30 megabytes. Control your file size by reducing your resolution. If, for example, you make an image four times

*Courtesy of* Scrapbook Retailer *magazine (Designed by Shalese Hinckley)*

*Courtesy of* Scrapbook Retailer *magazine (Designed by Melissa Maynard)*

Revising a traditional scrapbook page can take hours. With a few quick clicks of your computer's mouse, you can change the style of your digital scrapbook pages to convey a whole new look and feeling.

*The grand Catherdral in midieval Burgos*

*Hills above the Basque city of Bilbao*

**The Art of Spain**

Our excursions through the back-country of Spain took us to masterpiece after masterpiece. Not only where small villas filled with priceless memories, but the green countryside had us in awe of the beauty we experienced. Good thing our camera was handy.

We used our photo-editing software's filter tools to make these photos of Spain look like paintings (see Chapter 11).

*Courtesy of* Scrapbook Retailer *magazine (Designed by John Stratton)*

*Saving a photo of my*

*Great Aunt Eunice*

To repair this photo of Great Aunt Eunice, we reduced the opacity of the paint-brushed color to allow the original black-and-white shading to show through (see Chapter 10).

*Courtesy of* Scrapbook Retailer *magazine (Designed by John Stratton)*

# My Uncle's Boat

*This boat reminds me of something from an old movie. I always wanted to recreate this picture to make it look old. My Uncle Gilligan was always proud of his old ship, but I don't think it will set sail ever again.*

We aged the photo of Uncle Gilligan's boat by first converting it to duotone (see Chapter 11) and then using the Burning and Dodging tools to create "creases" (see Chapter 10).

*Courtesy of* Scrapbook Retailer *magazine (Designed by John Stratton)*

*beautiful*
(beau-ti-ful) adj.

Having qualities that delight the senses, especially the sense of sight.

Using the Grayscale option to convert a color photograph to black and white can produce a beautiful effect (see Chapter 11).

*Courtesy of* Scrapbook Retailer *magazine (Designed by Elizabeth Perez)*

Embellishments (see Chapter 11) such as these digital floral and button embellishments add interest and impact to this wedding page (see Chapter 14).

Manipulating the text (even just a little bit) can add excitement to your layout (see Chapter 12).

Each day, while we were home schooling for the first time in 2003, Grandma Grunts would come pick up the two little kids. She would always come in the little red car, honk her horn, come inside and say. "PRESCHOOL TIME!" Katie and Brynna would be so sad if the little red car was broken. They hated riding in the blue one. It just wasn't the same as Grandma's prized red one.

When they got to Grandma's house, it was the BEST! Katie and Brynna had BUBBLE BATHS and POWDER PUFFS. In the bathtub, they would have a fluffy Pepsi. Then they would rock, watch a movie, or play outside or in the toy box. Some days, the girls would just sit on Grandma's lap and rock. She would read to them or tell them stories. The girls wouldn't get off her lap. they would just sit there and LOVE her. These were some of their favorite days. Obviously, if you played hard, you needed a treat. There were popsicles or ice cream. Then the rest of the big kids would come over, and Grandma would make them lunch. The kids would watch Tom & Jerry, and Grandma and mom would have a big Pepsi on Ice. Then Grandma would hurry to get Makayla. It was a ball to be with Grandma and be spoiled so much. When Katie went to real school next the next year, she had quite the shock. It wasn't anything like GRANDMA'S PRESCHOOL!

This photo makes the large section of text seem more approachable (see Chapter 9).

We used a part of this photo to make an interesting page background (see Chapter 11).

*Courtesy of* Scrapbook Retailer *magazine (Designed by Melissa Maynard)*

*Courtesy of* Scrapbook Retailer *magazine (Designed by Sarah Johnson)*

This is Jackson climbing trees in Washington D.C. He wanted to climb higher and have a photo on each branch.

monkey business
June 2004

This hand-drawn tree makes a funky background (see Chapter 11).

*Courtesy of Scrapbook Retailer magazine (Designed by John Stratton)*

Using the Eraser tool on this baby theme page title gives the letters a worn, shabby chic look (see Chapter 10).

*Courtesy of Scrapbook Retailer magazine (Designed by Elizabeth Perez)*

We used digital sizing tools (see Chapter 6) to enlarge the image of the Arch and make it the focal point of our vacation page (see Chapter 7).

Text boxes (see Chapter 9) separate text from a busy birthday party background.

*Courtesy of* Scrapbook Retailer *magazine (Designed by Sarah Johnson)*

A child's scanned artwork makes this school-themed page stand out (see Chapter 11).

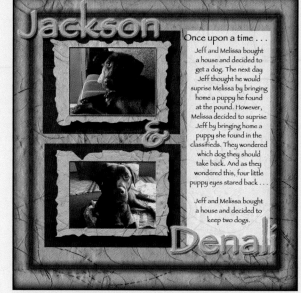

The Embossing filter tool (see Chapter 11) makes the border on this pet-themed page look three-dimensional.

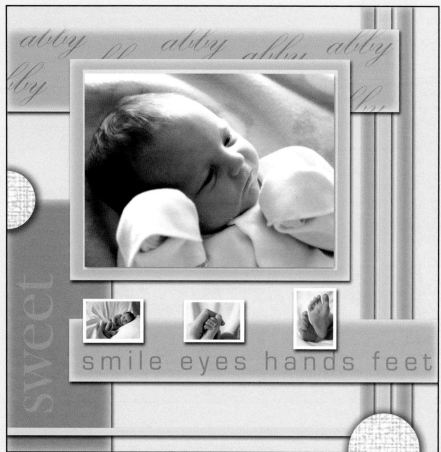

Adding small black-and-white images below the main color photo of this newborn allows you to include more images without overpowering the page (see Chapter 10).

Texture brings out the best in this page's foreground images (see Chapter 11).

This montage of buffalo blends diverse but related images into a unified whole (see Chapter 11).

The Clone tool (see Chapter 10) erases the seams between a series of regular sized images to create this impressive panoramic storm photo (see Chapter 11).

larger than the size you actually need, you can scan it in at 75 to 100 ppi and then change it to 300 ppi when you reduce its size.

Make digital "stickers" with your handmade artwork by scaling it or clipping it away from its background. If you enlarge a small drawing and the image doesn't look that great, place it on a light table and trace it onto a new sheet of paper; adjusting the drawing to get a crisp clean image. Then scan your drawing into the computer and alter it to fit into your design scheme.

If you don't have a light table, you can take an image into a computer-drawing program. Put the image on one layer and then open another layer to use for tracing it. After you finish tracing, throw away the scanned image layer and the tracing will be the only thing left in the file.

Lines created on the computer don't usually have the thick-thin characteristics of a hand-drawn tracing, so if you do a lot of this type of work, get one of the better computer tracing pads. You can make thick-thin computer-drawn lines on these.

## Creating embellishments from found objects

As you travel around, you may find many objects you want to use as embellishments on your scrapbook pages. Some of them will be yours for the taking; some you have to buy; and some you won't be allowed to touch, let alone collect!

Your digital camera can turn these "found" objects into great embellishments. Take a close-up of the object and then pull back so you get another shot of it in the context of its surroundings.

These photographs can serve as embellishments in a variety of forms. If you cut the background away from the object, you can use it as a sticker or as a piece of a collage, or you can take a group of objects and merge them together to form a montage.

## Scanning with 3-D embellishments

Some embellishments are more interesting when they're scanned. Just wait until you experiment with the great possibilities inherent in scanning 3-D objects!

Even though a scanner is built to scan flat objects, scanning dimensional objects can produce some very original effects. Try placing stiff white cardstock over your object to hold it in place at the angle you want. A colored or textured card might make things even more interesting. Or, try draping a cloth over your object before you scan it.

You usually leave the scanner lid up when you scan 3-D objects; consider the lighting in the room where you're scanning if you don't cover your objects. You may have to turn all of the room lights off.

## Making your embellishments look more "real"

With a little effort, you can make embellishments look like they belong on your layouts rather than like they're just "stuck on" design elements. The following sections provide a few digital tricks you can use to make your page elements work better together.

A big plus for digital scrapbookers who add embellishments to their pages is that they can easily clean up rough edges or other "mistakes" on scanned embellishments with digital tools (see Chapter 10).

### Using light and shadow to glamorize embellishments

If you ask photographers about the single most important element of their work, they invariably start talking about light. They tell you that early morning or late afternoon light is usually the best for photographing because the light at these times brings out the contrast in most images. After you start looking carefully at light, you can begin integrating its great effects into your design plans.

In traditional art, contemporary design, and photography, light implies, suggests, and demands shadow. The digital scrapbooker uses tools like filters to get the maximum light and shadow effects for layout designs.

To help make your scrapbook page look dimensional and visually consistent, try the following:

- ✔ Decide where you want to locate your light source. A light source from the upper right or upper left of your page usually works well.

- ✔ Use the lighting features in your digital editing program to highlight the embellishments on the light source side of the page.

- ✔ Position the shadows on the side opposite your light source.

In traditional scrapbooking, most embellishments are dimensional (string, buttons, clasps, hinges, ribbons, trinkets, and so on). The reason they look dimensional in the layout is because they cast shadows on the page. If you're working digitally and want to make a scanned item look dimensional, apply a cast shadow to it. A *cast shadow* is just the representation of what a shadow would look like if the embellishment were held over the page under strong light. Many programs allow you to add a cast shadow by selecting a cut-out object and then selecting the shadow function from the toolbar (use your program instructions to find the Shadow or Cast Shadow feature). Make certain the other page items look like they've been lit with the same light source coming from the same direction.

You can also use shadows on overlapped items. The thickness of the shadows suggests how far away an image is from the object on which its shadow is cast. If some objects cast shadows and some don't, the viewer will conclude (probably subconsciously) that the image isn't "real."

### Scaling embellishments

Attention to scale can also make your embellishments seem more "real." Showing a picture of a lightbulb larger than a lamp on the same page doesn't contribute to a realistic look. (This may be a good technique for advertising, but it's usually not so good for scrapbook page embellishments.)

Not that everything on your scrapbook page needs to be in the exact same scale. Just make sure there's a reason for scale variations. Sometimes, you can play with scale and reality to good effect.

Try taking photos of real objects, and then cutting the photographed images out of their backgrounds and scaling them down to make embellishments (see Figure 11-4). This technique, which was stepped out in the montage section earlier in this chapter, is an especially popular technique in heritage or shabby chic scrapbooks — although it's useful for other scrapbook styles as well.

**Figure 11-4:** One way to make an embellishment is to cut it out of a photo (left) and change its size to "fit" a page design (right).

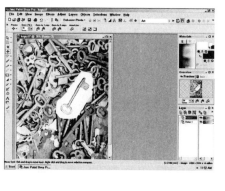

*Courtesy of Jasc Paint Shop Pro and Jeanne Wines-Reed (Designed by John Stratton)*

The distort filters are especially useful for altering embellishments to fit into your page design. Digital scrapbookers often use them to add a touch of fun to some of their photographs and designs.

### Filtering embellishments

Using filters to do a little texturing can often give a scanned embellishment just enough character to make it more believable (see Chapters 7 and 10 for some helpful information about digital texturing of photographs). Texturing the embellishment can differentiate it from the page background and make it more believable. These subtle changes can create dramatic effects. For more on filters, see the "Creating Special Effects with Filters and Plug-Ins" section in this chapter.

Putting a filter over embellishments sometimes helps integrate them more seamlessly into your design. Use a filter to change embellishment images to high contrast black and whites, convert them back into color, and then turn them into duotone or sepia-toned images.

If your image is a line drawing in black and white, you may want to change into an RGB color mode (RGB refers to the red, green, blue color system used by computers to create various colors) and fill your shapes with color. You can add filters to give the image an artier look or stretch it to fit into a certain size format.

# Creating Unique Backgrounds

A scrapbook page background is more important than its name implies. Scrapbookers enhance that importance by incorporating texture, color, contrast, and other design elements into the amazing backgrounds they create. In the following sections, we give you some good ideas for creating backgrounds you can be proud of.

Keep in mind that good background material is made of textures, patterns, and color. You don't want strong subject material in backgrounds; this only detracts attention from your scrapbook page's focal images. For backgrounds, you want images *without* a strong focal point. Look for interesting brick walls, patterns in the sand, a whole forest of trees, the sparkling water of a lake, and so forth.

The three main considerations with a background are to make sure it relates to the subject of the page, enhances the story being told, and coordinates well with the page's foreground elements. A good background doesn't have to be complicated; it can be quite simple and still serve its purpose.

Sometimes you see the same background throughout a whole album. Other times you find variations of the same background, or, as is most often the case, a variety of different backgrounds on the layouts.

Studying various background designs and finding out how they're made will influence your overall design decisions. Look at the background papers in your favorite scrapbook store to get ideas.

## Using your own photos as backgrounds

You can create exactly the kind of backgrounds you need by taking the photos for them yourself. You want images that relate to your foreground images, but that don't compete with them for attention. Images with subtle textures or patterns work well (rock walls, rippling water, sunsets, pastures, fields of corn, and the like). Apply filters and other photo-editing tools to your digital background photos. You can save big money by creating these background materials.

Here are a few guidelines that will help you do that:

- ✔ First, set your digital camera on its highest possible resolution — you need all the resolution you can get when you create background images.

- ✔ When you create backgrounds, give yourself some wiggle room. Don't fill the entire frame when you take photos for your backgrounds. If you compose a background shot using the entire frame, you may find yourself needing just a little more picture in order to fit the background on the page — and it won't be there.

- ✔ One category of background paper could be described as wallpaper — because it has a regular and repeated pattern. Look for objects that can create a wallpaper effect for you; perhaps the regular pattern of weathered wood from the wall of an old barn, a tall stone fence, or a thick green hedge. Impressive interior patterns are everywhere, too — the textures, colors, and patterns of an old plaster or a well-used wood-paneled wall come to mind. Even a wall of old wallpaper can become interesting.

- ✔ Use Mother Nature's interestingly consistent patterns — such as you find in a tide pool area, for example. The rocks and puddles are anything but regular, but there's a consistent color and texture to the overall area. By taking a wide shot, the individual elements blend together rather than demand individual attention in the photograph. Another example of this photo pattern concept is a wide shot of a crowd. If the shot is wide enough, the individuality of the people is swallowed up by the pattern created by the crowd as a whole.

✔ A large-patterned area accented by a few items that give extra character or embellishment works well for backgrounds. For example, you may find a large stucco wall with an interesting door or window in it. You could put scrapbook pictures or writing on the wall. The window or door would give the accent needed for interest and flavor. Shoot several versions of shots like this — by placing the door in the center of one shot, the lower right side of another shot, the lower left side of yet another shot, and so forth. You can then choose the design that best fits into your page design — or use all the versions as different background pages for a section of an album.

✔ Try using an object with "segments" in it. For example, picture an old building with two large dark windows. The windows would serve as segments in which you could place pictures or text. Although this type of background photo may create design challenges, it can be one of the most interesting when you get it to work; the photo's details help you create some great mood effects.

✔ It's usually best to plan your background shoots for early morning and late afternoon light. Midday shots can look washed out and flat (although this can be an advantage for some backgrounds). Early evening or even nighttime can also be a good time for taking background shots. Dark shots sometimes make great mood photos, and the large dark areas are a perfect background for lighter photographs or even light colored text.

✔ Use your photo-processing filters to make your background shots even more interesting. Applying a neon filter over a nighttime shot can produce some very strange and interesting effects. The same applies to many painting type filters or scratchy drawing filters.

✔ Using filters over background material can also help you overcome resolution problems that cause your background to pixelate and look fuzzy. You can apply a filter on a low-resolution background image, so it will look as if you intended the image to be funky-looking. Often, you may like the filtered background image better than you would have liked a high-resolution perfect image.

As you take more background and other special shots, you soon find yourself addicted to this kind of photography. It won't be long before your biggest problem will become how to store this material so you can find it when you want it. Here are a couple of suggestions:

✔ First, create some general categories, which can in turn be divided into subcategories. For example, you may choose to divide your background and embellishment materials into antiques, patterns, wallpaper, nature shots, vacation material, family material, work related, husband's hobby related, wife's hobby related, child related, and so forth.

✔ Next, rename all your shots, using descriptive titles instead of just numbers. You must be careful with this because you might accidentally name two files the same name. If that happens, simply put a 1, 2, or 3 at the end of the name.

## Selling your photos to papermakers

You may be able to sell your digital background photographs to scrapbook papermakers, who are always looking for unique and easy-to-produce backgrounds for scrapbook papers. You may not get rich this way, but manufacturers will usually agree to put your signature or mark on the papers. If you try this, remember two things: Be sure to make all your images high resolution (300 ppi) and send several ideas at once. Most buyers will want to select one or two designs out of twenty.

# *Texturing page backgrounds*

Textured backgrounds, such as the grass in Figure 11-5, flavor, enhance, and enrich a page's foreground images. Like patterns, textures contribute complexities of color and shape to a layout's base pages. They also create depth and/or the illusion of roughness or smoothness (though texture is most often thought of as rough or abrasive, it can also be smooth or liquid-looking).

Whether you use the texture options in your programs, scan and/or photograph your own textures, or find other ways to digitize textures, textured images can add intriguing new looks to your pages.

### *Using your program's background textures*

Most scrapbook editing programs come with computer-generated texture effects. You can create simple textured backgrounds with those effects and easily kick the textures up a notch just by altering their default colors.

CorelDraw and CorelDraw Essentials both offer a fantastic texture palette — basically a random texture collection. With a little adjustment of color and contrast, you can often make these textures look like natural materials: wood, leather, stone, and so forth.

### *Scanning in textures*

Real life texture items have a totally different graphic effect than computer-generated textures. You can scan almost any material (sand, sandpaper, weathered wood, painted surfaces) into your computer to make textured backgrounds.

Scanning your textured objects in super-high resolution allows you to enlarge these images and still maintain the resolution you need for high-quality printing.

Summer in Green Lake Wisconsin

Jackson's boundless energy was evident this beautiful summer day at Green Lake as he ran barefoot in the soft grass to his grandmother.

**Figure 11-5:**
The grass background brings out the best in this page's foreground images.

*Courtesy of istockphoto.com and Jeanne Wines-Reed (Designed by Ray Cornia)*

### Photographing textures

If you're interested in taking your own photos to use for background textures, check out some books on photography. Most photographers live and breathe texture and pattern. Studying the images you find in photography books may also help you know what to look for when you're on the hunt for texture with your digital camera.

You can photograph textures and then enlarge or reduce the images to the scale appropriate for use with your foreground material.

Look at the various cloud formations that pass over each day, for instance. Photos of the cloudy skies that precede a storm can make some very exciting backgrounds. This type of imagery also works well when combined with other images to create a montage background. For more on montages, see the section "Making the most of montage" earlier in this chapter.

### Contrasting textures

When you use two or more contrasting colors on a page, you intensify the impact of each of the colors. The same is true when you contrast textures. You increase the visual "feel" of each of the textures involved. It can be more difficult to control texture than it is to work with color contrasts because every texture is so distinct, and the specific differences in textures don't readily coordinate with those in other textures. But when you work with them, you can often get some really wonderful effects.

# Concentrating on background color

The background color or colors you choose can make or break your page design. You generally have a variety of elements on a page, and these can have a wide range of color variations. Choosing background color(s) that unify these variants will add polish, solidity, and cohesiveness to the page.

### Opaquing your background

One very effective technique is to place a translucent layer of color over the entire background. You can adjust the contrast and depth of your background by adjusting the opacity of the color layer.

### Coordinating hot and cool colors

Scrapbook artists often make dynamic backgrounds by contrasting background color(s) and color temperatures with foreground images. If your foreground images are primarily comprised of hot colors (reds, oranges, and yellows), build your background with cool colors (most blues, greens, and purples). Doing this will make the hot colors hotter and will give your background depth.

If your foreground images are made up of mostly cool colors, try to find background colors that are complementary but hot. Naturally, a neon blue or a bright lime green would fall in the hot color area, but these are exceptions.

Making a hot background can be more difficult than making a cool one. Because hot colors have a tendency to "jump" to the foreground, you often need to mute or gray them out a bit so they _stay_ in the background. Any color that is grayed becomes cooler, but it also provides less contrast and impact.

### Balancing lights and darks

A clear contrast between light and dark colors can make your colors brighter or richer. Imagine that you're looking at hot coals in a fire. In the daylight, the coals seem to be a dull red color covered with gray ash. At night, surrounded by the dark shadows of the evening, the same coals glow in brilliant reds and whites.

When you complete a background, squint your eyes almost shut. The color intensity of the background is dramatically reduced. Instead of color intensity, you see mostly contrast. If your images appear distinct and well-defined, you've made good artistic use of color and contrast. If your images blend into each other, you need to create more contrast. (When you want the background images to blend together to provide a uniform backdrop for the foreground images, do the same squint trick on the foreground images instead.)

## Finding other ways to create impressive digital backgrounds

Skim through scrapbook magazines (in print or online) to find examples of the best scrapbook pages. Then analyze why you like them. What elements do these pages have in common with other materials you like and how can you improve on the ideas you see in these examples? You can use those scrapbook page models and some of the following ideas as jumping off points for your own original backgrounds.

### Making watermarked images

In traditional scrapbooking, faint images were made by printing stamps with transparent or very light translucent ink. Digital scrapbookers have altered the original scrapbook watermark concept.

You can create this type of faint image digitally by either adjusting the translucence of an image or by adjusting its brightness/contrast. In some cases, you may want to change the image to black and white (grayscale) and then covert it to color (duotone) before you lighten it. These light images can be quite elegant when used over another (similar) color.

Another, entirely different, type of watermark used by scrapbookers would better be termed waterdamaged. Heritage style or shabby chic style scrapbookers (see Chapter 5) often use a technique that makes images look like they've been damaged and/or spotted by water or other liquids.

# The origins of the watermark

When paper manufacturers wanted to mark their papers with their logos, they used a watermark. A watermark had to be visible, yet invisible — because people didn't want to see logos on the papers they were using for their documents. Paper manufacturers solved this problem by printing their logos onto the papers with water rather than ink. When the paper was held up to the light, you could see a manufacturer's logo, but it was "invisible" at most other times.

To create this effect for backgrounds, mark paper or cardstock with drops of water. You may have to damage several sheets of paper in order to get the exact effect or pattern you want. Scan the waterdamaged paper into your computer and color the "spots" to complement the images. Another paper-damaging technique is to add a drop or two of black or brown dye into the water. This will give the water damage some color. Some people use weak tea or coffee to "age" their images.

## Looking to the ad industry

Advertisements in publications and other media are a great source of ideas for scrapbook page backgrounds:

✔ Find inspiring ads in magazines and study the backgrounds in the design ideas you particularly like.

✔ Look through one or more of the many advertising annual awards books at the library. Almost always: the better the ad, the better the background!

## Checking out the art and film worlds

Spending some quality time in bookstores, libraries, and museums studying art and art books can help you upgrade your design skills in a hurry. Look at a good painting, for instance, and try to separate the foreground (subject material) from the background. Then ask these questions:

✔ Did the artist create a deep or a shallow background?

✔ Do you see texture in the background?

✔ How do the background and the foreground of the painting work together?

Films are another source of background ideas:

✔ Study the introductions in '60s and '70s movies. Some of the designs in these opening credits are stunning (many of them were more interesting than the movies themselves). As you'll see, these designers had a field day with text styles, backgrounds, animations, and color.

When you view a film's opening credits, pause the movie every so often to study what the designers were doing to create their special effects. You can duplicate most if not all of those effects with your digital photo editor.

✔ Animated movies are heavily concentrated on backgrounds. The animated movie backgrounds from the '50s, '60s, and '70s, for example, may give you some great ideas for color schemes — as well as dramatically demonstrating the concept of contrasting cool and hot colors.

# Chapter 12

# Trying Your Hand at Artistic Text Techniques

**In This Chapter**

▶ Making sure your software stands up

▶ Wrapping and curving text

▶ Experimenting with other fun text techniques

▶ Integrating journaling

Designing with text is an art that scrapbookers love — and love to experiment with (refer to Chapter 9 for information about basic text operations). They use patterns and textures in place of text color fills, letters with reflective gold or other metallic colors, dimensional letters, text bending and stretching, *and* they constantly dream up innovative techniques of their own.

Although most scrapbooking programs can do a fair job with fancy headlines or titles, the possibilities with body copy are more limited (unless or until you're willing to purchase a more feature-rich program). You can, however, use some tricks to enhance your body text without upgrading your program.

## Souping Up Your Software

You can produce some very nice text effects with standard scrapbooking — even though they're not as fancy as the ones you can get with the more expensive graphic programs. Consider the following information before you decide what software (or software combinations) you want to use to create special text effects:

✔ Remember first that your text design decisions aren't limited to what your scrapbook program (even a standard program) tells you it can do. As a general rule, most programs can do more. If you see a text effect you want to duplicate, you can often find a way to do it. We show you some common text work-arounds later on in this chapter.

✔ Scrapbook Factory Deluxe, Paint Shop Pro, and CorelDraw Essentials 2 are the only scrapbooking programs that are considered to have really advanced text capabilities. Even Scrapbook Factory Deluxe is limited in certain areas.

✔ Some programs offer pre-made special text effects, and others require you to create them yourself. Scrapbook Factory Deluxe and Microsoft's Digital Image Suite have more of these pre-made effects than other programs. These effects are easy to create: simply highlight your text, and then click on the text effect you want from a pull-down menu. The program makes all the changes for you.

✔ Pre-made effects work great for headlines or subheads, but not as well for body copy. (If you want a big variety of special body copy effects, CorelDraw Essentials 2 is the only scrapbook program that can meet your needs — Paint Shop Pro comes close, but is more limited.)

✔ When dealing with body copy, remember that good word processing programs do a great job of cutting and pasting copy, checking sentence structure, deleting extra spaces, and running spell checks. These are all things that most scrapbooking programs *don't* do well. After your word processing copy is clean, just copy and paste it into your scrapbook program, then adjust the font, the font size, and paragraph style.

✔ For top-notch text handling, the professional designers use Photoshop, Illustrator, CorelDraw, and Freehand. (Quark and InDesign manipulate text in multipage documents, but these programs don't have as many special text effects as the other programs do.)

✔ If or when you want a more feature-rich program for creating special text effects, spend the money for a flexible, useful program like Adobe Illustrator. The new versions of the program sell for about $500, but older versions can be purchased for much less. This program can create stunning font effects. There are many classes and how-to books available to help you learn the program (such as the latest edition of Wiley's *Illustrator For Dummies*).

# *Wrapping Text*

The Text Wrap feature can wrap text around other elements in the design so that the text doesn't intrude on your layout's important images or shapes (as shown in Figure 12-1). Wrapping text also helps fill any holes in your design.

Text wrapping is a design trick that many people overuse — which results in distracting attention away from the overall page design or making the wrapped text too hard to read. So be careful not to get carried away with this wonderful text effect by using too much wrapped text on your pages.

## Jackson at the Sculpture Garden, Washington D.C.

Dad, you, and I took a trip to D.C. in June of 2004. One of the things that has always bothered you since you were little is making a mistake in your drawings. We have always said, "that's what erasers are for." So this big eraser was a grand teaching moment for you. You see no one is perfect and what matters in life is that we all do our our own personal best. We walked through the modern art yard looking at all the modern art placed in the park. You loved exploring and discovering all the different things Jackson. You're such a creative person. Ever since you could hold a pencil - you have been drawing. You're my little artist and Dad and I love you. You are the most incredible creation we have ever experienced. Love Mom

**Figure 12-1:**
This text wraps around but doesn't obscure the photos on this scrapbook page.

*Courtesy of Jeanne Wines-Reed (Designed by Sarah Johnson)*

## *Wrapping text automatically*

A good text-handling program such as Quark or Illustrator can wrap text automatically. This works a little differently in different programs, but basically, you place a text box on one layer and then put another page element (such as a picture box) on the layer above the text box. With both layers selected, you activate the Text Wrap feature in the program and the text flows around the picture box. The Text Wrap feature lets you determine just how far away from the picture box to offset the text. Selecting a program that can make an odd-shaped text box such as CorelDraw Essentials 2 is the key for easily wrapping text.

## *Wrapping text manually*

Usually, automatic text wrapping works well, although occasionally the text goes awry when you hit the button to activate the text wrap. You can, of course, then undo the automatic text wrap, and if you get frustrated, it may be easier to create the text wrapping effect manually instead.

Designers who use programs with automatic Text Wrap functions often opt to wrap text manually — primarily because they can make some things happen faster that way. Here's how to do this:

1. **Select the Text Box tool and click on the little arrow that activates a "fly out" menu.**

2. **Choose the icon from this menu that looks like an odd-shaped (rather than standard square, rectangle, or circle) text box so that you can create a text box in any shape you want.**

3. **Click to place *nodes* (little squares that create your text box points) wherever you need the text box to change directions.**

   After you identify the shape of your text box and place your cursor over the first node, the program recognizes the shape as a text box and allows you to put text in it.

4. **You can either type in your text or paste text (from a word processing file or elsewhere) into your text box.**

5. **After you place text in the box, use the white arrow selection icon to control the location of the text box by adjusting the positions of the various nodes.**

   This adjustment process allows you to properly position your text in your layout and to adjust the way the text flows within the text box.

If your program doesn't have automatic text wrap or the odd-shaped text box icon, you can still wrap body copy manually. Just follow these steps:

1. **Put the body copy into several text boxes based on the requirements of your text wrap.**

   For example, in Figure 12-1, we wrapped the text using three text boxes: one text box for the copy in the upper right corner, one text box for the copy between the photos, and the final text box for the copy in the lower left area.

2. **Adjust the size of the text boxes to fit the requirements of your design.**

   As you adjust the text box sizes, you may have to cut text from one box and place it in another text box.

3. **Position the various text boxes so that the spaces between the lines of text look consistent.**

# Creating Curvy or Wavy Text Lines

Curvy or wavy text lines that follow the edge of a round picture or wavy page element can create a great effect. The concept is to make text follow the path of an invisible line. This line may mimic an existing line in the design or it may be a design element all on its own.

Most scrapbooking programs allow you to create curvy text lines — although often in a simplified form. Usually, the programs show you a shape and allow you to put the text on that shape. For example, you can put your text on a circular path that will cover the entire circle.

In many programs, you draw a line and activate the text-to-curve button while it's highlighted. Then type in your text and make whatever font, color, or size changes you need. Some programs provide standard curve options. You simply choose what curve you want and type your text.

Here are some tips for using this feature:

✔ As a general rule, text looks good on a wavy or *gently* curved line, but not one with dramatic curves.

✔ If you want to wrap text around a curved page element, you may have to put each line of text in its own text box.

✔ If the line bends too sharply, the letters bump into each other or tilt drastically away from each other. Sometimes, you want that effect (pop-style artists use it) — but not often.

# Stretching and Skewing Text Boxes and Letters

*Stretching* your headline (or other selected) text makes it stand out significantly from the body text — giving the headline movement and interest. Even though the letter spacing and the word spacing remain untouched, stretching produces an interesting effect. Try it by following these steps:

1. **Type in your text and select your font and font size.**

2. **Click your text box with your arrow — you'll see *nodes* (little squares) appear on the corners and in the middle of your text box.**

   Some programs have two kinds of arrows (a black one and a white one), and sometimes only one kind of arrow works with text boxes.

3. **Click on one of the nodes and pull it up, down, right, or left and see how it affects your text.**

   The text will expand or contract in some manner depending on the direction you move.

This easy special effect gives you some really nice options for headlines or titles (just don't overdo it). If you use the same font for your title as you do your body copy, stretching will make a title look different from your body copy, but you still retain design consistency because all of the text is in the same font.

*Skewing* allows you to move one text box node at a time. For example, you can use the Skew tool to move the center node on the bottom of the text box and make the text come up in the middle in an arch. This effect is especially useful for placing over a round visual.

Another great skewing effect is to select all the nodes on the top of the text box (push down the shift key while you click on each node). After you click on the last node, keep your finger on the mouse and let the shift key up. Move the mouse to the right and watch the letters tilt to the right. This tilting gives the illusion of movement or speed.

One especially dramatic text effect is to make your text look like it's stretching back into the image (see Figure 12-2). To do this, select your Skew tool and move one bottom corner node directly up toward the top of the text block. This produces the illusion that your text is being viewed in *one point perspective* (all lines seem to converge on one common point in the distance — called the *vanishing point*).

Another way to give your letters the illusion of depth is to duplicate the text and place the duplicate text image slightly to the right or left of your original text block. You can get a nice effect by making the top text block in a strong color (or perhaps black) and the back text block in gray to create a shadow effect.

You can also use the Skew tool to create a variation of the curved effect. Leave a text block active, and then bend or alter the text box as you see fit by nudging the box with the Skew tool. You may have to experiment with this tool to get exactly what you want.

**Figure 12-2:**
The Skew tool can make your text look like it's stretching back into the distance.

# Outlining and Filling Letters with Patterns and Colors

Scrapbookers often alter their titles by filling the letters with patterns or photographs. Scrapbook programs are being revised and improved to make it easier for users to achieve this type of special effect. In this section, we go over a couple special effects that are especially popular with digital scrappers.

## Outlining around a letter in whatever color you choose

If your program allows you to create an outline, you will see two large color boxes in your color selection palette. One box controls the fill color and the other controls the outline color. Letter outlining is usually a two-step process. First, you select your outline color, and then you select the thickness of the outline.

If you can select both a fill color and an outline color in your program, you can also choose No Color for either the fill or the outline. Try using a thick colored outline and a no-color fill. Your background will show through the letter and produce a glasslike effect.

## Filling the letter with a pattern or with a photo

This is slightly more complicated, but the results justify the effort. Here's how you do it:

1. **Select a very bold type font — one whose letters have an ample area to display your pattern or photo.**

2. **Convert the letters from a font into a shape by highlighting the text and then selecting Convert Text to Curves or Create Shapes from your Menu bar.**

   Not all programs have this function.

3. **With the letters (shapes) still highlighted, insert your image or pattern into the shapes.**

   Each program seems to have chosen a different term for this step, so you need to refer to your instruction manual to see exactly what term your program uses.

4. **If you want to put a different image or pattern into each letter, click onto the letter (shape) or letters you want to affect and insert the image or pattern you want to apply.**

   Be aware that after the letters are changed to shapes they're no longer connected to each other. If you want them to stay together, you must group them together using the Grouping command in your Menu bar.

## Rotating Text

Not surprisingly, you use the Rotate tool to rotate the boxes that contain your text. This can be useful because it lets you adjust and readjust the positions of your text boxes until you get them to conform to your layout design plan.

Every scrapbooking or photo-manipulation program comes with a Rotate tool that works in one of two ways:

✔ In one method, you select a page element and then click onto the Rotate tool. A box appears around the selected element. You can then grab a corner *node* (little square) or the rotation bar made visible when the Rotate tool was activated to rotate your element to the desired position.

✔ With the second method, you select the item and then double click on the Rotate tool. A control box appears — into which you must enter a numeric value to indicate how much you want to rotate the selected item. A positive value rotates the image to the right while a negative value rotates the image to the left.

In the case of rotating text, make sure the text looks the way you want it to look before you rotate it. Things don't always work out so well when you try to change the text after it's been rotated.

# Changing Text from a Horizontal to a Vertical Format

Vertical text is very hard for most people to read, so use this effect sparingly. Type fonts used for this format should be bold and clear. This effect only works well with one or two words — usually these words are titles that you place on the right or left side of the page.

To activate this feature, do the following:

1. **Type in your text in a regular text window.**

2. **Highlight the text, and then click on the little arrow on the bottom corner of the text box.**

    This will activate the fly-out option box.

3. **Select the Vertical option and the text will reformat itself to a vertical format.**

If your program doesn't have a vertical text option, you have to put each letter of your headline in a separate text box and then arrange them all in a vertical design.

You could use the vertical text trick on a scrapbook page about a motel you stayed at. Because motels often advertise by spelling out "motel" in a vertical format, people have learned to read that word and recognize it easily. But stay away from using long or unusual words in this format.

# Shadowing Your Text

The Drop Shadow function is available in most scrapbooking programs. Use it to give dimension and character to your letters. Drop shadows can also help you separate your text from whatever image is behind it. Here's how to do it:

1. **Select the text block you want to modify.**

2. **To apply a gray drop shadow to your text block, choose the Drop Shadow button.**

   You can usually find it on your Menu bar, although different programs put it in different places. Look in the Effects or Filter areas first.

3. **Some programs allow you to adjust the opacity of the shadow (how dark or light it will appear), and some allow you to position the shadow (right, left, above, or below).**

Sometimes, you can also shadow the letters of your body copy text. The text shadow effect works best when the shadow appears very close to the letters. If the text and the shadow are too far apart, the text may be hard to read because the shadows appear in strange places in and around the letters.

# Applying Filters

When you begin to experiment with applying filters to your text, you enter an artistic paradise that presents you with endless choices and possibilities. When you browse through your editing program's filter menus and apply some of the filters to your text, you'll be amazed at what the filter programmers have dreamed up. For more info on filters, see Chapter 11.

To use filters on text, highlight the text and then mouse click on the desired filter. Some programs will filter text directly, and others require that you convert your text to shapes before the filters will work.

The way a filter works on text depends on the color or pattern of the text, the font type used, and the particular filter selected. Some filters won't make a noticeable difference in the look of the text, while others will really change it. (See Chapter 11 for more information about using filters.)

When you find a filter effect you especially like, write down how you did it. Surprisingly, you can quickly forget the steps you took to make some of your best-looking text.

# Designing Your Own Fonts

The designing-your-own-font buzz is getting louder by the minute. Scrapbookers like getting their handwriting made into a proper font so their electronic journaling looks like their own handwriting. There's also a lot of experimenting going on in the designing of specialty fonts that follow scrapbook layout and album themes. You can go about designing your own fonts in two ways:

✔ The first and simplest is to have someone else make your font for you. At www.fontifier.com, you can get a special template to write in the letters of your proposed font. Send in this template and for $9 you get a font of your handwriting or specialty font.

✔ The second way to get customized fonts is to purchase a program for making fonts yourself. The leading font-creation program on the market right now costs about $2,500. You may be able to do certain things with an inexpensive program, but if you haven't mastered all the font info and lingo, "cheap" could easily translate into "trouble."

If you're working on a PC, you can get a program called Font Creator. This program costs $65 and can be purchased at www.high-logic.com/index.html.

Mac people use a program called Fontographer from Macromedia. Actually, there are versions of Fontographer for both Mac and PC and the cost is about $350 for either. This is a highly regarded program, but it hasn't been updated recently so it only works on Mac OS 9.2.2 and below or Windows 95, 98, and NT. Another available Mac/PC font creation program is Font Lab. It retails for about $550.

# Waxing Poetic: Incorporating Long Journal Entries

When you scrapbook digitally, you can easily type and insert more text — and in doing so, tell more of the story. *Journaling* is the scrapbooking term used to refer to the writing done in scrapbooks (and you can find out more about what basic journaling entails in Chapter 9).

Though digital scrapbookers often keep journaling to a minimum so that it doesn't detract from graphic design elements, significant numbers of scrapbookers *do* create longer computer-generated texts. If you include these longer journal entries in your albums, you want to make sure the text is easy to read.

Following these suggestions can help make your text more readable:

- **Select a *clearly readable* font that fits in with your design scheme.**

    A font menu that shows you what the font looks like *before* you select it can save you many hours of design time. (Scrapbook Factory Deluxe, Perfect Scrapbook Maker, My Scrapbook 2, Creative Scrapbook Assistant, and Paint Shop Pro all have this feature.)

- **The greater the space between lines of type, the easier your text is to read.** Most people type single-spaced text and leave an extra line between paragraphs. If you use a fancy or hard-to-read font, you may want to double space all the text.

    With computers, the standard spacing between text lines (called the *leading*) is automatically applied. If you want more or less space, you must specify the changes you want; many scrapbooking or photo-manipulation programs don't allow you to make this type of adjustment. (For more information on leading, see Chapter 9.)

- **Place a tint over a portion of the page so it's easier to read the text you intend to put in that area.** This works as well with handwritten text as it does with typeset text.

- **Indent paragraphs only two to three instead of five or more spaces.**

- **Put one space between a period and the capital letter of the next sentence.**

- **Increase the size of the type if you want to accommodate the visually challenged.**

- **Use a drop cap.** A drop cap is the *first letter of the first word* of your text and is usually three text lines tall. Drop caps help make text more approachable by serving as signposts to the reader that you're beginning a new idea or section.

    CorelDraw Essentials 2 can do a drop cap automatically, but in most other programs, you must manually insert the drop cap in one text box and the rest of the body copy in another. Just put the drop cap text box in position over the body copy text box and make certain the letters don't overlap each other. Enter some spaces or place a tab space at the beginning of the line.

- **Use bullets in place of numbers or letters at the beginning of each item in a list.** Many people like to format these bullets into a *hanging indent* — an indent that keeps the text lines in the list from going back to the left margin until the list is finished.

CorelDraw Essentials 2 can make a hanging indent you can use with bullets (and for other purposes). With most other programs, however, you have to make your hanging indent manually with various text boxes — one for the bullets and one for the indented text.

✔ **Alter (just slightly) the color of the text in each column.** This effect isn't used much because a color change can greatly affect the readability of the text. If the color you choose doesn't work well with the page background, the text can become difficult to read. Still, it's an effective option when used with the right background.

✔ **When working with text, always be mindful of the background on which you plan to place your text.** A vellum or parchment background can make the text look rich and elegant. Colored backgrounds can make it fun and playful. Picture backgrounds can relate the text directly to the image in an intimate way. (For further information about these effects, see Chapter 11.)

✔ **Size the text.** Usually, body copy is set in 11- or 12-point type. This is just a rule of thumb because font size varies greatly from one font to the next. Start your design in 12-point type and then see how it looks when you print it out. The great thing about computer typesetting is that you can adjust text so easily if you want to make it smaller or larger.

✔ **Add small graphics.** Review your text to determine where you can intersperse it with some small photos or illustrations.

If your journaling turns into one or more full pages of text, the blocks of text can seem unwelcoming and intimidating. In addition to using ideas from the previous list, you need to use other techniques that will encourage people to read it. Some scrapbookers print journal entries, put them into protective sleeves, and intersperse them among the more graphic-intensive pages, positioning them strategically so that they relate well to a specific section of the album. We've also seen scrappers put their longer stories in appendices at the end of their albums. Some even reference the material in the appendices on relevant pages throughout the album.

Here are a few more ideas for making longer journal entries more approachable:

✔ **Place the text in columns.** People can read short lines of text more easily than they can read long lines.

✔ **When you put large text entries on a page that has several other elements, don't make your text lines any longer than ⅔ of a page's width.** But don't make the lines too short either. A fully *justified* text (evenly lined up on both the right and left margins) looks strange if the line length is too short.

✔ **Use *call outs:*** Extract a quotation or an interesting passage from the text by copying and enlarging it. Incorporate these call outs into a text block to attract the reader to your story content. Some people put flourishes around their call outs. Others just make certain there's enough space before and after the callout so these oversized words don't appear to be a mistake in the text.

✔ **Establish a size for your headlines or titles and your subheads.** Subheads are usually 2 to 4 points larger than body copy. It sometimes helps to bold them so they look different from the body copy. You don't need to have subheads, but they're useful if you switch topics, locations, or points in time. If you choose to include subheads, then make your titles or headlines significantly larger than your subheads.

# Chapter 13

# Incorporating Sound and Video

*In This Chapter*

▶ Scanning the fast-moving multimedia scene

▶ Preparing a multimedia scrapbook

▶ Sharing your work with your "audience"

*Y*ou may be considering incorporating audio and/or video into your digital scrapbooks. If so, the following information gives you a little peek at where a decision to "go for it" may lead you!

In this chapter, we review some of what's out there in the multimedia world and run you through the basics of creating a multimedia scrapbook. We also list the options for sharing your completed albums.

## Looking At Multimedia Merchandise

If you're new on the audio/visual scene, we recommend a basic audio/video software program like PowerPoint (so you can get your feet wet without soaking your wallet). If and when you decide you really like this work, you will probably begin buying a few pieces of audio software or some extra tools such as tape recorders, digital video cameras, lights, and so on. Here are some very general merchandise guidelines:

The beginning multimedia scrapbooker needs:

- ✔ A basic presentation program (such as PowerPoint; for more on PowerPoint, see the section "Microsoft's PowerPoint" later in the chapter)

- ✔ A digital camera and/or camcorder (for more on digital cameras, see Chapter 2)

- ✔ An audio source (computer microphone, CD player, and/or cassette recorder; for more on audio technology see the "Audio clips" section later in the chapter)

- ✔ A CD burner for saving presentation programs (see Chapter 2)

The more skillful multimedia scrapbooker will need a few more things:

- ✔ A better presentation or movie creation program that offers more special effects and movement (see the section "Other popular software options for advanced beginners")

- ✔ A DVD burner (see Chapter 2)

- ✔ A sound-editing program (if the presentation program doesn't have one; for more on this see the "Audio clips" section later in the chapter)

- ✔ Digital cameras and camcorders with good lenses and light meters (see Chapter 2)

- ✔ Tripods, lights, and sound equipment (see Chapter 2)

- ✔ A laptop computer (see Chapter 2)

## Keeping it (relatively) simple with presentation programs

Although slide show programs aren't equipped with the tools necessary for producing full-blown audio/video presentations, they do offer a level of sophistication adequate for many scrapbookers. Here's how they work:

- ✔ Each frame (comparable to a scrapbook page) in a slide show presentation may contain text, images, a video clip, and/or sound that you have cut or copied and pasted from one or more sources.

- ✔ Background templates are provided with most presentation programs. PowerPoint comes with several templates you can use to paste in titles, images, and text (though you can easily make custom backgrounds if you prefer them).

- ✔ Transitions between each of your frames (slides or digital scrapbook "pages") are simple to make. You can choose from several kinds of dissolves, cuts, or fades. If you're short on time and using PowerPoint, you can just choose Random Transition and PowerPoint puts various types of transitions between each of your slides.

- ✔ Still images can be made to seem to move. Pans, fades, and zooms can give the illusion of motion for still images. If you zoom into an image, you have to save it in a higher resolution so it holds together as the zoomed portion of the image enlarges. It takes several frames to make these special effects, and you have to carefully choose your transitions — but the results justify the extra time.

- ✔ You can time your slide show presentation by determining how long each frame will stay on the screen and then choose whether you want the frames to advance automatically or only when you press a computer key.

# PowerPoint's practical past

PowerPoint was built as a slide show format program to be used by business people — so that rather than projecting slides with a slide projector, they could project digital frames from their computers onto a full external screen or to a computer monitor (depending on the size and nature of their audience). As PowerPoint was upgraded, it became possible to include sound and even short video clips in the program's presentations.

## *Microsoft's PowerPoint*

PowerPoint is far and away the most popular program for presenting graphics, sound, and video together in a simple digital scrapbook form. For one thing, it's a *cross-platform program* (a PowerPoint presentation built on a PC will play on a Mac — and one built on a Mac will usually play on a PC). For another thing, many people already know how to use this program. Even if *you* don't, you can get easily get someone to help you with your first couple of PowerPoint projects. For more info on PowerPoint, see the latest edition of *PowerPoint For Dummies* by Doug Lowe (Wiley).

Not only does PowerPoint "walk you through" the steps for making your "pages," it's also very forgiving, allowing you to make corrections and changes quickly and easily. It also accepts a wide variety of image, audio, and video file formats. Because of this flexibility, PowerPoint isn't especially efficient in its use of memory and you can easily overpower the program and/or make huge program files. Those who prefer other presentation programs to PowerPoint can quickly detail these program faults, but if asked, most of the same people will admit to making their first presentations with PowerPoint.

## *Other popular software options for advanced beginners*

You can purchase an instruction book and try Photoshop Elements 3, Windows Movie Maker, or Mac's iMovie to make digital scrapbooks that really move. All three programs can also make a slide show or video presentation with audio clips and dissolves (their functionality levels depend on the capability of the computer you're using; what works on one computer won't necessarily work as well on another). Still, these programs are great for figuring out how everything (audio, video, and graphics) goes together.

Some digital scrappers are trying two relatively recent releases: Photo Story 3 (Microsoft) and Slideshow Magic (Apple). Others recommend PicturetoTV (which gives you lots of control and syncs the slides to the music) and the inexpensive Simplestar Photoshow.

Other programs you may want to check out include: ProShow, PSE3, Photo Album (and similar programs with some slide show capabilities), and InDesign by Adobe (this one has a big learning curve, but it allows you to add a video file to your digital layouts).

## Over the top with authoring programs

Authoring programs are high-end audio/video editing programs. You'll find reviews for these programs in publications that cater to digital video enthusiasts. The best authoring programs offer sound mixing capabilities and come with sound effect files, music backgrounds, and other audio "clip art" files. Their video editing tools are also impressive and as with the audio files, there are plenty of video images available for use in your audio/video scrapbook projects. To set yourself up with the programs and equipment required to run an authoring program, you need at least $1,500 (probably more).

Although the learning curve is steep for most good authoring programs, the results are impressive. You can actually make mini-movies with professional-looking cuts, dissolves, pans, zooms, and fades.

If you're serious about video editing, check out a Web site such as www.gnu. org and look through the video editors they offer. When you get ready to purchase a commercial video editing program, look for editors that allow you to control three things:

✔ The color palette

✔ The frame rate

✔ The type of compression used to keep the video files a reasonable size

A video editor with all these features will let you process your video clips and combine them with audio material. You can make some awesome audio/video presentations that will play correctly on your computer and convert appropriately for use in Internet applications.

For this type of work, a desktop computer is preferable to a laptop because you have to install various extra pieces of equipment and (sometimes) specialized expansion cards.

High-end productions don't work well on regular computers, but they can be played on common DVD players (the most universally accessible method of sharing your programs).

## Additional stuff you may yearn for

As with most hobbies, one level of capability usually tempts the hobbyist into trying the next level of sophistication.

When multimedia scrapbook albums become a passion, scrapbookers upgrade their computers with extra memory or larger hard drives and buy high-end DVD burners so they can share their work with family and friends. If *you* get to this point, you will have reached the serious hobby level and should seek out all the technical assistance you can find.

Get educated before you buy a new computer with an extra large amount of memory, huge hard disks, video capture cards, and special audio equipment like a high-quality DVD burner.

For scrapbookers who want to go all the way with full-blown authoring software and professional quality productions we suggest taking classes and searching the Internet for more technical information.

# Creating a Multimedia Album

The challenge in doing scrapbooks as presentation programs comes in properly using the medium. We recommend that you start with a simple program and a simple project. After you master that, you can gradually increase the complexity of your presentations.

In this section, we give you tips on how to organize your digital media, tell you how to resize images, and go over some of the basics of adding video and audio.

## Organizing your elements

Organization is probably more important when creating a multimedia scrapbook than it is in creating a conventional album. But the basic organizational approach is pretty much the same: decide what story you want to tell, collect and categorize your images and other elements, find a theme to follow, and then put everything together in a logical order.

The presentation program you choose determines how you need to prepare your images and sound files (refer frequently to your program manual). Your decision to print out a hard copy of the pages will also factor into your image manipulations.

Prepare and categorize the story (which may be in the form of a voice-over script) and all of the other elements you plan to include (scanned photos, audio and video clips, clip art, and so forth). Put these items into logically labeled folders for quick access — such as voice-over recording (your story), original images, sized images (to fit your layout and/or your sharing mode), audio clips (music or other audio), video clips, embellishments, and so forth. Here are some tips:

- ✔ **A voice-over recording:** This is an audio file that you create to tell your story — and a great way to "ground" and organize your multimedia album. Write your story out before you record it. It can provide a framework for your scrapbook (as you key your elements to the narrative) and determine the length as well (it can continue throughout the presentation as a background for the changing images).

  If you don't have enough images to last for the entire time of the narrative, it's simple enough to create more graphic slides (using close-ups or section shots of the images you *do* have or bringing in external graphics). You can also use fades and other special effect transitions to slow down the presentation time of your graphic slides.

- ✔ **Original and sized images:** Keep these folders separate from each other. You want to be able to access and resize an original image any time you need to — and that's easier if you have all of the original images for your album in one folder. After you alter an image, put the resized copy of an original image in your Sized Images folder, with an extension that indicates its size and resolution (or make a separate folder for distinctive resolutions, such as 72 ppi, 100 ppi, and so forth).

- ✔ **Other elements:** Digital accessories, embellishments, and other graphic items can go into one miscellaneous folder or into separate folders — depending on your materials. Then they'll be readily available for you when you want to paste them into your pages — and you'll know exactly where they are!

Use large (18 to 40 point) easy-to-read fonts on your presentation slides *and* keep text on your image layouts short. In this medium, people want to see an image for only 3 to 8 seconds; not much time to process text. If you absolutely have to do a significant amount of journaling with your presentation, you can incorporate many pages of text into the slide show presentation by making a link on your layout page to a journaled story (perhaps a biography of someone whose image you're featuring on a page). The text isn't on the layout itself, but if someone's interested, they can click on the link and read the story.

## Adjusting sizes of digital images

Most slide show program instructions list the image requirements in terms of overall pixel size rather than inches. The overall image size and the resolution both affect the number of pixels in an image. Computer screen and Web resolution is 72 ppi, so the program gives you the needed pixel size of the image at that resolution.

Saving your images at 72 ppi reduces file size and makes your presentation program run more smoothly — even though you lose image detail. Although 72 ppi is the resolution norm when you work with presentation programs, saving your image at a slightly higher resolution (100 ppi) makes your images look cleaner — especially if they're viewed on a high-quality monitor. This is a personal choice each scrapbooker must make. And if you plan to print your images, you may use even higher resolutions (200 to 300 ppi).

To convert your print-quality images to digital slide show resolution:

1. **Lower your resolution to 72 ppi.**

2. **Look at your image size in pixels and adjust it to the size stated in your slide show program instructions.**

This sounds complicated, but it really isn't; just one of those technical things that you have to master in order to work in this medium.

You may import an image into the slide show program and find a 1-pixel white line on the left side of the image. If so, go back to the original program and save the image 1 pixel wider than specified by the presentation program. Why some programs measure pixels differently is a mystery to us, but it happens.

## Adding sound and video

It's true that including audio or video in your digital scrapbooks isn't *quite* as easy as some people claim. And it's also true that raw audio or video clips often make very large, very troublesome files. Many have found, however, that an exciting multimedia scrapbook is worth the time it takes to understand the variables involved in digital audio/video processes. In this section, we give you a few helpful hints.

### Audio clips

You can easily insert audio clips into your presentation. Many people like to include subdued music that doesn't compete with the voice-over but provides an additional level of support to the story and theme. Sites such as www.photofun.com can help you add music to your digital pictures.

Most computers sold within the last five to ten years can process or record sound. You can hook up your cassette recorder, digital recorder, or CD player to the computer's sound jack with a patch cable (read your computer manual to see exactly how to do this). Then you can digitally record whatever voice, sound effect, or music you want — just use the sound recording software that came bundled with your computer software. If you purchase an inexpensive computer microphone, you can digitally record your voice directly into the computer.

Audio files, like image files, are usually pretty big. An audio mixing program helps you with this problem because it allows you to cut out the pauses, mistakes, and other parts of your recordings that you don't want. It also lets you compress the size of the audio file; a process that reduces the quality of the audio file (though compressed voice recordings can still sound good). You may want to buy a good audio mixing program. Or go to www.tucows.com, type in *audio mixing* and download some really good ones for free.

A mixing program also allows you to alter a recording so that your voice can resonate like those voices you hear on the radio or TV, put in a music background, and then place your voice-over on a different *track* or audio layer, adjust each element separately until you get the effect (the *mix*) you want, and save your audio file to the file format you need for your presentation program (yes Virginia, there *are* different kinds of file formats for audio recordings just like there are various file formats for images). If you're working on a PC, try saving your audio files in the WAV (pronounced wave) format.

### Short video clips

You can import short video clips into a presentation — as long as you remember that the key word here is *short*. Even in programs such as iMovie and Movie Maker, long video clips can make your computer choke and start dropping frames.

Video clips are no harder to insert into PowerPoint than any other graphic image, *but* video clips usually make huge files. If you have an older computer, you may need to purchase a special computer expansion card in order to import video from your digital video camera.

For the beginner, just being able to put one or two very short video clips into PowerPoint is enough, but if this is something you want to do on a regular basis, you eventually want a digital video-editing program. These programs allow you to cut and *splice* (put together) your video clips, add or edit the sound for your video clips, adjust image size, set frame rates, and delete frames so you can compress the overall file size of your clip.

---

## Streaming video

If you want to put individual scrapbook pages on the Internet as Web pages, many of the programs we have featured in this book can save your scrapbook page to HTML (the Internet-compatible format). Then all you have to do is go through the process of mounting your page on the Internet as a Web page.

Putting digital scrapbooks containing video clips directly on the Internet can be a whole different story. Usually, you can't control frame rate when you use a video clip on the Internet. That's because the download speed varies from site to site. Rather than deal with this problem, the Internet people just ignore it. Instead, they have invented a term they call *streaming video*, which basically means that the video clip runs as fast as your computer can download the images. This technology tries to adjust things so the video at least runs consistently, but the results are often far from perfect — so be warned.

---

If this sounds like something you want to do, take a class or course, or find someone who already does video editing and have that person walk you through the process. When it comes time to purchase an editing program, get the one that your video-expert teacher or friend uses or suggests. This process is technical enough that the best program for you is the one you can get help using.

Many colleges, universities, and adult education programs offer classes on video editing and/or video production, as do the manufacturers (these tutorials can often be found online). Check out `storycenter.org` if you want to sign up for a great digital story training session that will make you comfortable with video editing and production.

# Sharing Your Album

You've gone to all this work, so we bet you want to share your work with others. You may even want to display your material in more than one way. The most inexpensive alternatives are those that are computer-based. Printing hard copies is easy, but not always the most economical choice because of the cost of quality papers and inks. Burning your presentations to CD or DVD is cheaper, but requires an additional level of capability. If you want to play your programs on a DVD player and show it on a regular TV screen, then you add yet another level of complexity. In the following sections, we go over some of the main ways that digital scrappers share their work with friends and family.

### Printing out your slide show

If you've created a slide show, you may want to simply print out your work to share with your friends who don't have computer capabilities. Decide before you begin whether you're going to share your album by creating printouts. If you want to make hard copies of your slide show, you can prepare your images with a relatively high resolution (150 to 200 ppi). (Just remember that inserting higher resolution images makes your show run significantly slower on a computer, because high resolutions make larger files.)

### Using e-mail to share your slide show

If you want to send a presentation via e-mail, you need to make the file user-friendly by making all the images and other files as small as possible before you insert them into the presentation program. You can send the presentation as an e-mail attachment providing its size doesn't exceed the size limits set by your e-mail provider (or your recipient's inbox).

Another option is to send your presentation in the read-only PDF format (see Chapter 18 for information on this process).

### Sharing your presentation over the Web

Sharing your work over the Internet is an easy way to get your story out to a multitude of people. If you want to show your presentation on the Internet through a Web browser, you need to save the PowerPoint presentation in HTML format and post it on the Web so that it can be accessed through the URL you give it. Just copy the URL and send it via e-mail to whomever you want. The person on the receiving end clicks on the URL or cuts and pastes it into their browser window. For more on hosting your own Web site, see Chapter 18.

---

## Paying someone to create your multimedia album

So you want a fancy digital scrapbook but don't have the time and/or energy it takes to learn how to put one together? One solution is to organize your materials and pay someone to do the work for you. The more organized you are, the less you pay. You'll also be more satisfied if your personal scrapbook style and themes are included in these projects.

The two big questions about this approach are: (1) Where do I find people who can do this kind of work? and (2) How much should I expect to pay? To see what a full service group can do and what they charge, check this popular site: www.redshirt.com/honor. Other Web sites offer this same service, but redshirt is a good place to start. They'll put your scrapbook on CDs or DVDs in most popular formats. If you want to work with someone local, look under *Multimedia* or *Scrapbooking Services* in your phone book. You can also check out the local universities and computer tech schools.

Use a 72 ppi resolution version of your files (that's all you need for the Web) and a Web-safe color palette (indexed color) of the 256 colors that have been tailored for use with Internet browsers. Doing these two things helps your images work better with Internet browsers. Subtle color combinations are often lost during this color conversion, but you can sometimes counter this color loss by upping the contrast in your image before you convert it to presentation-program resolution.

Establishing a lot of contrast between your background and your foreground images really helps the look of your slide show.

### Burning your presentations to CD or DVD

Generally, you're better off saving an audio/video scrapbook on a CD or DVD than converting it to a Web-based program and disseminating it over the Internet because people who want to view it may not have a fast enough connection to accommodate the downloading of large audio/video files. Let your receivers know that they should copy your digital scrapbook onto their computers and play it from their hard drives rather than trying to play it directly from the CD or DVD.

To make advanced multimedia presentations, you need to have the appropriate programs, an extra hard drive, the right computer with a very fast processor, a lot of RAM cache, a fast enough connection for the hard drive, and no worries about memory problems. Then everything will work — but only on your machine! If you want to share your material with other people, you can save your audio/video presentation onto DVD, which compresses your material so others can play it properly too.

Saving your work to the type of DVD that can play on your video DVD player will make it user-friendly, but you need to purchase a special DVD-burning program to do this.

The newer DVD burners include software for burning DVDs in a format that can be used in a regular DVD player. The single biggest difference in these newer formats is that the software makes a selection screen that can be used with the DVD player.

# Part IV
# Getting Creative with Fun Projects

The 5th Wave    By Rich Tennant

"Remember, if you're updating the family digital scrapbook, no more animated files of your sister swinging from a tree, scratching her armpits!"

## In this part . . .

In this part, we show you how to try your hand at creating albums in three of the more popular scrapbooking styles (classic, heritage, and pop). We also show you how to use scrapbook themes to your design advantage. We're confident this will get you out of the beginning digital scrapbooker category *and* give you three (at least) finished digital albums to share. How you share them is up to you. We give you the options and you make the choices: print out a coffee table version, send the pages as attachments via e-mail, post them on a Web site, distribute your album(s) in a CD or DVD format, or take advantage of all of the above.

# Chapter 14

# Creating a Digital Wedding Scrapbook in the Classic Style

*In This Chapter*

▶ Figuring out your story

▶ Picking photos

▶ Choosing a color palette

▶ Using digital tools for your layouts

▶ Finishing your classic album

*T*he classic style, which we describe in Chapter 5, leaves a lasting impression. *And* it's not that difficult to create — especially if you remember its most basic formula: less-is-more! Scrapbookers often choose the classic style for wedding, anniversary, graduation, and baptism albums because its quiet elegance so perfectly commemorates these important milestones.

In this chapter, we show you how you can make an entire digital wedding album in the classic style. With specific digital tools and techniques, you can capture the classic mood in this wedding scrapbook. Using the following strategies will help you tell your story, choose your photos, create a unifying color scheme, and balance items on the pages — so that the end result is a treasured wedding album that has a cohesive, classic look.

## Sketching Out Your Story

Getting married very often means getting other things as well: a loan, an expensive dress, a reception facility, and a photographer to compile a high-priced album that tells the story of the wedding — mostly with photographs and occasionally with photos and text. But regardless of how wonderful a professional wedding album looks, no self-respecting scrapbooker can resist making one of her own — one that reflects her personal perspective and creative abilities.

When *you* scrapbook your own (or someone else's) wedding, you tell a story that's more personal than it is professional and more informal than it is perfect. But the importance of the vows, of the day and all it symbolizes, calls for a design style that gives the event its full due. And the tasteful, timeless classic style is the right choice — exactly what you want for a wedding album.

## Incorporating a journaled story into the album's overall design

As you express your insights and feelings about the wedding you want to scrapbook, try to find a unifying narrative thread for your story — something that will help preserve its significance as the years go by. For example, you might choose to repeat a phrase throughout the album: "We will remember this day because . . ." or "This day was special because . . ." or you might want to focus on incorporating many of the dreams and plans of the bride and groom.

The usual practice in creating a classic layout is to keep your page titles (if you use them) short and well positioned on your pages. You don't want to limit the story part though. If you have a story to tell (and you do), tell it! You can create whole pages of text if the muse is with you. Then either intersperse them with your feature photo pages to elaborate on the images, or put all of your written text at the end of the album. For more on incorporating long journaling into scrapbooks, see Chapter 12.

Of course, you can make the wedding story as short or as long as you think it should be. But the text itself (the way it *looks*) is always a crucial part of your design. The size, color, font style, and length are all important issues that deserve careful consideration.

You never want to lose sight of the fact that the story is itself a part of your design.

## Finding the right font for your story

Whether you write by hand or with the computer, the text will be digitized for this album. If you write it by hand, you can scan it. If you write with the computer, you may want to choose a font that looks like handwriting and will fit well with the classic design style of the rest of the album.

Fonts that work well with classic wedding album designs include Roman, Century, and Palatino — they *sound* like they would go with classic-style design, and they do. These and other *serif* fonts (font types that feature letters with "tails") are all good choices for classic wedding album pages (see Figure 14-1). You may also want to check out the Garamond, Bodoni, Bookman, and Goudy type faces for other classic-look options.

**Figure 14-1:**
Any of these classic typefaces would work well on this "Daddy's Girl" wedding page.

You can see your program's different font options after you put text into a text box. Just scroll through the font menu and your text will change to show you what each different font looks like when it's applied to your text. Remember that you can also change the text's color and size when it's in the text box.

In Photoshop, you just click the Text box and type in a few letters or words. Highlight the text and manipulate your text as you wish. Holding down the shift key instead of highlighting the text will also show you the font changes in the text box.

## Making a quick mock-up for your wedding album

When you plan your digital pages, we recommend that you make a pencil and paper mock-up book (described in Chapter 4), similar to one a publisher might make for an illustrated book project. Sketch your pages quickly. (You don't want to spend too much time on them, because they change continually as you work.)

You can use your story as a starting point for this hard-copy mock-up. Shrink the text so you can fit it into a small sketchbook, or make your mock-up pages full size. We prefer the latter option because it gives us more editing room.

Your story should help you decide which photos to include in the album. Estimate the number of photos and elements you think you're going to use and sketch out their placements on each of your mock-up pages. You can also make notes about colors, backgrounds, and other aspects of the design. (We save our sketchbooks and sometimes put one in the back inside pocket of the finished copy of a digital album.)

# Choosing Photos for Your Classic Album

You recognize classic photos when you see them (Figure 14-2 is an example). Just thumb through a few magazines and notice how easily you can identify the classic-style photographs and images. Their common characteristics include simplicity, balance, meaningfulness, and strength of character. You can find good examples of classic wedding photos in magazines and advertising brochures for the bride-to-be.

---

## Is it classic?

Many classic paintings (wedding and otherwise) portray strong and stately characters, often in the context of a significant historical moment or in luxurious settings. But not all classic photographs have to suggest luxury. It's the portrayal of human perseverance and triumph that's important. The subjects in classic wedding photos frequently convey a spirit of seriousness and commitment.

*together*

*forever*

*Courtesy of* Scrapbook Retailer *magazine (Designed by John Stratton)*

**Figure 14-2:**
This classic-style wedding photograph achieves balance by centering the focal image.

## Creating your own classic photos and images

In any scrapbook style, the photo is the main thing. That's why it pays to work on taking good photographs, no matter what style scrapbook pages you make. For more on taking strong photos, see Chapter 6.

Create your own classic photos (clean and simple, yet elegant looking) by taking the pictures with a good digital camera. Remember that classic-style photographs aren't candid shots. In fact, they're often staged with deliberate props and poses. Your subjects need to look successful and in control.

## Classic embellishments

Because the classic style is so simple, many people assume that there's no such thing as a classic embellishment. This isn't true. It's just that classic embellishments are understated and subtle — some tasteful photo corners or a simple double line around a photo of a wedding party's flower girl and a photo of its ring bearer, for example.

Scrapbookers sometimes use light pastel words to embellish the backgrounds of their wedding album pages, or a simple flourish centered under a horizontally rectangular group photo.

If you do choose to include embellishments in your wedding album, see them always as quiet supporting elements that won't upstage your photos or text. (See the color section for an example.)

## Altering your photos to suit your design

Look at the wedding photographs you've chosen in the context of the whole album. Then use your photo-editing program to make your photos as classically perfect as possible: by cropping, cloning out imperfections, and doing the overall color correction that's sometimes needed to get a fitting classic-style image. (The photo in Figure 14-3 has been significantly altered to fit in a classic wedding album.) For more on working with photos, see Chapters 6 and 10.

**Figure 14-3:**
We had to heavily retouch this classic photo (left) to repair, restore, and recolor it (right).

*Courtesy of Scrapbook Retailer magazine*

Here's how to get a regular photo into shape:

✔ Use the Clone tool to *weed out* unwanted elements in the photographs. You can get rid of an unsightly electrical outlet on an otherwise nice-looking wall, a tree branch right where you don't need it, or even a person (who really belongs somewhere else).

✔ *Insert* people or objects into a photo that weren't there in the first place. (For details on how to do this, see Chapter 10.)

When you're erasing part of a photo to get a minimalist classic look, make sure you save the original photograph — either in your digital library or photo album or on a CD.

## Collecting classic photos and images from other sources

You don't have to limit your album's images to the photos you take. Many scrapbookers include other images that enhance the design and style of their albums:

✔ Commercial CD and DVD collections often come with a brochure that includes small pictures of the images — so you have some idea about what you're getting when you buy the collection. For this wedding album project, you're looking for classic photos and images, so start your search with the CDs that seem to favor the classic style.

✔ Scan images from old books that go with your classic wedding design scheme and your color palette. You may find images that are perfect for your pages — but are surrounded by other stuff you definitely don't want. The classic less-is-more rule applies here. The Selection tool gets rid of what you don't want by extracting the "good" image so you can paste it onto your layout (see Chapter 10). After you "brush" out (cut out) and paste the image, you can feather its edges and apply a shadow.

✔ Try online sources if you can't find the photos you want, such as the royalty free zone at www.gettyimages.com.

## Selecting Your Wedding Album's Color Palette

Look carefully at the photos you've chosen to get ideas for your album's color palette (discussed in Chapter 4). You may use variations on the wedding colors (the colors in the wedding party outfits or the colors in the bride's bouquet). Or choose something that's meaningful to the bride and coordinate your design palette using that color (those colors) as your base. Pastel or muted colors work well on classic-style layouts. You might even want to use sepia tones or color-tinted photos for your wedding album.

Your photo editing program will let you bring up a color selection box. After that, choose your color(s) by clicking on the ones you want to use. You can further adjust your color(s) by entering numeric values in a related section of the color selection box.

Colors look different on a computer monitor than they do on printed pages. If you're going to make both CDs and hard copies of your album, plan on spending some extra time adjusting the colors in these different media.

Some more tips on choosing a classic color palette:

- ✔ Choose a three-color palette — two that are close in hue and one that contrasts (but not too much) with these other two colors. A good three-color palette for a classic wedding scrapbook might be a pure white, an off-white, and a pale pink.

- ✔ Find a classic design you like in a book or magazine and copy the colors.

- ✔ Create a few page spreads in pastels and then insert a few intermittently spaced spreads with stronger classic colors. This sudden contrast contributes a highly dramatic effect to your scrapbook. It can also establish a powerful rhythm based solely on color.

- ✔ Use your color palette to coordinate your design elements (backgrounds, photos, memorabilia, accessories, and embellishments).

# Designing the Classic Wedding Layout with Digital Tools

A simple, clean, well-proportioned classic scrapbook design has its roots in ancient Greece, where artists tried to create perfect forms based on harmony and proportion. It was the Greeks who developed the "rule of thirds" or the "golden mean" as a guide for artistic composition. It goes like this: Designs are more pleasing if focal points are placed in areas that are less than half and greater than two-thirds of the space being designed (refer to Chapter 7 for details about the tic-tac-toe grid — the scrapbooking version of this "golden mean" design principle).

The Guide Line (see Chapter 7), Snap To Grid (later in this chapter), and Sizing functions in your editing program can also help you achieve the design and placement balance that's so crucial to the classic style. Scrapbookers use these positioning tools in designing scrapbooks in other styles, too, but the functions are used most often in creating classic pages — where symmetry is such an important and fundamental design factor.

## Lining up classic page items with the Snap To Grid feature

Using the Snap to Grid feature is a quick and easy way to line up your scrapbook page elements so they conform to standard classic-style composition conventions (you can find the Snap to Grid feature under View). The program responds to this command by placing floating grid lines on your page (they don't print or show up on your finished digital pages). You line up your items close to the grid lines (you can lock the lines in place) and the program will do the rest. The top and left sides of your page elements jump (as if by magic) from one grid line to the next to get to their "proper" positions.

The disadvantage of this feature is that the bottom and/or right side of an item doesn't always line up as well as its top and left side. To compensate for this, you can either adjust the overall size of your page element (see Chapter 6), or take off the Snap To Grid feature and line up your images using the Guide Line tool discussed in Chapter 7.

If your images aren't where you want them when you proof print your pages, return to your digital copy and use the arrow keys to move the elements on your scrapbook page up, down, left, or right until they print correctly on your computer. Experienced scrapbookers leave enough margin on all four sides of the page to absorb any printer variation. To avoid alignment problems, use the same printer when you proof print and final print your pages.

## Using the Sizing tool for balancing your classic composition

Weight and balance issues are particularly relevant in classic design (refer to Chapter 7 for a discussion of these design principles). The classic stylist is very concerned with creating balance in a layout, and does this by manipulating the *weights* of elements and carefully placing them at strategic design points. Classic stylists use the Sizing tool to resize page elements during this process. (Find the Image section on your program's Menu Bar and select the Image Size feature — then adjust the image size of the photo to match the desired size for your photo.)

Your page photo(s) need to look right in relationship to each other and to other design items on the layout. You may often find yourself enlarging and reducing the size of all the page elements to get them to look "just right."

As the size of your page elements change, so does their placement on the page. When their placement changes, you have to adjust your sizes again — which makes it necessary to readjust the placement. Sounds maddening, but when the page comes together, it's really worth the effort.

# Assembling Your Wedding Album

Referring to your handmade mock-up book, you can use your scrapbook program (see Chapter 3) to compile your album. You know how many pages your story will be and have some ideas about how to incorporate it into the album's design. You have the placement for your photos and other elements planned.

Now you need to decide what page size you want to use, how you're going to integrate your backgrounds, and what special finishing touches you need to complete your classic pages.

## Deciding on your page size

No page size is inherently classic, but as is the case in designing with other styles, technical factors make some choices better than others.

The classic concept of less-is-more suggests that you choose a size large enough to allow you to really show off your featured photos. That's why many scrapbookers would say that when it comes to deciding on page size for a wedding album — the larger the better!

The single biggest factor to affect your page size choice is your digital camera. The fact that almost all digital cameras have a rectangular picture format means that your images will be rectangular in shape.

If your photos are all taller than they are wide, they would fit nicely in an 8½-x-11-inch scrapbook format. But when your pictures are wider than they are tall, a featured photograph that takes up a healthy percentage of the real estate on a page will cover most of the 8½-x-11-inch page width. This isn't much of a problem with most scrapbook styles, but it becomes very much of a problem when you create a classic album — because it ruins the kind of negative space you need in classic design.

*Negative space,* the space around an image, object, or page element, is as important as *positive space* (the space the item actually occupies — refer to Chapter 7 for more on these concepts).

For a wedding album, it's generally easier (with normal camera shots) to adapt the 12-x-12-inch page format to the requirements of classic style. There's more negative space to work with and wide shots can be enlarged so they're more visible. After you become conversant with the classic style, though, you may choose to use the 8½-x-11-inch format and just adjust your photography style to match it, which is what many book and magazine designers do. (For a discussion on how your page size choice may be governed to some extent by your printer, see Chapter 4.)

In the classic style, any element that isn't absolutely necessary is taken out of the design. Shapes are simplified and smoothed, and everything possible is done to make the design elements harmonious, simple, and clean.

## *Bringing in your digital backgrounds*

The Brightness/Contrast feature of your image processing program is one you'll probably use often for making classic-style images — especially for those color images you use as backgrounds behind a strong focal point image (see Chapter 11 for information about creating backgrounds from your photos).

Here are a couple things you can do to add drama to your wedding album backgrounds in a classy way:

✔ Increase the brightness until the picture looks washed out and decrease the contrast until it looks flat.

✔ Get a similar effect by taking an image and then using the Rectangle tool to place a white layer over the whole image. Go to the Layer dialog box and reduce the opacity until you get exactly the washed-out effect you want.

✔ The ghost effect you can get with the Rectangle tool can be achieved by superimposing other colors as well. In certain situations, this effect can be used to ghost a portion of the image so you can use various shapes to act as "frames" for these areas of the image.

✔ The background image can be an earlier picture of the subject of your scrapbook page, or an object representing a favorite activity, and so forth. These faint images give the page an ethereal quality — very dynamic when properly executed.

# Putting on the finishing touches on your digital wedding album

As every scrapbooker knows, you build your layout from the "back" and work your way toward the "top" of your page. The same principle applies whether you work traditionally or digitally. Lay in your background, then your photos, page titles, design elements, and journaling (please flip to Chapter 4 for info on layering and Chapter 1 for info on flattening your work).

When you design a classic wedding album, you have a lot of "story" *and* you don't want to clutter the layouts with too much text — so the journaling will most likely be placed on its own separate pages.

The final adjusting steps take longer in classic-style design than they do when you design in other scrapbooking styles. The reason for this is that all the proportions of the page elements probably need to be adjusted and readjusted to create a perfectly balanced composition. This is the crux of classic-style scrapbooking.

Because the essence of classic style is to eliminate the fluff, the unnecessary, and the overdone, try to use filters sparingly. The filter effects work well only when they support the message of the page and your overall design scheme.

If you want to nudge your classic-style wedding layouts up a notch, you can try using some of the following digital tools and techniques:

- ✔ **Painting filters:** One finishing trick is to apply a Paint filter to your layout images to make them look like they were painted with oil paint. Paint Shop Pro and Photoshop Elements are especially good for this kind of effect because you can adjust the "degree" of painterly effect you apply. Wedding images usually look best when there's just the slightest suggestion of paint overlay (though for other styles, a heavy paint technique is often used to make an image look rich and "arty"). The Watercolor, Crystal filter, and Texture filters can add interest and character to your wedding photos, but be careful to understate these effects.

- ✔ **Lighting filters:** This is one situation where applying two effects on the same image isn't necessarily a bad thing. You can use your program's lighting filters to achieve some fantastic effects on your wedding photos (backlighting the bride, and so forth).

    You can apply a Paint filter to an image of the entire wedding party, put a color over it with the Rectangle tool and adjust the opacity until it's just right. Then you can add the Lighting Effect filter to subtly spotlight the bride and groom in the image and get a really nice 3-D effect.

## Framing experiments

Another classic-style convention involves using windows, columns, alcoves, and so forth to frame images. You can easily do this for your digital wedding album by using some of the effects found in the Layer Style dialog box in Photoshop Elements. Just select an image, and go to the upper right corner of your screen.

Select Layer Styles. Within the Layer Styles, select Bevels and then apply one of the Bevel Styles to your image. Next, select the Drop Shadows section in the Layer Style menu and choose a drop shadow for the framed image. This would make a nice frame for a parents-of-the-bride (and/or) groom photo.

Save your work in stages. When you get an effect you like, save it. Work on it some more, and when you're satisfied with what you've done, save the new image under a different file name.

# Chapter 15

# Putting Together a Digital Family Album Using the Heritage Style

......................................................

*In This Chapter*

▶ Picking out a story

▶ Tracking down your heritage treasures

▶ Coordinating colors

▶ Whipping up backgrounds

▶ Using embellishments

▶ Putting it all together

......................................................

*C*reating a digital scrapbook of your old family photos is a great way to preserve and showcase these important treasures. The heritage albums (some of the best scrapbooks we see) link one generation to the next, and make it possible for family members to get to know about their ancestors.

In this chapter, we cover some of the heritage scrappers' favorite tricks and techniques: writing and designing the stories; making older photos look new and newer photos look old; using digital tools to get the heritage colors just right; creating heritage backgrounds; and incorporating memorabilia, accessories, and embellishments that work well with the heritage style.

## Telling the Heritage Stories

The digital heritage album is a perfect place to preserve stories that might otherwise be lost or destroyed over time. It becomes a touchstone for collective knowledge about a family's history.

You are the researcher, the historian, and the preservationist who's compiling this important heritage document. Find out all you can about the people and places in your heritage photos — from every source possible. Your research will be stimulating and absorbing. We guarantee it! (See *Scrapbooking For Dummies* for more on writing heritage stories.)

Study those one-of-a-kind photos and find out as much as you can by interviewing people who may know something about them. These stories can be lengthy, so you need to decide how you want to incorporate them into your album. Interspersing journaled pages with graphic layouts is the usual solution.

## Focusing on a single ancestor, place, event, or time period

First, decide on a focus. If you choose to single out just one of your ancestors for this heritage album, consider choosing one whose life stories are fading fast. You want to get all of the information you can before those who know things about this person pass on.

You may want to focus on a place, an event, or a time period rather than a person. Doing this has an advantage in that you can sometimes get more photos and memorabilia from a wider range of people to enrich your heritage pages. Your narrative will include specifics about how this location, event, or historical time period affected your ancestors.

## Tracking down the stories

The best sources for stories about the people you highlight in your heritage scrapbook include family stories handed down from one generation to the next, relatives who knew those people, and old diaries, letters, and memorabilia.

You're looking for material that will bring the people, places, and events in your heritage album to life. Peculiarities, idiosyncrasies, and specific details can do that. When you try to extract such information from members of your family, you may get several versions of the same story (not at all unusual). Record all the versions in your scrapbook if you want, or check your stories against two or three other accounts and choose the version that seems the most plausible.

## And . . . everyone gets a copy!

Digital scrapbooking has turned out to be a boon to heritage scrappers. For one thing, it solves some of the sharing problems that can arise when families have to decide who gets to keep family heritage materials. Priceless photos and memorabilia can be photographed, scanned, made into digital albums, and then copied onto CDs that can be distributed to everybody who wants one. They, in turn, can easily replicate it and pass it on to future generations — who can reprint it over and over (and probably convert it to ever newer technological formats as the years go on).

If you can't find anyone who knew your subject personally, or if it's not possible to ask questions, you may have to dig a little deeper:

- ✔ Some of your family members have no doubt heard stories about this person, place, or event. Ask them to write the things they remember — in their own handwriting (which you can later scan and use on your album pages).

- ✔ If you need information about a certain place for your album, you can find interesting (and probably little-known) facts about it at the library. Try, too, looking in old newspapers for articles or published photos that may be useful in your documentation.

- ✔ Increasingly, back issues of many old newspapers are being incorporated into online database sites. Using a search engine, you can access the contents of these old newspapers in the comfort of your home. Hopefully, this info won't offend the sensibilities of the research purist for whom research isn't real unless it involves a certain amount of dust and mold. For the rest of us, these sites are just plain wonderful.

## *Using digital tools to enhance your writing*

You can use digital tricks to "set the scene" or create a mood for certain situations. Some of these tricks include using a charcoal filter to convert a photograph of an old house into a drawing. Or you could take the photograph and reduce the opacity of the image so it looks ghostlike.

If an old house or homestead that's important to your heritage stories is still standing, you might be able to show an old photo of the building alongside a photo of the updated (remodeled, modernized) version of the same home.

## Using a heritage album to showcase your genealogy

You may want to create a genealogy heritage scrapbook after you finish this album (refer to our *Scrapbooking For Dummies* for detailed information about genealogy projects). A genealogy album highlights the history of your family rather than just one event or place or person.

✔ Heritage scrapbooks that focus on genealogy are easier to do when you use one of the scrapbook building software programs (refer to Chapter 4 for more information about these programs). Scrapbook programs usually contain several pre-made pages that fit right in with the genealogy theme.

✔ Some scrapbookers begin by showing a family tree complete with pictures and names. Others show a family chart that clearly identifies where everyone fits in the family. Some just start a page with themselves on it and put people in the book as it suits them. If your family genealogy interests you, a genealogy scrapbook is a great way to record those things that make your family unique.

Maybe your heritage research turns up a story about a house fire (a much more common occurrence in the "old days" than it is today). You can use your Burn tool to make an image look like it's survived a fire by darkening its edges.

✔ Burn marks usually show up in photos in rounded patterns. The burn is darkest along the photo's edge and lightens as it gets further into the photo.

✔ After you have the dark spots looking good, use your Eraser tool to make the edge of the photo ragged and rough looking.

✔ When a real photograph burns, it breaks off in sharp, brittle, angular sections. If your edges look too sharp, you can soften them up a *little* with your Smudge tool.

✔ To give your image an even more believable burnt look, put a hole in the photo away from the ragged burnt edge of the image. Usually, these holes aren't large, but their edges are ragged. On some photos, you may have to go one step further and airbrush some black along the edges to make the burnt effect more realistic-looking.

# Choosing Your Photos

Now that you've decided who or what your scrapbook is about, the next step in creating a heritage-style album is to gather and select your photographs. Only when you go through the photos do you begin to understand how the structure of your heritage album will shape itself.

The photos for heritage albums choose you rather than the other way around. You and probably others in your extended family have a set number of photos from the family's collective past — and that's that. Nobody can go back in time and take more.

## Finding family photos

It's often difficult to find out what photos relatives have. Contact your relatives (include distant cousins, great uncles, and so on) and tell them you'd like to make copies of any old family photographs they have. If they're hesitant about finding and lending you their photos, ask for photos and information about a *specific* person, event, location, or time period. For some reason, people are more willing to share when you ask for specific items.

After you get your relatives feeling comfortable about sharing their photographs, ask them to join in on your hunt for more of the same from other family members or close family friends.

## Repairing photos

Don't worry if some of the photos you want to use are tattered and torn. A damaged or aged photo is interesting to look at. It has character, and suggests stories about its history.

---

## To scan or not to scan?

Photographic prints, and especially early photos, are prone to natural decay due to the chemicals used in processing. The silver used in most photo processes *oxidizes* (decays) at a very rapid rate. The hot debate over whether or not to scan these old photographs shows no signs of cooling any time soon. Traditionalists claim that old photos need to be placed in special tissue holders and protected from light and humidity and *should not be scanned* because a scanner's bright, harsh light will accelerate their decay.

Digital scrapbookers counter that these photographs are going to decay anyway, so that even if scanning is harmful, scanning is the only way to preserve them.

We think it *does* make sense to scan or digitally photograph these images in an effort to save them, even though bright scanner lights will accelerate their decay to some degree. The skill of the person using the scanner is an important factor here — you should only have to scan the image once if you scan it right the first time. Remember that after a photo is in the computer as a digital image, the image can be manipulated with your digital editing tools and you won't have to scan it again.

One or more photos that have been *too* damaged can, however, detract from the quality of your page design. Never fear! You can use digital tools to repair it to an age level that fits in better with your overall heritage album design (refer to Chapter 6 for specific instructions on repairing damaged photographs).

## Aging your photos to get a uniform look

Unify your heritage pages by altering some of your higher quality images to make them look consistent with the oldest photographs in your heritage album.

When photos age, they sometimes get spotted (with both white and black spots), bent, wrinkled, torn, and/or discolored. You can easily "age" your better looking photos with digital tools:

- ✔ Print the images out on photo paper.

- ✔ Cut the edges to get a white border around the photo (like an older commercial photograph would have).

- ✔ You can also crease, water spot, burn, or otherwise abuse the photo so it appears older.

- ✔ Rescan the image in this condition to create the look that will fit in with the other elements in your heritage design (for more on photo editing and coloring techniques, see Chapter 10).

### Adding spots

Most of the spots on old photos are white spots caused by scratches or by dust or lint on the lens. To replicate these spots on a perfectly good photo you want to age a little, do the following:

- ✔ Use your Pencil tool set with a small brush size (2 to 4 pixels). Make dust spots of different sizes on your photo. The trick is to make the spots in places where they don't interfere with the important parts of the image.

- ✔ Be careful not to make too many spots or make them too large; most spots on old photos are small and random.

Some old photographs also have dark spots, but these are difficult to replicate convincingly. They're also more distracting, usually larger than the white dust spots, and often have soft rather than hard edges.

### Creating spots

Many old photos are water spotted or spotted with grease. Using your Dodge tool, you can imitate a water spot by making parts of your image lighter. The Burn tool can create the grease spot effect by making the image darker.

### Creating fake folds with the Dodge tool

Of all the aging techniques, making folds is the easiest. Most folds or bends happen on the corners of a photograph. You can create this same dog-eared look by following these guidelines:

1. **Click your Dodge tool and select a very small brush size.**

   If you have the choice in your program, opt for a line style with a soft edge and an exposure of about 50 percent.

2. **Using a stop and go motion, start on one side of the photo and draw a jagged line at roughly a 45-degree angle to the other edge of the photo.**

3. **Try to drag your mouse over this line again.**

   You'll hit the line at some points, but will branch off the line in most cases. This is good because it creates a kind of crackled or spiderweb look to the lines.

4. **Start a new line close to but *not exactly* where you started the first line.**

5. **Draw the new line at a slightly different angle toward the second edge of the photo.**

   This makes the fold lines appear to have started at the point where you started your lines, but will give the impression that the fold was neither intentional nor finished.

6. **Make secondary crack lines coming out of your original lines (like tree limbs).**

   Lighten and thicken some areas of your lines while leaving other areas faint.

### Using your Eraser, Dodge, Smudge, and Burn tools to replicate the look of a torn photo

Here's a quick way to age a photo by making it look as though it's been torn:

1. **Create a crack with your Dodge tool.**

2. **Use the Eraser tool to make a ragged hole from one edge of your image along the path of the tear you created with your Dodge tool.**

3. **Soften the edges of the tear with your Smudge tool, so that the image now looks worn and handled.**

4. **You may decide to include more Dodge tool cracks coming off the tear area and going at 45-degree angles away from the "tear."**

5. **To finish off your tear, use the Burn tool to "discolor" the edge of the tear.**

   On real photos, this discoloration is never uniform along all areas of the tear.

## Protecting old photos from accelerated deterioration

As you look through your old photos, you gain a deeper appreciation of their value. If you're one of the people in your family who has heritage photos, consider yourself the steward of a priceless treasure. Guard your treasure by keeping the photos away from direct light, air pollutants, and extreme temperature changes. House them in your living environment, not in humid basements or hot attics.

# Creating the Color Palette

Heritage-style scrapbooks usually include the muted colors you see in artifacts from days gone by (actually, the old timers used a lot of bright colors, but black-and-white cameras couldn't capture them). Both black-and-white and early color photos have been changed (sometimes drastically) by time and sunlight.

## Choosing your colors

Loud, bright colors seldom fit in well with the heritage style. But even though many of your old photos are black and white, you don't have to limit the color palette for your album to just those two colors. Here are some other ideas:

- ✔ Note how some of your old photos have "aged" into different hues. Choose your palette from their neutral, subdued tones: brown, tan, sepia — even light blues, faded violets, or delicate pinks work well. Attempt to choose colors that complement all of your page elements.

- ✔ You don't have to limit yourself to a monochromatic or rust-and-brown motif. Actually, you can use any color you like. Just make sure it's muted and, for the most part, pastel-looking.

- ✔ If the original photo you're working with is in color, you may decide to turn it into a black-and-white image and then make it a *duotone* image (a two-color image; this process is described in Chapter 11).

- ✔ You can tint photos that have been damaged (either *really* damaged or "damaged" on purpose to make them look old). Make sure your image is in RGB mode (the color mixing system used on computers). Then use the Rectangle tool to overlay color on your image. Adjust the opacity to get the "right" heritage shade.

## *Using digital tools to get the colors you want*

Heritage photographs that look faded or have been stained may look multi-colored. This is the reason we scan these images (that aren't true black and whites) in the RGB color mode. After you open this color image in your photo-editing program, you can use the colors you get from the RGB image or you can work with it in black-and-white (grayscale) mode. This process (scanning in RGB and changing the image back to grayscale) often lets you preserve details that would have been lost had you scanned the image originally in grayscale.

Sometimes you may want *sepia* tone (the old fashion brown looking photo) or *duotone* (two-color) photos. Other times, true black-and-white photos may suit your purposes. You can create wonderful designs using sepia and duo-tones in your layouts. To change a black-and-white photo into a color image:

1. **Select RGB Color (instead of Grayscale) under the Mode feature.**

   RGB color has the added benefit for scrapbooking purposes of creating a smaller finished file by allowing the designer to decrease the color intensity — thus decreasing file size (see Figure 15-1 for an example of how to execute a Decrease Color Depth option).

2. **Select the Hue/Saturation/Light feature.**

3. **Check the Colorized button.**

4. **Slide the Hue button until you get the color you want.**

   Note that you can make just about any color. (In some programs, you have to change the image to a 24-bit image before you can complete this operation.)

5. **After you finish, bring the color level back down to save file space.**

   Refer to Chapter 10 for more information about selecting Hue, Saturation, and Light features.

Many of the filters you apply to a duotone image will appear totally different than they would on a full color image. This ability to make a *monochromatic* (one hue in different shades and values) image into whatever color you want can be a tremendous plus for your scrapbooking. Imagine being able to change your full color embellishments to a single gradient color or your black-and-white photos to colors that go well with your scrapbook color palette.

You won't be the first scrapbooker to get hooked on working with black-and-white images after discovering what you can do with both old and new black-and-white images.

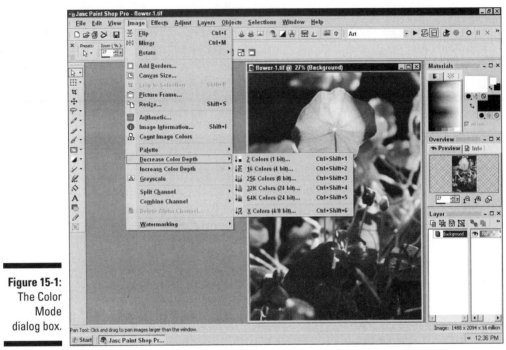

**Figure 15-1:**
The Color
Mode
dialog box.

# Designing Digital Heritage Layouts

Unlike the classic-style album, a heritage scrapbook can handle more page items. Memorabilia, accessories, and embellishments enhance rather than detract from the heritage look.

## Adding memorabilia and accessories to your heritage pages

Find some family mementos such as old letters, recipes, birth/death/marriage certificates, military medals, awards, tickets, and such. These can be scanned into your computer or photographed using a digital camera and included in your digital heritage album.

## Old chemicals and old photos

Many older black-and-white photos aren't really black and white. Before the days of colored photographs, photographic images were processed as continual tone images. Some photographic chemicals made the images black and white, some brown and white, and some came out in strange colors. The particular mix of variables depended on the (individualized) chemical solutions used to develop the images.

 Here are some tips:

- Place a few memorabilia items your ancestor owned and used and arrange them on a table in front of a plain background.
- You can also hang things into the picture from above or place your staged items in the center of the photograph and design around them.
- Photograph some accessories. Old lace from your grandmother's wedding dress or scanned pressed flowers would make great backgrounds or scanned elements on your digital heritage pages.

## Using and resizing embellishments and other items to fit your layout designs

Embellishments that fit "perfectly" into your layout scheme designwise often don't fit sizewise. Here are some tips to help you resize your embellishment items to fit your page layout requirements:

1. **Import your original image onto your page and decide what size you need to make it.**

   The original image is usually too large.

2. **Open the image in your photo editor and reduce it to the required size.**

3. **Lower the pixels per inch (ppi) resolution according to how the page will be printed (refer to the info about resolution in Chapter 2).**

4. **Save the resized image under a new name so you don't lose your original image.**

You can save memory by saving the smaller file and keeping the original on a CD (your computer will work faster and better, too).

5. **If your reduced embellishments still compete for attention with your primary subject material, use some of the filters in your photo-editing program to soften the embellishments.**

You want them to blend in more subtly with the heritage images and other items on your page.

## Assembling a Heritage Album

Now that you know what you're working with, you can begin the process of assembly. As always, you can use your scrapbook program to set up your new scrapbook. Here are a few other tips to keep in mind:

✔ As you work on assembling your heritage album pages, remember to envision them as two page spreads; that's how your viewers will be seeing the scrapbook when it's printed out.

✔ Start placing your page elements from the "bottom" layer and work your way up toward the "top" layer of the page. If you change your mind about the order of the page elements, just modify your layer order. For more on layering, see Chapter 4.

✔ When you finish your rough layout, put in your journaling — and then adjust the design and the elements to accommodate your story. Save the page, print it out and move on.

✔ You can add traditional embellishments to the printed pages if you want, so you have a combination digital/handmade album. This option is especially attractive for heritage albums.

✔ If you choose to leave your scrapbook in digital form, you may wish to save a copy of the file in PDF format so you can quickly and easily e-mail it to family and friends.

### Finding the right page size for your journaling

Heritage albums usually include a lot of journaling; one of the main reasons we create these albums is to preserve as much of the past (in image and in narrative) as we can.

The digital scrapbooker isn't subject to the traditional scrapbooker's page constraints. When you scrapbook digitally, you can make your pages any size you want. The size is limited only by the size limitations of the printer you used to print out your work.

With heritage-style scrapbooks, you can use a 12-x-12-inch format, an 8½-x-11-inch format, or even an 8½-x-14-inch tabloid format that duplicates the size of many old time weekly letterpress newspapers. If you use an 11-x-17-inch format (provided your printer can accommodate this size), you can fold it over, insert several pages together and make yourself an 8½-x-11-inch scrapbook pamphlet.

If you aren't going to print your scrapbook and opt instead to just have people view it digitally, the sky's the limit. You can restrict your "page" sizes to accommodate only that material you can see on the monitor without scrolling up and down or right and left — but you don't have to.

## Creating heritage-style backgrounds

The backgrounds in heritage layouts can be stunning. Try some of the following background techniques. If you create a background you really love, you can use it on more than one layout — or even on every page in the album. (Now there's a time-saver!)

- ✔ When choosing a somber background color for your spread — a dark brown, black, dark tan, or rust red, you can give your pages pizzazz by putting lighter colored images over this monochromatic base. Light colors such as light grays, tans, parchment yellows, ivory, or whites work well.

- ✔ Reverse the previous technique by using lighter monochromatic colors as background and darker images in the foreground. In this case, choose the lighter colors associated with the heritage style.

- ✔ Super enlarge common old-time images such as newspapers, tomato boxes, and old photos to use as backgrounds. These images look best when they're monochromatic or duotone.

- ✔ Make your heritage background stand out by using your Rotation tool to put images on a slant (see Figure 15-2).

- ✔ Enlarge old-fashioned handwriting (blow it *way* up), and use it as a layout background. Scaling back the contrast of the writing will give you an awesome look (see Figure 15-3).

✔ You can take embellishment photos of old doorknobs, hinges, boxes, paper tags, hooks, keys, watches, shoes, hats, tools, and so forth to use on your page backgrounds. A high-resolution shot allows you to enlarge these items so you can use them as backgrounds. Imagine a background shot of a huge old-fashioned telephone enlarged so much that it doesn't even fit on the page — just enough of it showing so you can tell it's a telephone. Most of what you see is the pattern of the wooden desk on which the telephone sits. The desk pattern makes a perfect background for your scrapbook pictures and text. The huge telephone gives the page the antique flavor you want. (Remember that this type of photographic effect isn't possible with a low-resolution image.)

**Figure 15-2:**
Heritage images set on a slant.

Betty
Ann
Boswell-
Jackson

*Friendships*

*Courtesy of Jeanne Wines-Reed (Designed by Michelle Guymon)*

**Figure 15-3:**
An old handwritten letter used as a heritage page background.

*Courtesy of Jeanne Wines-Reed (Designed by Michelle Guymon)*

# Chapter 16

# Celebrating the Here-and-Now with a Pop-Style Digital Reunion Scrapbook

. . . . . . . . . . . . . . . . . . . . . . . . . . . . . . . . . . . . . . . . . . . . . . . . .

### In This Chapter

▶ Focusing on your story

▶ Finding and incorporating pop images

▶ Choosing a color palette

▶ Creating pop layouts

▶ Finishing and sharing your unique piece of pop culture

. . . . . . . . . . . . . . . . . . . . . . . . . . . . . . . . . . . . . . . . . . . . . . . . .

A pop-style scrapbook reflects an interest in what's happening in today's popular culture — although what's pop in one part of a city, state, or country may not be considered pop in another. For instance, the red, white, and blue cowboy boots that everyone's wearing in some parts of Texas may not be popular in Washington, D.C. (then again . . . they may be!).

Your perspective of what constitutes pop art and pop style is bound to be different from someone else's. Revel in the difference, and create your pop-style album with the elements that *you* think are most up-to-date and culturally relevant.

Many events can lend themselves to a pop-style treatment. But in this chapter, we concentrate on a family reunion event — showing you how to choose and manipulate images that will "pop" your pages, how to create fantastic pop-style backgrounds, tell a hip story, and wrap it all up with cutting-edge digital tools.

One interesting aspect of this style of scrapbooking is that it dates itself. In years to come, your pop album will identify and showcase the particulars of this very specific time period — which is one reason why pop-style family reunion albums work so well. They showcase the special characteristics of this period and demonstrate how family members experienced it.

# Figuring Out Your Pop-Style Story

When you decide to create a pop-style album, you become a kind of historian. You emphasize the here and now by detailing its peculiar and unique characteristics — with pictures of course, but also with narrative and descriptive writing (known as *journaling* in scrapbook lingo).

Pop scrapbooks that tell a story about an event that takes place in a very short time period (such as a two-day family reunion) work well. You can include info about the day prior to the event, the two days of the reunion, and the day after — writing about how it affected you and the people close to you, what challenges had to be met, who you met and what the meetings were like, and so forth.

When you go to the event, take your recording tools (digital camera, digital video camera, a voice recorder of some kind, and perhaps a laptop computer). After you have your material, make your scrapbook quickly so you can remember those important details that seem to slip away if you wait too long to put them to paper.

This sounds like a lot of journaling — and it can be! It's imperative that you do a mock-up book that includes your story before you begin putting together your final scrapbook.

## Incorporating current pop trends

In pop-style journaling, you try to express yourself with the vocabulary of your time and tell about your experiences in the contemporary languages you know best. Your text can't be "wrong."

What do you wish your grandmother had written about in her journals or scrapbooks about the "pop culture" she was a part of? Write about those kinds of things in your pop album (your own grandchildren will be amazed!).

Our best advice for pop journaling is to integrate your view of what's important in the current pop culture with the people subjects on your page. For example, you may have photos of the younger folks at your family reunion. Do some of them have two or more earrings on each ear? If so, how does this reflect current pop culture? What does the phenomenon mean? How do you feel about it? How does your grandfather's Aunt Mary feel about it?

## Short stories? Long stories?

The length of the stories in any of your scrapbook albums will vary depending on some of the following conditions: How much material and how much time you have when you create the album; how much you like (or don't like) to write; and the design style you're working with.

Digital journaling gives you options: Make your entries as short or as long as you want. Remember that you can always create separate pages for long entries. Depending on your interests (and perhaps on your powers of observation), you may write a lot or a little about the "history" of the pop culture you describe in your pop-style scrapbook.

Short pieces of text fit in very nicely with pop design (see Figure 16-1), but if you find you're really interested in pop culture, you may find yourself writing pages of absorbing text about what's going on now on the pop culture scene. Plus, at a family reunion, you often get many, many family stories (sometimes in different versions) that absolutely *have to be* recorded and included in your album.

**Figure 16-1:**
Journaling in a pop-style text box. Notice how it is not like "normal" journaling?

*Courtesy of* Scrapbook Retailer *magazine (Designed by Shalese Hinckley)*

Special text effects that can work well with pop-style albums include fun fonts, tilting text boxes, skewing letters, using metallic overlays (to reflect the metal theme in pop culture), and so forth. For ideas on how you can get these and other special text effects, see Chapters 9 and 12.

# Choosing Your Pop Images

You may not find many pop images in the mainstream scrapbooking image market (in the form of stickers, clip art, and so forth). Even when you do come across pop art in digital form, licensing restrictions may limit the number of pop culture icons you can reproduce for your scrapbooks. What you *can* do is this: *Combine* your own digital materials with traditional scrapbook materials to build a cache of images that fit in with the pop style.

Never use original photographs or pieces of art in your scrapbooks, which is no problem for the digital scrapbooker, who can scan the original once and work with copies or save original digital photos and work with copies of those. Save and categorize all of your original images on disks. Your pop album photos may be recent — but they still deserve the same care you give your older photos. These pop photos are historical photos too, in that they reflect and record a certain time period.

## Creating pop photos and images

If you decide to make a pop-style scrapbook, take some pop-style photos (traditional, even, and equally balanced photos don't scream pop style). Tilt your camera. Take a few super close-ups. Get some weird angles and catch people being themselves. This doesn't mean you can't use regular pictures too, but "pop" wants you to stretch the envelope and get a little crazy.

### Try Posterizing

You can apply the Posterization or Poster Edges tool (on the Filter menu of your photo-manipulation program) to your photos. This quick trick helps you get a pop look on just about any image. For more info on how to use filters, see Chapter 6.

As you start applying posterizing and other filters to your photographs, you may notice that some filters work great on some images and not on others. The nice thing about the pop style is that it gives you more leeway to use filtered images than is the case with other scrapbook styles (note how the filters are used in Figure 16-2).

Courtesy of Scrapbook Retailer *magazine (Designed by Shalese Hinckley)*

**Figure 16-2:**
Check out these traditional images filtered to fit with a pop-style layout.

## Getting your images to "move"

Pop-style design incorporates and reflects high-level contemporary energy with movement. This kinetic aspect of pop can be found in images where cloth shapes flow in the breeze, mechanical contraptions have moving parts, or machines look like they're in motion.

✔ **Photograph and collect images that show movement.** Taking pictures of things that are actually moving is challenging, but it can be done. Get tips on how to accomplish this objective by reading about taking motion photos in a good photography how-to book such as the latest edition of *Photography For Dummies* by Russell Hart (Wiley). For your family reunion, think about photographing kids or balls and other things in motion.

- ✔ **Choose images that are associated with motion.** You could use motorcycles, jet planes, powerboats, and sports cars. For the reunion, you might want to use images of the transportation modes people used to get to and from the reunion.

- ✔ **Use filters to effect motion.** Try some of the filters in your editing program that give your images an illusion of movement. Look for filters with names like Wind or Motion Blur. Ripple or Shear filters can also produce the illusion of movement. This technique would work well for photos of games and other reunion activities.

- ✔ **Show distance to indicate movement.** If you're scrapbooking the long road trip you or someone else took to get to the reunion, find some ways to show how far you had to travel to get from one place to another. Combine the kinetic style with appropriate panorama shots. You can get a panorama shot by setting up your camera on the side of the road and showing the road behind you and the same road extending off into the horizon. If you get a picture of a big truck speeding past, so much the better.

- ✔ **Take time-lapse photos.** Set up your tripod so that you outline where the legs of the tripod need to be positioned and index your camera to take the same shot at different times. It's fun to see a flower grow or the day turn into night. This technique offers an interesting perspective on the movement of time. At a family reunion, you might use a time lapse to show different people sitting around a table at various times.

---

# Working with retro-pop images

You generally use your latest photos in a pop-style scrapbook — photos that show life as you see it *today*.

That's the usual approach to a pop album, but it's not the only approach. You can also choose to replicate the pop style of another era, an option we call designing with retro-pop — to reflect the "now" of a bygone day or to design albums about that period.

The pop art of any age glories in the temporary. Pop art from the '60s, for example, glorified the expendable — the paper dress and the cheap billboard sign. It spoofed the power of Madison Avenue and elevated mass-produced consumer items such as tomato soup. If you incorporate '60s pop style into your scrapbook, try to emulate this irreverent attitude and find and use the icons

that represent it. For examples, take a look at some of the works of the late Andy Warhol.

The pop style that flourished in the late '60s died out in the mainstream art world. But it's still popular with many scrapbookers, who characterize it with pop culture icons, bright primary colors, and comic book or poster-style drawings. You can use '60s pop design for a whole '60s scrapbook (with '60s photos) or as a design theme in a contemporary pop scrapbook.

When using pop icons, be sensitive to all copyright and/or trademark laws. It may be illegal to copy many of the images you want to use. Remember that you can't distribute certain brand images without express permission of their owners.

## Drawing on pop publications and characters

Notice how comic book artists design their panels, and set up your camera shots at the reunion to duplicate those effects. After you take your pop-style reunion photographs, you can add some comic book whams or bangs to the photos.

Let the kids pick out some of the photos and make pop reunion scrapbooks of their own. They find some great images in about sixty seconds.

**TIP**

Pop style is perfect for child-oriented scrapbooks. Kids love to see themselves as comic book heroes. They'll even pose for you if you let them know you're making a comic book about them. Get someone or something to play the villain and give your children the hero roles. And hey, pop styling is a good excuse to dress up your dog or the cat — an activity the kids are sure to love (although the dog and cat may not be so excited).

If you have any drawing skill at all, get yourself a comic book and practice drawing some comic pictures. It may take some time to get the hang of this style, but when you do, it's easy to make images to put in your pop-style scrapbook.

# Creating the Color Palette

Pop-style scrapbooking design, like pop art, often relies on shape, color, and line rather than realistic forms. It's freeflowing, impulsive, trendy, and current; sometimes brash, and almost always exciting. The colors you choose for your album should reflect this excitement. Ask yourself, "What color best describes the feelings I want to convey?"

## Using your photos to "find" a color palette

**REMEMBER**

The colors in your photos are the colors of your time. Use them to build the color palettes for your pop-style pages, combining them with the shapes and textures you find in your photographs — the visual elements of the "now" culture you want to capture.

Most pop-style scrapbookers take pictures of the things that surround them and use the color schemes they live with. Pop palettes can be created using modern colors or by identifying and choosing appropriate pop activities to photograph. The colors of the current cultural scene will show up in billboards, advertisements for hot pop products, movie ads, buzz words, fashion patterns, tight shots of automobile logos, or the newest electronic gizmo. Photograph these to find authentic pop colors you can use as the basis for your color palette choices.

## Getting your main color elements from your backgrounds

The pop scenery photos you take can all be used as backgrounds to set the ideal mood for your pop-style pages. (See Chapter 10 for suggestions on how to take background photographs.)

The easiest and faster way to construct a color palette for a pop scrapbook album is to use the background as the basis for your color scheme. With pop-style scrapbooking, most of the images are in full color. The background can also be in full color, but it needs to be dimmed so as not to create too much visual noise. Just pull out some of the dimmed colors in your favorite background, brighten them, and use three or more of them as the basis for your album's color palette.

# Designing Pop-Style Layouts

You can create a variety of design schemes that work well with pop themes. For a family reunion pop album, begin by determining what objects, colors, activities, and attitudes best represent your contemporary world and then decide what combinations will work best with the look and feel of your reunion photos and stories. In the following sections, we offer a few layout ideas for you to consider.

## Creating pop page backgrounds

You may want to use some of the following background techniques in your pop-design plans. For a look at a great pop background, see Figure 16-3.

### Popping foreground images with a monochromatic background

Pop backgrounds are usually simple. Although pop design is characterized by bright colors and interesting shapes and lines, toned-down background colors are typical on pop pages where scrapbookers have used them as a backdrop for bright foreground colors.

Try selecting or creating a monochromatic base layer for a page. Here are some tips:

- ✔ If you want to use an image of a building as a background, photograph the building in the shade rather than in bright sunlight — to mute its colors and make its shapes less dimensional.

✔ Apply a filter or two over the background shot to soften it and make it look even more monochromatic.

✔ Look at the colors that remain most prominent in your subdued building shot. Brighten these colors (without changing their hue) with the Hue/Saturation/Lightness feature (see Chapter 10) and apply them to the foreground elements on your page. They'll stand out without clashing with the background.

If you need more contrast and punch in your title or in the elements surrounding your foreground photos, you can use brightened complementary colors from the colors you find in the background.

**Figure 16-3:**
Here's an example of a simple yet fun pop-style page background.

*Courtesy of* Scrapbook Retailer *magazine (Designed by Shalese Hinckley)*

### Washing out a pop background

A variation of the monochromatic technique is to select a photo for your background, then lighten it and bring down the contrast with the Brightness/ Contrast feature in your photo-editing program (see Chapter 10). This creates a washed out looking background that works well with fully colored foreground images and other page items. Open the original background photo again to find and select accent colors you can use in your design.

### Applying filters to your backgrounds

Jazz up your backgrounds by using the filters in your photo-editing program. Adjust the color, polarize the image, or put a funky texture over the photo to add some pop to your image. Contemporary scrappers have been on a metal kick for a while now. You can key in to this trend by using filters that overlay a metallic look onto your background images. Photoshop, for example, has a Chrome choice under the Sketch menu in its Filter menu. This technique is especially useful for those background photographs that are less-than-perfect. For more on filters, see Chapter 6.

### Popping the old into the new

Some things in this brave new world of ours may look more classical than pop. You can spike such images up a notch with your digital tools when you want to include them in a pop-style album.

Say, for example, you'd like to use an exterior wall of your reunion's community meeting building as a background. The problem is that this particular building was constructed in 1911, and a shot of its exterior wall would reflect the early 1900s instead of your pop world.

You can make a 1911 wall into a pop wall by recoloring it — maybe even using a Neon filter! Or lean a skateboard against the wall. Or what about parking a brand new car or motorcycle in front of it? It's easy to transform the wall into a pop symbol appropriate for your pop-style background.

## Using the "non-art" pop style

There's a sector of today's pop art that's sometimes referred to as the "non-art movement." The designs work hard to *not* look like art, so that everyday items are presented in the most unartistic way possible. If you're interested in designing pop albums in this style, make certain you understand the current conventions (or non-rules) in this type of pop by doing a little research on the movement.

Although you may not want to use this non-art style for a whole scrapbook, you can experiment with it in a section or two of an album. Consider using it when your material is more informational than beautiful.

## A master's non-art

Picasso modeled the non-art style in his famous *Guernica* painting. Guernica was the name of a little Spanish village that Hitler bombed to test some new military ordinance. Picasso was devastated by this action, so he painted an ugly picture with distorted body parts and disturbing images to describe what had happened. This isn't a pretty painting, but it communicates clearly what Picasso thought about the unspeakable actions of the Germans and certain Spanish leaders.

Say, for example, you want to do a special section of the reunion album on the oldest family member there — perhaps a great-uncle who immigrated to the U.S. in the early 20th century. You could do that section in the non-art pop format by making it look like a report or legal document. Your design could include dates and times, quotes, pictures with date stamps, receipts, and so forth. Your journaling could resemble the terse language used in government directives.

## *Incorporating memorabilia, accessories, and embellishments into your pop design*

The pop family reunion album suggests many possibilities for memorabilia, accessories, and embellishments. Let people at the reunion know you want to include these things in your pop design. Then photograph or borrow and scan the items. You'll get a broad and interesting variety this way because you have items from many different people.

Here are some suggestions:

- ✔ Memorabilia can include tickets and other items associated with getting to and from the reunion or with the reunion itself.

- ✔ To accessorize a pop album, think of what accessories the advertising sector uses in its pop media ads. Here's an example: create and size bright blocks of color (using a digital rectangle and a Sizing tool) to make a pop frame for great-grandmother's beautifully aged face.

- ✔ Embellish your pop pages with 3-D items — you should find good candidates for embellishments at the reunion: old family treasures people have brought to share, decorations made especially for the reunion, and all kinds off amazing stuff. Just keep your eyes open and you'll find all the perfect stuff you need to embellish your pop pages.

You can use your digital filters to "pop up" the traditional items and elements you collect. Remember too, that you can print your digital reunion pages out and then include more "real" memorabilia, accessories, and embellishments on the pages. You can then scan the pages so they'll be ready for copying and sending.

# Completing Your Digital Pop Album

When working with other scrapbooking styles, there are some generally accepted norms we can refer to and build upon. With pop style, the whole point is that it is individual and personal. A pop-style book has no special page size conventions. In fact, some pop scrapbook designers use two or three or even more different-sized pages in one pop album. Your material and your own style sense will be your best guides in this department. Whatever page size(s) you decide on, here are a few pointers to review as you complete your reunion pop-style album:

- ✔ Remember the importance of the mock up book! Putting your pop album together is much easier if you've figured out how you're going to incorporate all of the reunion stories you've collected into one overarching reunion narrative. Keep that narrative simple and chronological and tuck the other stories in where you think they should go. Remember that you might have pages of nothing but stories in some sections of this album.

- ✔ Organize your photos to follow the narrative and the sub-stories. Then begin at the beginning by creating a title page and building each page from the "bottom," layering your way to the "top." For more on layering, see Chapter 4.

- ✔ Start with the background, and, again, if you're short on time, you can use one background or variation of one background for every page in the album. Lay in your photos, page titles, and other elements and when your page is roughly laid out, position your text. Then adjust the design and the elements until you're satisfied with the layout.

Because pop scrapbooking is all about what's new, you may want to experiment with incorporating audio and video elements into your pop-style album. (For more information on audio and visual scrapbooking, see Chapter 13.) The scrapbooking programs are offering more and better audio and video capabilities all the time, but it's still not a slam-dunk process.

Of course, you can find programs that allow you to transform your pop-style scrapbook album into a pop-style mini-movie, but you can also insert very brief audio and video clips to give pop scrapbooks that cutting pop edge they deserve.

# Chapter 17

# Working with Digital Theme Projects

### In This Chapter

▶ Finding a theme

▶ Collecting theme materials

▶ Designing themed digital spreads and albums

▶ Trying your digital hand at specific themes

**S**crapbook themes unify the pages in a layout — or in a whole album. A unified, cohesive album (digital or otherwise) is more aesthetically pleasing than one that jumps around from subject to subject. Plus, consistent themes help viewers understand the perspectives you have in mind.

In this chapter, we make some practical suggestions on laying out digital theme pages and albums, including the following: where you can find theme concepts, how to collect the digital materials you need for your theme layouts, and how to use digital tools to create themed layouts and albums that reflect your individual interests and priorities. We also cover some of the more popular scrapbooking themes you can use to jumpstart your projects.

## Choosing a Theme

Whether you're choosing a theme for a single layout, a particular section of a scrapbook, or for an entire album, you probably won't be surprised to find out that your theme options are endless!

Many themes are based on events we all share and generally recognize as special: graduation from high school, community or business awards, and athletic championships and blue ribbons are all candidates for themed scrapbooks. So are births, birthdays, holidays, anniversaries, school events, vacations, family histories, personal histories, weddings, graduations, businesses, and hobbies.

**TIP**

Remember, too, the special events that don't receive public notice; those milestones in every person's life that often pass quietly by and yet can be as important as those that receive wider acclaim. What significant passages in your life might serve as themes for a personal and very individual album — a period of struggle or illness, participation in a service-oriented group effort, or other experiences that significantly affected and changed you?

## On-the-spot themes

Always keep your digital camera handy! You can never tell when or where an idea for a themed scrapbook might grab you by the lapels. It may happen at a social or work-related event. But wherever it happens, you'll be glad you can produce and duplicate scrapbook page materials at digital speed. You can quickly put together the materials for a small, themed scrapbook of a baby shower with the ready-made templates found in your scrapbook program (see the accompanying figure). Print out copies of this mini-scrapbook and personalize them for your friends by including digital shots you took of them at the shower.

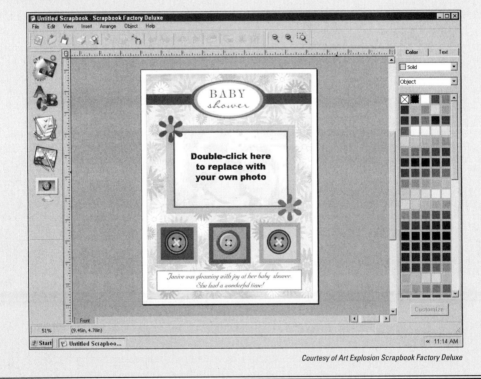

*Courtesy of Art Explosion Scrapbook Factory Deluxe*

When choosing a theme, look at the material you have on hand. Do you have more photos of your family's Yellowstone vacation than you have of any other family experience? If so, this might be the place to start: a vacation-themed scrapbook just about your Yellowstone trip.

Or not! Maybe you'd rather start small — with the 20 or so photos you have of your third child's first birthday party. A small, themed birthday party album (with lots of journaling to make up for the pictures you should have taken but didn't take of that third child) may be just the project you think you can handle. (See the color insert section of this book for examples of digital vacation and birthday party pages.)

No matter what theme you choose, you can find creative elements both online and in scrapbook stores that can help you express it. This chapter's "Gathering Scrapbook Theme Materials" section — and the appendix — can help you gather the materials you need to make a stellar theme album.

# Gathering Scrapbook Theme Materials

Because the market for themed albums is so humongous, you can find an abundance of material on most of the themes you want to work with. In the following bulleted list, we have some specific tips to help you in finding what you want:

✔ Many scrapbookers choose a scrapbooking program based on the type and number of ready-made theme templates it offers. Many programs include at least some theme templates, so you can put together a digital heritage, birthday, classic, or sports event theme-oriented scrapbook very quickly. The scrapbooking programs seldom, however, provide enough templates *that you like* on any single theme for an entire scrapbook.

✔ If you need more material that relates to a specific theme you're working with, you can borrow some scrapbooking program templates from a related theme and adjust them to your design — or you can add your own page designs to a program's basic templates.

✔ Scan the memorabilia, accessories, and embellishments that go with the standard scrapbooking themes and use the scans in your digital theme albums. Use ticket stubs, corsages, themed material from scrapbook stores, and so forth.

✔ Scrapbooking Web sites are full of digital theme materials you can download and use on your pages. Choose from clip art and other graphics to get a variety of themed material. (See Chapter 8 for specific information about downloading and using Internet graphics.)

# Designing Theme Layouts

Designing two-page rather than single-page spreads has become more than a trend in the past few years. One of the reasons that the two-page layout has become such a common staple of scrapbook design is that your theme can be so much better expressed in two adjacent pages than it can on a single page.

Try to imagine the spread as a little world unto itself and use your theme to help your viewer understand this world. Everything on the layout should support the theme.

No matter what theme you decide to focus on in a digital scrapbook album, your design process will be pretty much the same. Use a consistent procedure as you put together your themed album. The orderly approach will make the creation process more enjoyable than if you go at it piecemeal.

After you know what your theme and story are, follow these steps to create your digital scrapbook:

1. **Collect your photos, embellishments, and other page elements.**

2. **Sketch out the story you want to tell.**

3. **Select backgrounds that complement both your story and your theme.**

4. **Place your photographs on the scrapbook pages and see how they look.**

   If necessary, enlarge, reduce, or crop the photos. Arrange them with an eye for the space you need for your journaling. Analyze your photos to determine how (and whether) they support your theme. For example, if you're working with a Western theme, make sure your photos all support that theme (see Figure 17-1). Suppose everything looks Western except one picture. Try placing a Western-style frame around the picture, or cropping out its non-Western elements.

5. **Place your embellishments on the spread.**

6. **Use imaginary or real guide lines to better position your page elements on the layout.**

   Traditional scrappers mentally lay a tic-tac-toe grid over each individual page (see Chapter 7). Lay a larger grid over a two-page spread to accommodate and coordinate the two pages of the layout. Remember that when you scrapbook digitally, you can easily activate your editing program's guide lines to make your grids.

7. **Select an appropriate font and add your journaling.**

**Figure 17-1:**
A two-page spread with a Western theme.

# Exploring Popular Theme Page Ideas

The conventional themes that have become so important in traditional scrapbooking can easily be used to focus your digital scrapbook projects. As you contemplate what theme to tackle next, think about how you can best apply the various digital techniques in this book to support your theme.

Remember that scrapbooking is a highly personal activity and limited only by your imagination — so keep expanding your list of scrapbook themes to include subjects that interest, intrigue, surprise, and inspire you!

## School scrapbooks

Making a themed album to record the highlights of a particular school year is a scrapbooking favorite. Start simple by focusing on two major aspects of the school-year experience:

- Special activities or assignments that will still seem significant in later years.
- Specific talents a child demonstrated during the year.

After you collect the materials for these two general aspects of the school year, organize and evaluate them for design purposes. Be sure and consider the personality of the child. Some children like "brag books," but others don't.

## An unusual family story

Many years ago a man built his family their first indoor bathroom. Everyone in the family looked forward to the convenience and comfort this project would provide. When it was complete, the man realized that people in the house could hear the toilet flush whenever it was used. To him this was so embarrassing he continued to use the outdoor privy for some time until he got used to the operational quirks of the new plumbing.

Include photographs and notes from various people involved with the child's schooling. Get pictures of the teachers or a note in a teacher's handwriting that says something positive about the child. Many children are greatly influenced by principals, coaches, and other school personnel. Include these individuals in the school-themed album.

Most school-related scrapbooks chronicle an entire year's activity, so laying out the pages chronologically makes sense. Photos at the beginning and at the end of the year should illustrate change and growth. Your design style and color scheme can also reflect the child's age and current style choices.

Scan a child's artwork (see the color insert) or take digital group shots of children's oversized artwork and montage them into one image. The grouping should show a broad sampling of an artistic portfolio. (And don't forget to include samples of a child's handwriting!)

A school-themed album is a natural storage spot for audio and video clips (see Chapter 13 for more on adding audio/video to your digital scrapbooks). As time goes by, these voices and moving images from the past become more and more appreciated and treasured — especially your child's voice responding to his or her school experiences.

## Friend themes

How about a theme that emphasizes how important your friends are to you? Categorize larger groups of friends into smaller and more workable groups.

For example, you may see one group of people every Sunday for dinner. Another group may meet mostly to share hobbies such as golf or bowling. You may only see some people when you're out doing yard work, or when you go to your job. How can you subsection these people into scrapbook theme categories?

One suggestion is to plan some regular get-togethers with a group of your friends so you can record these events and show the progress of your friendships at regular intervals. If you like to play golf, for instance, do a golf scrapbook that chronicles what happened during the year. The characters in your story may drift in and out, but the theme of golf gives you a framework for your narrative.

## Family scrapbooks

Many scrapbookers make family-tree albums where they map out and define the relationships among members of their immediate and/or extended families. Every family has stories that make their members proud to bear the family name, and these family legends often set the bar for personal conduct. What better way to pass on these stories than with a scrapbook? In fact, scrapbooks about ancestors are so important, they have a scrapbooking style category (heritage) all their own. For more on the heritage style, see Chapters 5 and 15.

### Focusing on funny family stories

A scrapbook containing entertaining family anecdotes can make a wonderful themed album. Some of these stories may be merely humorous, but others can be strange or unusual. For an example, see the sidebar in this section.

Most families have funny stories they sometimes recount within the family circle, but wouldn't think of writing down. Those are the kind of anecdotes that make really interesting, themed scrapbooks. Getting pictures of various locations and of different family members to support the theme may take some time and detective work, but the results can be hugely gratifying.

Use the funny family stories theme with young children's scrapbooks. Write down the funny things your child or grandchild says and does. Keep these stories in an ongoing scrapbook.

### Grandparent scrapbooks

Many of our grandparents grew up in a time when horsepower came from real horses. Some of the things that greatly affected their lives are totally unknown to the modern generation. A themed scrapbook chronicling their experiences can introduce the younger generation to their ancestors *and* to the historical events and realities of their grandparents' time period.

When creating a heritage scrapbook about your grandparents, narrow the field by identifying an aspect of their lives you want to illustrate. For more on the heritage style, see Chapters 5 and 15. The family connections angle is certainly important, but some of the aspects we discuss in the following bulleted list can also make interesting albums:

- ✔ **Record their traditions.** Many of our ancestors have left us with ethnic and/or religious legacies that should be passed along. Use these cultural traditions as themes for albums about your grandparents. Younger generations who understand where family principles originated (and how they helped the family) are often more open to these traditions.

- ✔ **Tell their love story.** Use a courtship theme in an album about your grandparents. You can base the design of the themed album on their love letters, using a heritage style to emphasize the fact that this story happened to people in the past.

  • Because the original letters your grandparents wrote to each other are precious and irreplaceable, scan and then print them on the scrapbook pages instead of using the originals in your album. The digitized letters become less "real-looking" when they appear flat on the printed page, but you can use your digital tools to bring the letters back to life.

  • Print the letters on separate pages and then attach those pages to your background paper. Use digital filters as you see fit. With this process, you have preserved the original letters and then duplicated them in a way that gives them depth on the page.

- ✔ **Focus on their special characteristics.** Grandparents can be a rich source of inspiration for their grandchildren. Sometimes grandparents are remembered for certain qualities such as loyalty, or even for a set of idiosyncrasies that could provide enough material for an entire themed album. The stories illustrating such characteristics deserve to be recorded and remembered.

- ✔ **Highlight their vocations.** Explore the impact of what your grandparents did for a living by asking the following questions:

  • How and why did your grandparents get started in their vocations?

  • Did they choose vocations in an attempt to distance themselves from the lifestyle of their parents? If so, what were the results?

- ✔ **Recall the challenges they overcame.** You could also create an album about your grandparents' hardships, their challenges, and even their weaknesses. How they dealt with failures isn't only a measure of their characters, but a lesson for the younger generations as well. A heritage scrapbook can be used to pass down the wisdom of people who have dealt with disappointment.

## Pet scrapbooks

To some people, pets are family; no two ways about it — and that's one reason a scrapbook about a person's pets can be interesting, informative, and funny.

The hard part of doing a scrapbook about pets is putting together a focused story. After you do that (maybe something about how the pets interact with the people in their families), the rest is easy, especially because animals aren't camera shy . . . so you can often get good shots of their antics.

Photographing pets can be challenging. First of all, a pet's color can cause major contrast problems. Black labs with dark eyes may be very difficult to photograph because you can't get enough contrast between the dog's overall color and the color of his eyes. Cats and camera flashes don't go together well either. Fish like to hide in the reflection from the aquarium glass and horses tend to point their noses at you when you try to photograph them so it looks like their faces are two miles long. Even with all these problems, you can get a good animal shot if you're patient and remember to take multiple shots.

Pet theme scrapbooks can be especially fun if you allow yourself to get creative with your camera. Ask yourself these important questions:

- ✔ What different camera angles might show the world from the pet's perspective?
- ✔ How can you catch the pet's personality through pictures?
- ✔ How can you visually demonstrate the relationship between the pet and the family?

## Vacation scrapbooks

Vacations are popular themes because they represent an easily defined period of time. People are usually having fun and feeling free, generating the great photographs, memorabilia, accessories, and embellishments that make for exciting scrapbook pages. For a look at a detailed step-out of a traditional vacation scrapbook, see *Scrapbooking For Dummies*.

## Business scrapbooks

Many people make scrapbooks about their businesses. A business-themed scrapbook is often best approached by breaking the project into chunks: one scrapbook about how you got your business started, another one about the growth of the business, a third scrapbook on the history of the products, another about the challenges faced by the business, and a fifth scrapbook highlighting key employees.

These scrapbooks often serve the serious purpose of charting the business and providing a historical record from the owner's point of view. Descendants or outsiders often need this information. Without critical records and facts, such info can forever remain a mystery.

## Hobby scrapbooks

Hobbies fill a special niche in the lives of many people, and it's not unusual for a hobby to take on increasingly heightened significance in someone's life.

Case in point: The Wright brothers' interest in aviation was a silly hobby until their contraption flew; then it became a marvel of science and a wonderful business opportunity. We've been taking bets on whether or not Mrs. Wright was likely to have made a scrapbook about her boys' hobby.

## Remodeling projects

Documenting a remodeling project can be one way to take some of the sting out of the process. The expectations, disappointments, setbacks, and triumphs of such an undertaking are all fodder for a potentially great scrapbook.

You may organize a remodeling project album based on the timeline for completing the project. As the pressure mounts, defuse the stress by using your camera to record the "process." Before long, you'll probably have enough material for several scrapbooks.

You can also use this scrapbook when it comes time to sell your house. Showing potential buyers before-and-after photos is a great way to increase the market value of your home.

## Public building projects

Documenting community or regional construction projects can be very rewarding. Major construction projects are often controversial, and they don't get properly documented. If you choose to record some of these community construction events, you can offer your perspective about the project to the whole community.

# Chapter 18

# Sharing Your Scrapbooks

*In This Chapter*

▶ Printing your scrapbook pages

▶ Converting traditional scrapbook pages to digital form

▶ Sharing your digital pages over the Internet

▶ Creating and copying your scrapbook CD/DVDs

*I*n the past, people had to use their hands to hold and look through scrapbooks. The advent of digital tools changed all that. You still can print your pages and share hard copies, but now you also can share your scrapbooks with family and friends electronically. Granted, a digital scrapbook viewed on a monitor won't have the tactile quality of a handmade album, but it will be wonderful just the same.

When you print your digital scrapbooks, you can then duplicate them as many times as you like!

In this chapter, we tell you how to make digital copies of traditional scrapbook pages by scanning or photographing them and how to share your pages in the same way other digital scrapbookers share theirs: printing them, e-mailing them, publishing them on the Web, or saving them to CDs and DVDs.

## Printing Your Digital Pages

Whether you scan your pages, photograph them with a digital camera, or create the pages digitally in the first place, one way to share them is to print them out.

The printing procedures for getting nice-looking and long-lasting pages are the same as those for getting good photo prints:

- ✓ **Use a good printer, ink, and paper.** For those concerned with getting the longest-lasting printed image, we recommend Epson brand printers, inks, and paper. As various printer manufacturers make improvements, this advice may change. If you want to keep up with the newest and the best printer/ink/paper research, visit `wilhelm-research.com` periodically. Also, refer to Chapter 2 for more advice about selecting printers and supplies.

- ✓ **Make sure your images are high-resolution.** For detailed information about resolution issues, see Chapter 2. We discuss preferable file types and sizes for printing pages in the following section.

Photography stores will make full color prints of your completed scrapbook layouts. These prints will have the same archival quality as color photographs. Some shops just use an inkjet or laser printer for work such as this, which only gives you the same quality print you could get at home with your personal inkjet printer. If you pay an extra price (the cost will vary from store to store), make sure the store is printing your work using the same kind of photo paper and procedures they use to process color film. By the way, many shops offer quantity discounts — but you may have to ask for one.

## Resizing and saving

Suppose you make a 12-x-12-inch digital scrapbook page but you don't want to print out a page that large. Because the page is digital, you can easily resize and save it so you can print it in a smaller size (without losing your original page, of course). Here's how you do it:

1. **Open your finished scrapbook page in a photo-editing program.**

   You may use Photoshop Elements, Paint Shop Pro, Digital Image Suite 10, or some other program.

2. **Select the Image Size or Resize Image feature from the Menu bar and an option box appears.**

3. **Select the size you want for your printed scrapbook page and the page is automatically resized.**

   If you change your mind about the new size, find the Undo feature on your Menu bar and resize the image again until you get what you want.

4. **Save your resized scrapbook page *with a new name*.**

   This is important because if you save the file using the old file name, it will overwrite your original file. By renaming the file, you will create a new file and your original file will remain unchanged.

As you save your scrapbook files for printing, remember that some file formats work better for your printer or the photo store than others. Most places that do high-quality printing work would prefer a TIFF or a JPEG file (although some outlets are beginning to ask for EPS or PDF files). Whatever format you use to save your files for this purpose, make certain you give them an image with enough resolution (300 ppi works best for printouts). If your image is saved in a lower resolution (150 ppi for example), the resulting print will not be as clear or colorful as it could have been (see Chapters 2 and 6 for more information about resolution).

## Adjusting your printer settings

It's important that you check a few specific printer settings before printing out your scrapbook pages:

- ✔ First, push your paper guide snugly, but not tightly, against the side of the paper in your paper feed. This is how the printer indexes or positions your paper to print properly. (Sometimes you may adjust the printer to accommodate special situations; for example, moving your image or your paper to one side to create an extra large margin for binding your page into a book or space to punch holes for a binder).

- ✔ Use the settings in the Printer option *within* your scrapbooking program to make the following adjustments: Choose the number of pages you want to print; select color or black-and-white printing; and indicate the print quality and type of paper you want to print on. Using these important settings will help ensure that you get the best images possible.

If you're only printing draft copies, you don't want to use the maximum amount of ink or take a long time printing out a page — in which case you don't have to use the Printer option in your editing program.

Naturally, having your printer user's manual handy will help you make your adjustments. You may also need to refer to the manual for printer maintenance and trouble shooting.

## Binding your pages

Most scrapbookers (both traditional and digital) are very particular about how they bind or construct their scrapbooks. Digital scrapbook paper is usually thinner than the cardstock papers typically used as base pages for traditional scrapbooks because the digital page doesn't usually have to hold as many heavy embellishments. If you *do* want to put a lot of embellishments on a printout of a digital page, just mount the printed page onto a piece of quality cardstock.

---

## The evolution of the printer cartridge

When color printers were first manufactured, they came with two cartridges: a black ink cartridge, and a color cartridge that contained red, blue, and yellow inks. These printers performed remarkably well, and some printers using this color system are still being sold — even though the system has two major drawbacks: First, if you use all the blue ink, you have to replace the whole color cartridge — even if your red ink and yellow ink are almost full. And second, some colors such as brown and the various shades of gray don't look good because the mixing elements for these difficult colors have limitations.

As photo printers became popular, the printer manufacturers decided to add more colors and put them in individual cartridges. The print quality was better, *and* you could use all the ink in every cartridge. Photo printers have improved dramatically in recent years. If you've shopped for (or already own) a photo printer, you know they come with up to seven different ink cartridges.

---

If you use the proper brand ink and paper to match your printer (and if you allow the print to properly dry), the image should be quite stable.

How you bind the printed pages of your digital albums is up to you. We give you all the information you need about your binding options in *Scrapbooking For Dummies,* including the latest research about scrapbook binder types, protective page sleeves, and admonitions against laminating your pages.

# Digitizing Your Traditional Album Pages

The best digital scrapbook layouts emulate the depth of traditional scrapbook pages. Those real buttons, tags, snaps, strings, and other materials on a handmade page give it character and dimension. The dimensional quality is what makes digitizing these pages a challenge, but you *can* scan a traditional page and do it well with a little planning.

In this section, we give you the tips you need to turn your traditional scrapbook pages into quality digital pages by using a scanner or digital camera. Then you can share these pages electronically with family and friends and/or print out numerous copies of your digitized scrapbook pages.

## Using your scanner

Scanning is probably the easiest and most straightforward method for making a digital copy of your traditional scrapbook page. There are, however, a few minor drawbacks to this method. The most obvious problem is when the scrapbook page is larger than the size of the scanning bed. You can either resize your pages (see the "Resizing and saving" section, earlier in the chapter) or quickly scan your page in sections and then put the page back together digitally. In the following sections, we give you details on exactly how to use your scanner. (For more info on scanners, see Chapters 2 and 6.)

### Scanning smaller scrapbook pages

If your scrapbook page is 8½-x-11 inches or smaller, scanning it is a pretty easy process. Just set your scanner settings, put the page on the scanner, scan it, and save it in the file format that will best suit your needs (see the resizing and saving section in this chapter).

If you're committed to creating traditional scrapbooks, but know you also want to digitize your pages so you can share them with others, consider choosing an 8½-x-11-inch or even an 8-x-8-inch page size format for your hand-made pages. These sizes fit easily on your scanner bed. After you scan your pages, you can enlarge them to 12-x-12 inches or larger in the digital version of your scrapbook (see Chapter 6 for details on how to enlarge or reduce the size of a digital image).

Alas — even lining up a small page on your scanner isn't as simple as it should be. The scanner's line-up marks don't always correspond to the edge of the scanner bed because many scanners don't scan to the edge of the glass. To solve this problem, you can cut a thin piece of wood to match the exact width of the space between the edge of the scanner bed and the scanner's index placement mark (as indicated on the plastic edge next to the glass on your scanner). Using the wood strip will help you quickly and *exactly* square up your page with the edge of the scanner (as shown in Figure 18-1).

**Figure 18-1:**
A thin piece of wood can be used to position a page properly on the scanner.

*Courtesy of Epson America, Inc.*

---

# The skewed scanner story

To understand why your scans don't always line up is to understand how scanners work. A scanner has a curved lens that serves to focus the image onto the image-gathering mechanism in the scanner. Because the lens is curved, you see more distortion the further out you go from the center of the scanner bed to the edges.

---

## *Sectional scanning for larger scrapbook pages*

When the page is larger than the size of your scanning bed (the bed is usually 8½-x-11 inches), the scanning procedure becomes more complex. You have to scan the page in sections and then digitally "stitch" those sections together. We walk you through this process, but want you to know that it can be frustrating and time-consuming at first.

In fact, the work involved in scanning larger handmade scrapbook pages into digital form is one reason some people decide to start creating their scrapbooks digitally rather than making a traditional scrapbook page and then scanning it. (You can solve the large-page scanning problem by buying a scanner with a larger scanning surface, but they cost upwards of $5,000!)

The sectioning procedure consists of two main parts: You scan your page in four separate sections, and then you open these separate sections in your photo-editing program where you stitch them together — thus creating one digital image from the four scans. Here's how:

1. **Place the top portion of your scrapbook page face down on the scanner, positioning it 1 inch down from the top of the scanner bed before you start the scan.**

2. **Place the wooden spacer on the left side of the scanning bed.**

   Use it to line up the left side of your page. (For more information on creating a wooden spacer to position your pages more exactly on the scanning bed, see the section "Scanning smaller scrapbook pages" earlier in the chapter.)

3. **Scan the image and save it.**

   For most situations, saving the file into a TIFF format is the best, but many people prefer a JPEG format because it usually makes a smaller file. With many of the programs, the image just appears in the program from the scanner and the operator doesn't know what file format it is in. When they save the scrapbook page, the image is embedded into the proprietary file format of the program.

4. **Now switch sides, and move the wooden spacer to the right side of the scanning bed.**

   Line up the right side of your page with the wooden spacer.

5. **Scan the image and save it.**

   When you scan both your images in the same location in this manner, the distortion should be identical for both sides of your scan. Also, by using your wooden spacer on both sides of your scanner bed, you can keep the top and bottom of the images in the same relative position on the scanner.

6. **To scan the bottom section of your page, remove your scanner lid and slide the page over the back edge of the scanner so you can get the bottom part of your page on the scanning bed.**

7. **Place your wooden spacer on the left side of your scanning bed and line up the bottom left side of your page with the spacer.**

8. **Scan the image and save it.**

9. **Move the wooden spacer to the right side of your scanning bed and line up the bottom right side of your page with your wooden spacer.**

10. **Scan the image and save it.**

Now you have the four scans you need to stitch together. Here's how to do it:

1. **Open one of your scans in your photo-editing program.**

2. **On your Menu bar, choose Resize and then Image.**

   The dialog box lets you adjust either the image (your page) size or the canvas size (the canvas is your working area).

3. **Select Canvas Size and make the canvas size really large.**

   Make it significantly larger than the size of the page. You need this large area because your scans can take up a lot of space beyond the edge of the page. Having plenty of space around your page makes it easier for you to handle this extra image size without bumping into the edge of your canvas. Later, you can crop your image, getting rid of that huge canvas size, but for now, you want a large canvas on which to stitch your scans together.

   If you're using Photoshop Elements, the easiest way to finish this task is to select File and Create Photomerge. Again, you open all four scan files, but it's not necessary to create an extra large canvas. Select the File and Create Photomerge to open a dialog screen with all four files, and the program will automatically find the intersecting points and pull the image files together into one.

4. **Open the other scans one at a time.**

   Copy and then paste them onto the first image (section number one of the four separate page sections) with the large canvas. (The Cut and Paste features are under the Edit section on the Menu bar.)

5. **Place each of the four scans on a separate layer so you'll be able to move each of them independently without moving the other images.**

   Some programs place each scan on a separate layer automatically. If yours doesn't, when you move one image the others will move as well.

6. **Adjust the scans until they line up properly with each other.**

   You may have to open the Layers feature in your photo-editing program to switch back and forth from one scan to another. This feature is usually found on the Menu bar. For more on layering, see Chapter 4.

7. **After you have all the images in position, flatten the image if your program allows you to.**

   This will lock the four scans together so you won't accidentally bump something out of alignment.

8. **Crop away any excess so your page is properly sized and the extra canvas eliminated.**

   Use the square selection icon found on the side toolbar and select Cropping, which is located under the Image section on the Menu bar.

## Using your digital camera

Another way to get your scrapbook pages into digital format is to photograph them with a digital camera. This method works well provided you do two things: use the proper lighting conditions, and position your camera directly above the scrapbook pages you're going to photograph.

In the following sections we explain the pros and cons of photographing out of doors and inside, and we tell you exactly how to set up for each of these environments.

### Shooting outdoors

Using outdoor light is usually the best option because (for one reason) indoor lights can turn your images green (florescent lights) or yellow (incandescent lights).

To take photos outside:

1. **Attach your camera to a tripod.**

2. **Take your scrapbook page outside, and lay it on the ground in good sunlight.**

3. **Place the tripod over the scrapbook page and position your camera so it's pointing straight down.**

4. **Square the camera up with the scrapbook page, making certain that no shadows are falling on the scrapbook page.**

5. **Take the shot.**

6. **Place the next scrapbook page in place, and do it all again.**

   After the initial adjustments are made, similar shots can be made very quickly.

This process sounds simple enough. And it is. But before you begin shooting, you should know about the following important variables:

- ✔ **Consider the irregularities of light.** Morning and evening shots are a photographer's favorites, but the angle of the sun can create shadows on your scrapbook pages. High noon shots can sometimes wash out the colors of your page, and cloudy days can make it look dull.

- ✔ **Check your tripod.** Some tripods aren't designed to let you position a camera perpendicularly to the ground (most photographers don't do much ground shooting, so they don't need that feature). Also, it's more difficult than you can imagine to keep the tripod legs from casting a shadow on your page. And too often, after you get rid of those shadows, your own shadow finds a way to get into the shot. If you set your scrapbook page on an easel, you'll find that the page leans back a little and you get a trapezoid-shaped digital scrapbook page.

Sorry if all of this sounds complicated! It's really not. After you set things up, eliminate ominous shadows, and find the right light, it's pretty easy. Understanding the variables is half the battle.

You could use a music stand to hold your scrapbook pages — as long as the music stand is made of natural wood or painted flat black. A silver stand reflects too much light. A stand painted another color could reflect that color onto the edges of the scrapbook page. You must also be careful to line up your camera perpendicularly to the scrapbook page so that the edges of your page appear square when you bring it into your computer program.

### *Shooting indoors*

Outdoor light is usually the best option, but you can also shoot indoors — where you may find other lighting challenges. For one thing, indoor shots are almost always underlit, and incandescent lights make a scrapbook page look yellow and fluorescent lights make it look green.

You can use a copy stand to avoid some of these problems. A copy stand, an adjustable device that holds your camera in position above the object being photographed, has two adjustable hooded light sockets with photo white lights you can use to light your pages (see Figure 18-2).

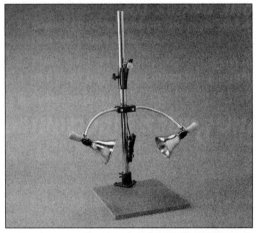

**Figure 18-2:**
A copy
stand.

*Courtesy of Testrite Instrument Co.*

Here's how to take indoor shots:

1. **Mount your camera on the copy stand's adjustable bar and turn on its two photo-grade lights.**

2. **Place your scrapbook page on the stand table and adjust your camera and your lights until everything is just right.**

3. **Take the picture.**

4. **Place the next scrapbook page on the copy stand table, and do it all again.**

   After the initial adjustments are made, similar shots can be made very quickly.

If you don't want to buy a copy stand, just get some photo-grade lights at a photography store (they look like regular light bulbs). Put them into some shop light fixtures with adjustable stands (the kind with aluminum light reflectors built in). By using an adjustable tripod and the shop lights, you can duplicate the function of a copy stand — plus you have some lights to use for indoor shots with your digital camera.

We don't really know of a good way to take quality indoor shots of your pages without having to buy any extra equipment, because indoor shots are almost always underlit. Perhaps if you had a huge skylight and you waited until the right time of day.

# Transmitting Your Pages Electronically

One of the big advantages of digital scrapbooking is that scrapbookers can share copies of their material electronically — through e-mail, over the Internet, or on CDs and DVDs.

## Preparing your pages for e-mail by using PDFs

When scrapbookers e-mail their pages, they want to be sure of two things: that their pages won't be too large to send (most e-mail programs can handle at least a 1 megabyte file), and that the person receiving them can view the pages. Adobe's PDF file sharing software, which compresses files, meets both of these requirements. In the following sections, we show you how to use this program.

People using their e-mail for the first time often have difficulty making it work. If you're having difficulties, find someone who knows your e-mail program, or call your provider for help. After you realize how easy it is to use e-mail, you'll have no trouble.

### Creating and sending PDF files

If the software program you're using to make scrapbook pages allows you to save your scrapbook pages in the PDF format, you simply save your pages in the PDF file format and then attach them to your e-mail. Refer to Chapter 3 for information about which programs can save scrapbook page files in PDF format.

The PDF format is the best format for sharing scrapbook files as e-mail attachments not only because it's the most universally used, but also because it compresses files (the Optimizer in Acrobat 6.0 compresses files up to 45 percent). Here's how to create a PDF file:

✔ In most programs offering PDF creation, you simply select the PDF format instead of a TIFF or JPEG and then you have a PDF file, which the program puts in a file folder or on the desktop. In some programs, you can choose how you want the PDF file saved: at a high-resolution PDF (large file size), a medium resolution (medium file size), or at a low-resolution PDF (small file size). Select the low-resolution option if you're sending the file as an e-mail attachment, and medium or high resolution if you want to print the PDF file.

✔ Programs vary in the way they indicate image resolution. Some programs ask what ppi (how many pixels per inch) you want and give you a selection anywhere between 72 ppi and 300 ppi. Other programs just ask you to select from "small file" in steps up to "large file" — basically 72 ppi (small) to 300 ppi (large). Select the resolution you want and the program does the rest.

Sending your files over the Internet using one of the lower resolution settings will speed up your upload *and* the download time for your receiver.

✔ After you make a PDF file, check its size. Many Internet providers won't allow you to send or receive an attachment larger than 1 megabyte. In the past, some Internet providers have also stripped off the file extensions so they can compress files even more. Hopefully, no one does this anymore, but if it should happen to you, try typing .pdf after the file name and see if that allows you to view the file properly. If that doesn't work, you can sometimes copy the PDF file and paste it into your e-mail message box. If that doesn't work, you have to copy your files onto CDs or DVDs, which we discuss in the "Burning Your Books on CDs and DVDs" section.

If the program you're using doesn't allow you to adjust the size or resolution level of the PDF file, you can still adjust your PDF file size by altering the resolution of the original file. See adjusting size and resolution in Chapter 6 for further information on this procedure.

Use the Attachment function on your e-mail program to send digital materials (see Figure 18-3). Simply click on the Attachment tool and then browse through your computer files until you find the PDF file you made and then select it. It will automatically be included as an attachment on your e-mail. Because scrapbooking programs make each page (or in some cases, each two-page spread) separately, each page (or spread) must be made as a separate PDF file.

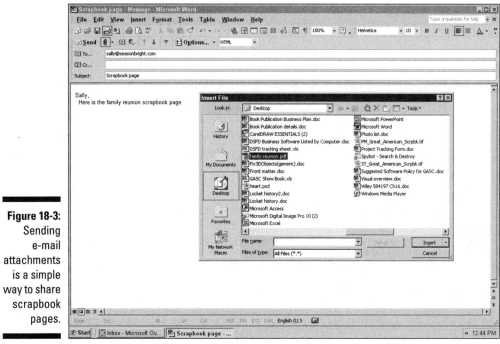

**Figure 18-3:**
Sending
e-mail
attachments
is a simple
way to share
scrapbook
pages.

### Reading PDF files

Because the Adobe Acrobat Reader program (which reads those PDF files
you sent) is installed on most of the computers sold in the last five or six
years, your receiver just clicks on your PDF attachment, which automatically
opens the Reader program and the file so the person can see (and even print
out) your scrapbook page.

Sharing file attachments with other people via e-mail can certainly be more
challenging if the sender and the receiver are working with different programs.
(If the PDF version of your program doesn't match your friend's version of
the Acrobat Reader program, she can download a new version of Acrobat
Reader from the Internet for free — but other program differences between
sender and receiver will pose different problems.)

Even when receivers *can* open a sender's files, they may have different fonts
than the ones the sender used to create the files — which can also cause
problems. With PDF files, the receiver won't have a problem if the sender
has embedded the fonts in the files (*embedding* means the fonts have been

converted to graphics and that the source fonts don't have to be accessed by the receiver to be displayed in the files). Many programs do this embedding automatically. (If your program has an Embedding feature as an option, always choose to embed your fonts.)

## *Publishing your pages on the Web*

You may enjoy sharing your scrapbooks by mounting pages on a personal Web site so your family and friends can view the scrapbooks whenever they wish. The following sections tell you how to do this.

Always keep a copy of your Web pages because Internet companies have computer crashes too. You'll most surely have to *remount* or reinstall your Web site periodically. For instructions on saving these files to CDs or DVDs, please refer to the "Burning Your Books on CDs and DVDs" section later in the chapter.

If you want to display your scrapbook pages on your own personal Web site, you need first to ask your Web service provider for Web space. This usually costs a few extra dollars a month. You also need to get a program for constructing Web pages and another program for sending your newly made Web pages to the server where your Web site is connected to the Internet. You can do all this yourself or hire a techie to help you. After you're set up, the Web site process is pretty straightforward and you should have no trouble using your site.

## Reading attachments

Several years ago, Adobe decided to do something about the problem of attachment files that couldn't be opened and read or viewed. They developed a protocol that would let people view most e-mail attachments — *regardless of the format* the attachment files were originally created in. They introduced two programs (Acrobat Distiller and Acrobat) and offered these programs in Windows, Mac, Unix, Linux, and other configurations. Now people could view (though not edit) text and image files. Acrobat Distiller converts your file into the portable document format (PDF) and Acrobat lets you view the PDF file. Adobe charged for the Acrobat Distiller program, but the Acrobat (viewer) program is offered free over the Internet (go to www.adobe.com) and

is also included with most new computers and many software programs.

Over the years, the Acrobat programs have been refined and features have been added. You still can't edit a PDF attachment, but you can add review notes to it so documents can be sent back to the original creator for adjustments. You can also embed fonts into the document so that it can be viewed in its original form — even when your viewers don't have these fonts installed in their computers. The color profiles have been improved to the point where you can now print many color PDF file attachments with very good results.

### Saving your pages in an acceptable size and format

Save pages you want to display on the Web in HTML format. All your Web graphics are displayed as either GIF or JPEG images and most people tell you to save these images at 72 ppi (pixels per inch). However, we find that saving images in the JPEG format at 80 or 90 ppi seems to make the images look better on the screen than a 72 ppi image does.

You may have to adjust the size of your scrapbook page to fit your Web page format. (See Chapter 6 for further information on this procedure). When working with Web pages, it's usually easier to size your pages in terms of pixels rather than inches.

### Finding Web space

Ask your Internet provider whether it offers a Web page option with the basic Internet package. Many, if not most, of them do allow their customers to put a Web site on the Internet, but restrict it to 1 or 2 megabytes of material. This is enough space to let you get started so you can determine whether you like presenting your scrapbook pages in this manner.

Find a Web page designing program that you can download for free. There are many good ones and a lot of free Web page design programs are quite simple and work well for scrapbook pages or spreads. Ask your family and friends which programs they use (we like Dreamweaver). They'll probably be more than willing to show you how these Web programs work. Or, you can pick up the latest *For Dummies* book on the program you decide to go with.

If you decide you like sharing your scrapbooks on a Web site, you may choose to rent a larger Web site from your Internet provider. The cost for a larger site is nominal.

### Transferring your files to the Web

Most people use a file transfer protocol (FTP) program to transfer their files to the server that will mount these files (their pages) onto the Internet. After your files are *transferred* (copied) to the remote server, they can be viewed on the Internet.

You can download a free FTP program from the Internet or you can purchase a Web page design/FTP program that comes with an instruction book. These are a little easier to work with because everything is contained in the same program. Plus, these programs usually offer more possibilities for page designs.

Web page design programs usually use Web-specific terms, so having a friend to help you through this process can be really helpful. Also, see *Web Design For Dummies* by Lisa Lopuck (Wiley) if you want to become more familiar with the FTP lingo.

### Linking your pages

As you go about designing Web pages, you first create a home page to which you can link all your other Web pages; your *home page* is also your primary URL address. Viewers go here first to find out how your site is organized so they can access all of your other pages. After viewing one of your scrapbook pages, viewers most often return to the home page and select a different page to view. You must update (change) your home page every time you mount a new Web page. Otherwise your viewers won't be able to find the new Web page.

You can also link your scrapbook pages together in sequence, so viewers see the first page, and then hit a Next button — continuing in this manner all the way through the scrapbook. This system works well when you don't have too many pages.

Another issue you should be prepared for is other people wanting to link to your site. This is a common request after you have a Web page mounted. Other people will want to have you provide space for a link to their sites. If you don't watch out, your Web site may become cluttered with links to other sites. Make a policy concerning this and stick to it. Your policy might be one of the following:

- ✔ Set a limit as to how much space you will allow for links. After it's full, don't accept any more links.

- ✔ Rotate your links so that the links you allow on your site only stay for something like two months.

- ✔ Just say no to all link requests.

## Burning Your Books on CDs and DVDs

Another method for sharing your digital scrapbook pages is to save your scrapbook pages as PDF files in the high-resolution format and then burn them to CDs or DVDs.

When you share your scrapbook pages on CD or DVD disks, your friends can put your disks into their computers and view your images using the Adobe Acrobat reader program (get the latest free install version from Adobe's Web site). They can print out the pages you send them, but the quality of those printouts will depend on *their* printers, inks, and papers. If your scrapbook pages are larger than the paper size of the person's printer, they can often use a fit-to-paper sizing option on their printer control panel to print out the page. (See adjusting size and resolution in Chapter 6 for further information on this procedure.)

One advantage to sharing your scrapbook pages on CD or computer DVD disks is that you can save your PDF files at higher resolutions such as 300 ppi, which in turn makes the printed copy of the file sharper and more colorful. However, if you save your files in 300 ppi high resolution, some people may not be able to open them on their computers because they may not have enough random access memory (RAM).

When burning CDs or DVDs, make certain you follow the instructions that came with your computer, or with the CD/DVD burner if you installed it in your computer as an add-on feature. You must also use the type of disks the manufacturer recommends.

You can purchase CD/DVD labels at all good stationary supply stores for use in your printer to make labels for your CD/DVDs. Ask the salesperson about software you can install on your computer to make this process easier. The software is brand-specific for the labels you buy and provides backgrounds and templates for making professional looking labels.

Several new printers come with a built-in feature that lets you print labels directly onto CDs or DVDs. You can buy special disks for the purpose of printing labels. Using this system, you won't have the problem of conventional CD labels coming unstuck and gumming up your CD or DVD player.

# Part V
# The Part of Tens

The 5th Wave                    By Rich Tennant

"Oh Ted, take a picture! It'll be great for our scrapbook."

## In this part . . .

The four short lists in this part give you a clear, comprehensive view of some important (though often overlooked) digital scrapbooking points. Review the pointers, check the digital scrapbooking pitfalls list, try one (or more) of the ten creative ways to integrate digital techniques into your traditional scrapbooks, and discover ten great ways to get kids involved in digital scrapbooking activities.

Check out our appendix too. Its up-to-date Web resources list introduces you to fast-moving digital scrapbooking action you don't want to miss.

# Chapter 19

# Ten Tips for Every Digital Scrapbooker

*In This Chapter*

▶ Getting ready for digital scrapbooking

▶ Attending to hardware and software issues

▶ Making memory room

▶ Organizing, caring for, and sharing your files

*I*f you're fairly computer savvy, you can probably breeze through this chapter. Even so, we hope you can still pick up a tip or two to add to your knowledge about digital scrapbooking basics. For newcomers to things digital, the going may be a little slower — but that doesn't mean you won't end up, like the tortoise, at the same place as the hare.

## Pinpoint the Kind of Digital Scrapbooks You Want to Create

Before you make any other decisions about scrapbooking, figure out what types of scrapbook projects interest you. This decision affects all the other decisions you make regarding equipment, programs, and materials. For example, people who make video-only scrapbooks need video oriented equipment and programs, but can get by with just an inexpensive printer. In contrast, those who use digital tools to make standard scrapbooks need to have a high-quality printer — because their final product usually consists of printed pages.

Look at some of the digital pages, layouts, and albums in scrapbooking magazines and on digital scrapbooking Web sites to discover more about your range of choices regarding the kinds of albums you want to create. We suggest that you also read Chapter 5 in this book for detailed information about style options — so you can imagine how your choice of design style determines your choice of materials, techniques to use, and so forth.

After you have some ideas about what you want to do, it becomes easier to decide which of the scrapbooking programs best meets your needs (we list and discuss these programs in Chapter 3).

# Work with the Hardware You Already Have

Instead of rushing out to buy an all-new computer and accessories system, make a commitment to use the equipment you already have (at least during your first forays into digital scrapbooking). Your printer, scanner, and digital camera need to work with your computer, but you don't have to start replacing old and purchasing new equipment right away. If you can't wait to buy new stuff, you may end up with things you don't need or can't use — or things that you need to upgrade again very soon. As you go along, you figure out what specific kinds of equipment you really want and need.

Sometimes, an older computer won't run properly with graphics programs such as the ones you purchase and install for scrapbooking. But when you're starting out, you can often just add memory to your hard drive without having to replace the old one. Adding more random access memory (RAM) than the program recommends may help your computer run more smoothly (see Chapter 2 for more info on adding additional RAM). When you select your digital scrapbooking software, make sure to read the text on the program's packaging before you buy. It will list the recommended system requirements and amount of RAM your computer needs to run the product properly.

# Select Software That Meets Your Needs and Skill Level

To get a general idea of which programs to consider for your digital scrapbooking needs, refer to Chapter 3 where we list the various features of the most popular scrapbooking programs. When choosing a program, carefully compare the features of the programs in your price range and then select the one that best suits your needs. Make certain you check to see that the system requirements listed on the software box match the capabilities of your computer.

If you decide to purchase a new or a more advanced scrapbooking program, be able to justify its cost by knowing that you can handle it and that you *need* it to do more with digital scrapbooking. For example, if you want to digitize traditional scrapbooks and make them into books to share, or put the same material into digital scrapbook form to send to friends and family over the Internet, you want the programs that will help you do these things in the best and fastest way possible. The advanced programs offer a wide range of creative possibilities for you — you can even use them to add video clips to your scrapbook.

# Master Your Hardware and Software

Most people have an understandable aversion to instruction manuals. But we promise you that the effort you make to carefully read the manuals that come with your programs really pays off. Delve into all your programs as thoroughly as possible so you can get the most out of them. In some cases, just understanding how to work with a simple program can save you the cost and frustration of upgrading to a more advanced program.

Take the technique of text wrapping, for example. In Chapter 12, we explain how to wrap text around a picture or graphic manually rather than automatically. If you don't use this effect frequently, there's no need to pay for an expensive program with the Automatic Text Wrap feature.

If your program manuals are poorly written or the information in them seems just too difficult to absorb, buy a third-party book or manual that clearly explains how to use your programs (the *For Dummies* computer books are especially helpful). After you know what an operation is called and where to find it in your manual, you can use the appropriate program features to make your digital pages easily and correctly.

# Keep Your Computer Healthy

An ounce of prevention is worth as much in the digital world as it is in medicine. Keeping your computer healthy can prevent all sorts of frustrating slowdowns.

Run the disk check and defragmentation programs regularly (once every two months) to cut down on disk errors and to make your computer run faster. (See Chapter 2 for additional information about boosting your computer capabilities.) Both the disk check and defrag programs are usually found in the System Tools area of your computer. They help keep your hard disk organized and running efficiently. Some people like to run these programs automatically by setting up their administrative tools to activate them on a pre-set schedule, but others prefer to run these programs between major projects.

Computer viruses can get into your computer through e-mail messages and downloads from the Web (and even sometimes from CDs or DVDs). Although some viruses are easy to remove, others aren't. A good virus protection program and careful e-mail and Web browsing habits are your best lines of defense:

✔ Download only from reputable sites and then check the downloads for viruses before installing or using the downloads on your computer. The reputable sites usually work hard to keep viruses off their sites, but sometimes no matter what they do, a virus gets through their defenses. Checking everything you download can help you avoid a lot of problems.

✔ Delete unsolicited e-mails without opening them. This is a major means by which viruses get onto your computer. If you don't open the suspect e-mails, the virus can't get into your system.

✔ Run your virus scanning software often. At least once a week. You should also update your virus detection files on a regular basis.

Even when you purchase a popular virus protection program like Norton AntiVirus or McAfee, the program will only be effective if you keep it updated to protect your system against new viruses that can come from new program installations and other sources. Some of the protection programs offer to automatically update for you at a cost of about $40. We think the automatic update is well worth the price.

✔ Check new CDs or DVDs for viruses by running them through your virus software before you download anything. It doesn't happen often, but when there's a virus on a commercial CD or DVD, it's usually a nasty one.

# Set Up a Workable File System

Do set up a workable file system for your scrapbooking activities. Most digital scrapbookers create a new file folder for each scrapbook project. Placing all relevant files in this folder keeps them organized and happy.

## The amazing memory stick

A memory stick (sometimes just referred to as a flash drive) fits into a USB port on your computer. Your computer sees it as an external hard drive, so you can copy and delete files on it just as you would on a regular hard drive. These little sticks are great for keeping an extra copy of your work-in-progress, super easy to carry in your pocket or purse, and they make it possible for you to share your files with anyone, any time, anywhere.

Your digital photos also need to be well-organized and cataloged or they can overtake your computer as surely as hard-copy photos can take over your closets, drawers, and shelves. Catalog your photos to make them as easily and quickly accessible as possible.

Most photo album programs let you view thumbnail images of your photos, so you can easily select the one you need. Here are some tips:

- Create a new folder for each different event you photograph and label it with an event name and date.

- At least once each year, make a folder for that year and put all the year's folders into it. If you group your photos into year blocks, your individual folders won't get too unwieldy.

- Every so often, you should burn your organized photos to a disk (CD or DVD). In this way, you won't have to keep so many images on your hard drive.

- Organize photos by subject. If you had three sons named John, Tom, and Fred, you could create a different subject folder for each son (each subject) or you could make a folder entitled "Sons."

- Because files can be categorized in so many ways, some people use a series of descriptors when they name their files. One file might have an event descriptor (for instance: vacation), a subject descriptor (John), and a date. The file name might look something like this: VACjohn6-99.

You can use a tiny memory stick as you work on a project, and then put the finished project onto a CD or DVD. File these disks alphabetically by project, or by year, or in whatever way best suits your organizational purposes. We recommend you have at least two sets of backup disks. Keep one set at home so you can access and use the images, and a second set somewhere else — so it will be preserved in the event of a home disaster.

# Take Advantage of Your Digital Camera

One of the best things about digital cameras is that you can take as many photos as you need to get those "perfect" shots without having to worry about how much it's going to cost to develop film. If you don't like the shot, delete it and take another picture using different light or angles. If you're not sure which shots you want to save, save them all and choose the best when you see them in your editing program.

Select a resolution for your images that will allow you to create large images (when you take small images, it always happens that you need them larger). Because you can't save as many pictures when you save large images, you may also want to get extra memory cards for your camera. When your first memory card is full, just extract it from your camera and slip in a new one.

Remember that digital cameras use up batteries quickly. Always have spare batteries so that you can take all the shots you want and view them on the LED screen (located on the back of most digital cameras).

# Back Up Your Files

A computer hard drive can go bad at any time with little or no warning. Some hard drives last for years while others go south soon after they're purchased. Develop a system for backing up your work and your materials and use it consistently. Here are a few helpful tips:

- Save your work frequently. Many people save their material to their hard drives every 5 or 10 minutes. In this way, the maximum you can lose at any one time is a few minutes worth of work.

- When you finish working for the day, save everything you've created or altered onto a backup disk — such as a CD, DVD, or memory stick.

- Watch out for power surges, which may cause your hard drive to crash and wipe out important files or images. Get a surge protector with a battery backup. These units also catch power spikes that can damage or destroy your computer. (They don't work against lightning strikes, but then, nothing else does either.) Here are a couple of things you can do, depending on whether you have a desktop or laptop:

  - If you have a desktop computer, you may want to get yourself a battery backup or *universal power supply* (UPS) so that if the power blinks, your computer will stay on. The size of the battery backup must match the size of your computer and computer screen (most desktop computers can be fitted with a battery backup for $50 or less).

  - A miniature *laptop* power surge suppressor that acts as a backup system if the power is cut off will cost you $10 to $15. The surge protector fits right into the transformer and will protect the transformer and the computer from most power surges.

# Manage Your File Sizes and Resolutions

Today's computers and home printers can produce top-quality images for scrapbookers — providing you pay attention to the sizes and resolutions of your files. Saving an image at 300 pixels per inch (ppi) will make it magazine-quality, but the significantly larger file size will also require more computer hard disk space as well as RAM when the file is open. For more information on RAM, see Chapter 2.

You can save file space on your computer by reducing the size of your images whenever possible. If, for example, you have a 6-x-4-inch photo image file, but you only need it as a 3-x-2-inch image for your scrapbook page, reduce the size of the image in your photo file to 3-x-2 inches.

Reducing the ppi level of an image to a level you consider acceptable will also help save space. If your printer can make your scrapbook page look just as good at 200 ppi as it does at 300 ppi, then use a 200 ppi resolution on all your images.

# Share Your Scrapbook Pages

One of the best reasons for creating digital scrapbooks is that you can easily make and share copies of your work. In sharing your scrapbooks, you're sharing a family-oriented perspective — an outlook on life that can't help but uplift and inspire other people.

When you plan to share your pages, save them in the PDF format instead of in your program's file format. The program file format preserves all the layers, links, and commands and lets you make changes whenever you want, but it also makes a large file. If you flatten the final version of a page you've created and save it in PDF format, you'll be able to print it faster (for more on flattening your images, see Chapter 1). It will also be easier for other people to open PDF files on their computers — even if they don't use the same programs you do. For more information on sharing your scrapbook pages, turn to Chapter 18.

# Chapter 20

# Ten Digital Scrapbooking Pitfalls to Avoid

*In This Chapter*

▶ Shopping up a storm

▶ Failing to plan ahead

▶ Falling into a rut

*L*istening to the advice of those who have had experience with digital scrapbooking can save you time, money, and frustration.

In this chapter, we give you the benefit of our own experience with digital scrapbooking and also share tips we've collected from others who have been at this for some time. What follows is a list of things successful digital scrapbookers wish they'd known when they started out.

## *Don't Rush to Replace Equipment*

When you decide you want to get on the digital scrapbook bandwagon, you may be tempted to immediately buy a brand new printer or computer or digital camera — or all of the above. Wait! Analyzing your scrapbooking goals before you replace your old (and perhaps perfectly good) equipment can mean big savings. Too many scrapbookers have purchased equipment that wasn't a good match for their needs and been sorry later.

Study the market for a while and see just what's going on with digital equipment. *When* you buy your equipment can make a big difference in cost. Christmas is the time when digital equipment and software are most expensive, so late January and February are good times to get deals on the software and hardware that didn't sell during the holidays. You can also save money buying equipment and software in late summer and early autumn when items are put on clearance prior to the Christmas push.

Sometimes, the newest technology can be buggy and unreliable. Purchase a piece of equipment or software after it's been tested and reworked. By that time, the bugs are out and there's something new on the market that drops the price of the "older" technology.

Know why, how, and how much you're going to use a new piece of equipment even before you comparison shop for it. Armed with this information, you can make wiser decisions. You may wish to look at one of the many comparison-shopping sites available on the Internet, such as www.froogle.com.

For more information on choosing equipment, see Chapters 2 and 3.

# Don't Put Too Many Programs on Your Computer

Collecting and installing several programs on your computer to meet your digital scrapbooking needs sometimes causes problems. In fact, trying to run too many programs may even cause your computer to rebel. It's generally true that the fewer programs you install, the better your programs and your computer will run. For more information on running the right programs, see Chapter 3.

# Don't Forget to Bring Your Camera

In the old days of larger and harder-to-operate cameras, you had an excuse for leaving your camera at home. Today, you don't. One of the best things about our contemporary technology is that the equipment is smaller, easier to use, and easier to transport.

How many times have you seen an unexpected photo opportunity and chastised yourself for not having your camera with you? Why keep regretting the shots you missed? Instead, get in the habit of taking your camera wherever you go, so you won't miss those great photo ops. Some people even purchase two cameras, a larger one for taking extra good pictures (perhaps with removable lenses and filters) and another, very small camera that can be taken anywhere.

# Don't Forget to Create a Morgue File

Trying to track down digital material you really want to use, even when you do know where to find it, can be extremely time consuming. Believe us. You need a *morgue file* where you can keep your collection of magazine and newspaper ads, scrapbook page samples, patterns, and other elements that attract and inspire you. In fact, you may decide to keep two morgue files — a digital one and a hard copy one.

Color combinations, special effects, interesting textures, style ideas, and type fonts are some of the items you might save in your morgue file. Categorize the materials as you collect them — perhaps according to element types, styles, or colors. You'll find, too, that you'll become more and more selective about what you choose to include in your file.

Periodically (once every year or two), you should make time to reorganize your files and make clean copies of all your material. As you do this, look for ways to streamline your system and keep track of your saved images and other elements. Also, find out how other people organize their file systems and categorize their materials to get ideas on ways you can better address this difficult task.

# Don't Ignore Copyright Laws

As you get more involved in the digital world, you may find that many people openly ignore copyright laws. But prosecution of piracy and copyright infringement is considerably more aggressive than it has been in the past. For details about how to avoid illegal use of other people's ideas, see Chapter 8.

When you share your scrapbook pages, you need to be aware of the potential risks involved in using unauthorized materials. No one is likely to bother you if you use a "borrowed" font on one of your scrapbook pages. But using a Disney character could get you into trouble. Images, logos, and trademarked items are off limits; mainly because many companies are struggling to keep their intellectual property under control and have developed legal strategies to sue violators. If you happen to show up on a big company's radar (and digital radar is pretty powerful), you can get into a legal hassle even if there's no real basis for the lawsuit.

Copyrighted material should be designated as such on the material itself, but this doesn't always happen. Sometimes the trademarks or copyrights are left off when materials are put on the Internet. Other times, you may be using a digital image that someone has taken from a copyrighted image and neglected to attribute. Because there's no clearinghouse through which you can check to make sure you can freely use the material you want, try to go to the original source or creator of the image. If that's not an option, use your best judgment — or create your own image!

You'll find plenty of materials clearly specified as authorized for personal use. Some items are old enough to be designated as in the public domain and therefore usable without penalty, but be aware that even though the original copyright or trademark on such material has long since expired, new copyrights can be attached, and the material re-copyrighted. In this case, the new copyright may not be attached to the image you want to use. Although this situation may give you partial protection, you can still be prosecuted for unauthorized use of copyrighted material.

# Don't Start Too Many Projects

The excitement of a new idea for a digital scrapbook project can carry you through the demands of its initial stages. But as with so many other worthwhile things, it takes a certain amount of discipline to see the project through to completion. We often have more ideas than we have time. The result is a series of unfinished projects that wait forlornly for *someone* to work on them again. Try to plan and finish one small, manageable project first and move on to others *one at a time.*

Another way to keep yourself from too many starts and not enough finishes is to do an organization of *an entire album* in page protectors (see *Scrapbooking For Dummies* for a complete description of this process). That way, even if you can't resist getting started on some fabulous new album idea, you have the other project all laid out and ready to go when you come back to it.

# Don't Print on Colored Paper

The white "color" in most pictures comes from the paper. Printers generally identify white as *a lack of printed color.* For colors that need white as a mixer, a certain amount of the white paper shows through so that it's really your eyes that "mix" the color.

When you print on colored paper, colors are altered because they don't have the white paper to "mix" with. If you print on a pastel colored paper, you may like the effect of its light tones mixing with the color, but darker paper colors don't usually work very well. There are exceptions, of course, and some designers can get interesting effects printing certain images on colored papers.

# Don't Abandon Traditional Scrapbooking

You don't have to be *either* a digital scrapbooker *or* a traditional scrapbooker. You can be both. The important thing in scrapbooking is that you follow your creative impulses. Combining digital and traditional techniques is a great way to complete the greatest number of scrapbook albums in the least amount of time. Many scrapbookers digitize (by scanning or photographing) their finished handmade scrapbook pages so that they can share them electronically (we describe this process in detail in Chapter 18).

Another reason for using this approach is that you can use embellishments from both realms — the traditional and the digital. Sometimes the paper (or other item) you want is only available in a traditional format (or vice versa). Take what you can get where you can find it. Get materials and ideas from everywhere.

# Don't Get into a Rut

Don't get locked into just one style or method of scrapbooking. Try new ideas. Look around to find out where the action is. Stop in at your local scrapbooking store, go to scrapbooking conventions, and see what's going down online. Do your scrapbooking with a buddy to get some synergy happening! Invite other people to get involved in group parties.

Digital scrapbooking is an ever-expanding field, with new possibilities developing all the time. Perhaps incorporating audio and video clips into your digital scrapbook pages is too difficult for you right now, but in the not-too-distant future, we bet somebody will put together a program that will make it easier. Be open to the possibility.

Don't be afraid to ask people you don't know to show you how they put their scrapbooks together. Most of them are willing to share. You can get out of your rut in no time — and you'll find that each of your albums will have its own wonderful, distinctive identity.

# Don't Give Up

Digital scrapbooking involves a certain amount of study and it can be frustrating to go through this discovery period. Don't give up just before everything is about to come together for you. If you run into challenges and problems, resist the temptation to throw up your hands and quit. Help is everywhere!

Look at `http://groups.yahoo.com/group/ComputerScrapbooking` if you're having digital scrapbooking difficulties. This discussion group is made up of people who have overcome digital scrapbooking problems and are willing to help you and others who now face the same challenges.

Most people who work in the digital scrapbooking field understand your questions and situations (whatever they may be) and they're more than willing to help you. Ask your questions and you'll soon have enough information to make the wisest of decisions. For more information on receiving help from "old hands," see the references in the appendix for scrapbooking sites. Pay special attention to scrapbooking chat rooms or sites that offer training materials.

# Chapter 21

# Ten Creative Ways to Integrate Digital Techniques into Traditional Scrapbooks

## In This Chapter

▶ Creating digital design elements

▶ Making digital copies of priceless originals

▶ Cataloging traditional elements with digital tools

*T*raditional scrapbooking is a wonderfully fulfilling creative activity, but it does take time, and many who are used to making scrapbooks by hand are interested in the fact that incorporating digital timesaving techniques into their projects means they can scrapbook more efficiently. At recent convention crop parties, we've noticed that even the most tech-shy scrapbookers are becoming curious about digital tools and techniques.

At this summer's round of convention cropping parties, we expect to see more and more traditionalists taking advantage of the digital techniques we describe in this chapter.

## Print Out Digital Images

Use digital tools to improve the quality of your photos. When you scan a photo and put it into a digital editing program like Photoshop, you can then adjust its brightness, contrast, and sharpness, remove unwanted elements, combine it with other images, or whatever you think needs to be done to make it a better photo. When you're through, print out the image in the size you need for your traditional layout (see Chapter 6 for more info on scanning and printing).

If you want to further enhance the quality of your images, take them to a photo store and have them printed on commercial photo paper at the exact size you need. Printing out copies on your home printer can help you decide exactly what size you want *before* you make a trip to the photography shop.

You can also find photo services on the Internet where you can upload your images and have the prints delivered directly to your house. Some services such as www.snapfish.com or www.ofoto.com even allow you to store images online as long as you make an occasional purchase.

# *Customize Special Background Papers*

When you purchase scrapbook papers for the base or background pages of traditional albums, you're buying the same paper that thousands of others are using in their scrapbooks. With digital tools, you can produce unique and professional-looking background papers that reflect *your* individual taste. (See Chapters 7 and 11 when you want to experiment with digital backgrounds.)

Creating custom background papers means you can also create custom spaces for journaling. Make some areas of your background lighter or darker to serve as text boxes where you can write your stories and support your themes.

Traditionalists who make their own digital background or base pages often use the filters on their digital editing programs to create original designs. They sometimes take an image into a photo-manipulation program and invert the colors. This is one of those effects that works really well occasionally. If you do this with a portrait, you'll recognize it as an effect used in the 1960s and '70s to make rock posters or album covers.

Creating posterizing effects is also fun. This particular filter is one that usually looks good and simplifies a background considerably. Similar effects can be created with the Crystal or Watercolor filters. Or, try a very slight blurred effect to create perceived distance in the background — the foreground will appear sharper and more defined.

# *Support Your Embellishments*

Embellishments are the extras, decorations, and assorted doodads (and we do mean assorted) that many traditional scrapbookers use to dress up their pages and support their design styles. Scrapbookers generally try to coordinate the embellishments they choose for their albums with their stories and themes. (For more on embellishments, see Chapter 4.)

Try combining digital 2-D with traditional 3-D embellishments to get some "wow" effects. Here's an example: Make a digital 2-D image of a spool of string on your background paper and another 2-D spool of string image in your foreground. Then stretch some *real string* from one 2-D spool to the other. Or, use piles or stacks of 2-D tag images and then put a real 3-D tag as an embellishment on top of the pile.

Mixing your traditional 3-D embellishments with 2-D digital embellishments pops life into your layout. Be careful!! Once you start doing things like this, you may find it hard to stop.

# Print Stickers

Digital tools can make life much less expensive for those scrapbookers who can never have too many stickers and cutouts. There's no end to the number of stickers you'll be able to find and create with your photo-editing software. And, you can use the same software to make these images bigger or smaller — just exactly the size you want.

 You can add a self-adhesive backing to your stickers if you purchase special label paper for your inkjet printer. Another option is to use a scrapbook adhesive to adhere these items to your scrapbook pages; see *Scrapbooking For Dummies* for a detailed discussion about the use of adhesives in scrapbooking.

# Make Your Own Headers

When you want a professional-looking page, layout, or album headline for a handmade album, you'll be grateful that you have your computer and a big selection of fonts. Traditional scrapbookers print out digital header text and then cut out the letters to place on their layouts. A sharp craft knife with a replaceable blade works well for this; scissors work too, but they may bend or crease the letters when you try to get into tight spaces.

Computer type is great when it comes to making colored headlines. You can easily choose the proper color and even outline the letters if you need to. If you misjudge the color slightly, just alter it and print the header out again.

You can't get every conceivable color from your printer. Because of the mixing qualities of the inks in your printer, some shades of color are impossible to match to the colors in your design. What you *can* do is find a color that will be just slightly darker or lighter, but one that still blends well with your design colors.

A color can be greatly affected by the paper it's printed on. If a paper is shiny, you'll be able to get colors that you can't get when you reproduce your colored images on a matte paper.

# Scan in Handwriting or Drawings

Many traditional scrapbookers use digitally scanned handwriting and drawings on their handmade pages. You can enlarge or reduce these scans to fit in with the designs you create.

Although many people print out the handwriting scan and then cut it out and adhere it onto a page element, it's easier to just print the scanned handwriting onto the scrapbook page you're using. If the scrapbook paper is too thick for your printer, print it on paper that *will* work and adhere that paper to your scrapbook page.

You can also print the signature onto a clear label and then place the label where you need it on the page. You may want to frame some printouts (such as children's drawings), and then adhere them to your scrapbook pages. The frame hides the edges of the paper and looks like a seamless part of your design.

Be selective about where you apply adhesive because even the most scrapbook-friendly glue can discolor photos and special papers. If you're combining traditional scrapbook techniques with digital material, please refer first to the information about adhesives, buffering/neutralizing agents, and acid-free materials in *Scrapbooking For Dummies*.

# Make Iron-Ons

Try making iron-ons for a traditional scrapbook by transferring digital images from your computer onto cloth. This transfer process usually involves heating the special digital decal with a hot iron to transfer the image onto the fabric.

You can use the fabric with your image on it as a traditional scrapbook page. This is an especially useful technique for use on a scrapbook cover. Scrapbookers often sew lace or other embellishments onto these cloth covers, creating very personal and unique designs.

You can also use this technique for printing images on T-shirts. You just need to invert the image so that when it's ironed on to the T-shirt fabric it prints the correct way. This is also a good solution for printing the titles of your scrapbooks on the spines of those albums you cover with fabric. Just remove the spine, iron on the label, and replace the spine.

# Replicate Letters and Documents

Many original documents are too precious to use in a scrapbook, but sometimes, you really need those documents to tell your story. The solution is to scan them and, if you want, age or "damage" the copies so they look more "real" when you put them in your layouts. Even if people recognize these items as copies, they appreciate the effect you've created. For more on making images appear older, see Chapter 15.

# Use Digital Tools to Share Traditional Scrapbooks

If you enjoy making your scrapbooks in the traditional manner, you can still share them digitally. As explained in Chapter 18, stitching together a scanned 12-x-12-inch scrapbook page isn't too difficult.

You can scan and print copies of your album pages or put the pages in PDF format and send them as e-mail attachments. The newer programs make this process easy: Just load your scanned images into the programs and print them off or save the images as PDFs with just a few clicks of your mouse. After you put your images on disk, you can also take your work to a photo store for printing.

If you don't have a computer or a scanner, you can still digitize your scrapbooks. Many photo and computer stores have services that perform these functions. (Another option would be to find a friend who has the right equipment — and who will probably do this for a fraction of what a commercial shop would charge you.)

After you start sharing your scrapbooks in this manner, you can look at similar material from others, easily viewable with a simple Acrobat program. If you don't have this program, you can download it off the Internet for free from www.adobe.com. Older computers may take longer to load the file, but almost all computers are able to handle it.

# Catalog Your Images

Digital tools and techniques can help you with the job of cataloging elements you use (or think you might use) in making traditional scrapbooks.

If you're working with a digital camera, or if you scan your images, you can save and catalog them with a digital album program. Saving and finding photographs has become less of a problem now that album programs let you file your images and then review them quickly in thumbnail format. Naturally, the more pictures you file, the more material you need to review, but with some forethought, you can organize your digital photos into a system that will help you find exactly what you need, when you need it. We organize by year and event by creating folders (one for the year 2005) and categorizing by event under each main folder.

After you have your digital photographs cataloged, you may also want to digitize your slide or print photographs. Prints are easy (though time consuming) to scan. Slides can be a little more difficult. There are some flatbed scanners that scan slides, but you usually have to special order them. They work well, but it's time consuming to set the slides onto the scanner to make sure they're straight. If you have many slides to scan, you can get specialty slide scanners — you insert the slides in slots and the slides are indexed automatically. If your slides are larger than 35mm (or if you have strips of negatives to scan), the special order flatbed scanners are the best. For more on archiving photos, see Chapter 19.

Of course, you could go to a photo store and have your prints, negatives, and slides scanned by professionals, but doing this is costly. If you decide to take this option, make certain you ask for a quantity discount. If you can be patient and allow the photo technicians to do your job during a lull in their regular work, they may give you an additional discount.

# Chapter 22

# Ten Fun Ways to Involve Kids in Digital Scrapbooking

## In This Chapter

▶ Giving children access to digital tools

▶ Providing ideas and instruction

▶ Linking digital scrapbooking to a child's interests

Children love to participate with adults in "grown-up activities." But for one reason or another, many such activities are off limits. Not digital scrapbooking! In fact, digital scrapbooking is so child friendly that you won't have to do any convincing when you plan a second session. The kids will be ready to go.

Children come in so many shapes, sizes, and temperaments that we just assume you'll adjust the information in this chapter to suit your situation. We can, however, mention at least a couple of across-the-board generalizations:

First, kids of any age need some "rules" when they're going to do digital scrapbooking: limit their number of printouts, for example. Depending on the printer and the paper and inks you use, a single color page could cost as much as $2 to $2.50 to print. (Using different combinations of paper and ink quality levels for different purposes can cut down on printing expenses.)

Second, children under 10 should probably not be allowed to go too far on the computer by themselves. Parental supervision can keep them from becoming frustrated or doing something that may adversely affect the computer or its programs.

Now, you'll want to try some of the following ideas as you encourage your children or grandchildren to "work" with you on this fascinating, productive, creative, (and let's not forget educational) hobby. Digital literacy (which includes learning the "grammar" of digital processes so that children can learn to author with digital tools) is, increasingly, integrated into school curricula.

# Give Your Child a Digital Camera

Kids enjoy the magic of making pictures, and they often use cameras in fascinating (if not always totally appropriate) ways. *And* they're famous for taking lots of really bad photos. When you give them digital rather than film cameras, they can take pictures all day long — and it's not going to cost you a dime to develop their little masterpieces.

You can find several good cameras available for as little as $30 that work very well for children — even very young children (the best buys are at the camera bars of most discount stores). However, these inexpensive digital cameras don't have an LED screen on the back to view the images as the child takes the pictures. You can now get a low-resolution full-featured camera for a very reasonable price.

Kids come up with some really clever and original ideas. If they're clever enough, try publishing them. The school newspaper's a good place to start, but look for other outlets as well. Many kids like putting their creations on various Internet sites. Provided you monitor which sites they choose, this might be a fun experience for your budding digital artist.

# Help the Kids Download Free Clip Art

Children love to "design" with cartoon figures and other kinds of clip art. Teach them how to download free images from selected Web sites. Have them save the images, paste them on their pages, and color them in with your editing program's drawing tools.

# Scrapbook School Assignments

Scrapbooking school assignments actually works quite well, and when you train your children to do school reports in digital scrapbook form, you give them a valuable skill set that involves both visual and verbal communication.

Because digital scrapbooking and magazine page design are so similar, have your children think of their digital layouts as magazine pages — with graphics and text arranged to relate to each other and to look good together. Kids can produce very professional looking work when they put together a school assignment using a magazine format.

# Scrapbook a Special Event

Help your children make scrapbooks of special events such as birthday parties. The best children's scrapbooks highlight what *the kids* think is significant. Seeing an exciting event come alive on a scrapbook page helps children understand the purpose and joy of scrapbooking. By sharing their scrapbooks with family and friends, children relive happy events, gain self-esteem, and make the connection between the art of scrapbooking and their memories.

Children often want to add more "stuff" to their scrapbooks later. This is easy to do with digital scrapbooks and can teach children many valuable lessons — including how beneficial and fulfilling editing and revising can be. Printing and sharing the new versions of scrapbooks is a cinch in digital-land.

# Create a Child's Family Tree

Family tree albums can help children understand and integrate the moral values that are important to their families. When they explore and focus on positive attributes they see in their relatives, they gain added incentives for following those good examples.

This is the perfect opportunity for teaching your child how to scan old photos and to import them into a photo-editing program in order to repair and restore them. They can write some text about their ancestors using a word processing program like Microsoft Word and then copy/paste it onto their family tree pages.

# Photograph and Write about Favorite Possessions

Use photos or scans to help children record ten or so of their favorite possessions. Have the children explain why these items are so cherished. This project does more than teach children about scrapbooking. It also lets them know that you're interested in their treasures — and that you're interested in *them*. Plus, knowing what's important to children can help you respond to them on positive and meaningful levels.

These scrapbooks will be very entertaining when your children revisit them later in life. Until then, you may want to protect these masterpieces, because at certain life stages, the scrapbook artist might want them destroyed.

If you have several children, encourage them to help each other with this particular project. As they work together, they may discover why various possessions are important to their siblings and, as a consequence, may be more understanding and supportive of each other.

# Make Gift Scrapbooks

Help your children make digital gift copies of their work for one particular person or for several. They can customize copies of these gifts by including individual messages in the backs of the scrapbooks or by rearranging or redoing pages using the same basic digital album. Even if they do the original scrapbook in a traditional manner, digital reproduction (scanning) of the scrapbook will allow you to share the work with several sets of grandparents or great-grandparents.

One scrapbooker bought a blank calendar and helped her child adhere family pictures on the calendar's large graphic area — a different image for each month. She and the child hand-lettered family birthdays and anniversaries on the appropriate dates. You can have your child personalize these calendars for family members, scan them, put them on a CD, and give them in both formats as Christmas gifts.

# Avoid the Doldrums

Ever hear a kid complain about being bored? Just how someone could be bored in today's world may not be clear to us, but children seem to have no trouble understanding the concept. To combat this complaint, you may want to sign your children up for one or more of the many digital scrapbooking classes (or scrapbook-related digital-skill classes like Photoshop Elements) being offered in your area.

Meantime, you can spice up a rainy day or a lazy summer afternoon if you keep a little list of kids' digital scrapbook projects handy. You may even get the youngsters to help you with one of your own projects — especially if you ask them to arrange and journal about pictures of themselves.

You can choose projects that will expand the children's digital and design skills. Another plus: They're sure to have a feeling of accomplishment for helping with something important — even if they don't admit it!

# Make a Group Scrapbook

A high profile sports event or any long-term group effort is a good candidate for a group album. Because young people seem to have a great deal of enthusiasm and extra time for new experiences, get them going on creating audio/video event scrapbooks. In this way, your kids (who are probably *very* computer literate) can experiment with the high-tech scrapbooks and then show you how to make them.

More than one young person has turned out interesting video productions with some friends. These young people often continue to experiment and study media arts and may even forge a career from their interests. But even if your little geniuses never become movie directors, the skills they develop in scrapbooking and photography can help them in other aspects of their lives.

# Teach Scrapbooking at Your Local School

Sometimes, the best way to get your children interested in something is to get their friends interested in it first. Try offering your services to teach a scrapbooking class at your local school.

You can teach a classroom full of school-age children about scrapbooking by helping your child's teacher implement a book-building project. Teachers are generally happy to have their students create books because doing so helps foster appreciation and respect for books.

In the past, making storybooks was more difficult because the printing and binding costs were often prohibitive. Digital equipment like cameras, computers, and printers, along with low-cost binding machines have made class bookmaking projects much more affordable.

One kindergarten teacher made a class book by asking her students to give her their recipe for cooking a turkey. The children dictated their recipes, and the teacher wrote them down and collected them into a book. You can imagine the results! Consider compiling this type of book for a school fundraiser. Most parents will pay big bucks for such unique publications.

# Appendix

# Web Resources

● ● ● ● ● ● ● ● ● ● ● ● ● ● ● ● ● ● ● ● ● ● ● ● ● ● ● ● ● ● ● ● ● ● ● ● ● ● ● ● ● ● ● ● ● ● ●

*W*eb resource sites and digital scrapbookers are naturally compatible, and you can easily find plenty of digital material for your pages. But because finding the *best* resources can be challenging for the digital scrapbooking novice, we've provided you with the URLs of some of our favorite Web sites.

If you follow our lead (and your own interests), you can find some really great material for your scrapbooking projects. Visit www.freebyte.com for site URLs that offer free scrapbooking materials for your projects (not all the material on this site is free, but much of it is). You get the site list of places where you can find these materials by clicking on clipart, images, and photos.

To begin your search for free software (known as freeware) that you can download, go to www.gnu.org and www.tucows.com.

Whenever you find a good site, be sure to check out the links they suggest you visit; good sites often link you to other sites with similar objectives.

# *Exploring Scrapbook-Specific Web Sites*

You can find digital materials for your scrapbooking projects at several sites on the Internet. These Web sites offer a wide variety of scrapbook information and digital paraphernalia, including page templates, background "paper," and embellishments. Many of these sites charge for their services, but others offer free scrapbooking resources. Some even provide a helpful combination of both.

To check out what's new in digital scrapbooking land, put on your traveling hat and get ready to visit some of the following active Web sites:

✔ **CB Digital Designs** (www.cbdigitaldesigns.com) offers a variety of materials for sale, including (at this writing) two CD collections and many smaller digital scrapbooking packages. To see exactly what you get for your $35 CD investment, you have to scroll through several screens, but they give you a good idea of what you'll receive when you order. Images are 300 ppi resolution.

- ✔ **Computer-Scraps** (www.computer-scraps.com) sells two CDs for $25 each. They post a visual listing of exactly what you get on each CD. Resolution is 300 ppi. This site offers some nice freebies for download.

- ✔ **Design Butcher** (www.designbutcher.com) appears to be a new site with limited offerings, but the designers also do work that's available for sale on the Scrap Girls Web site mentioned later in this list. The single CD ($33) contains 50 papers and more than 100 embellishments. You can tell by their name that they don't take themselves too seriously.

- ✔ **Digital Design Essentials** (www.digitaldesignessentials.com) offers two CDs priced at $35 each (or both for $60). You can also buy individual kits for $6. All material is clearly shown so you can see exactly what you're buying. This is another site that believes in offering freebies, and you can take advantage of some interesting material just by visiting the site.

- ✔ **Digital Scrapbook Design** (www.digitalscrapbookdesign.com) offers various layout kits, backgrounds, elements, and templates (or *ploppers*) at very reasonable prices. All material is furnished at 300 ppi. They also have some free material you can evaluate and download if it meets your needs.

- ✔ **Digital Scrapbook Pages** (www.digitalscrapbookpages.com) has been set up to sell the work of various digital scrapbook artists. Images are 300 ppi unless noted otherwise. They categorize all of the digital scrapbook materials.

- ✔ **The Digital Scrapbook Place** (www.digitalscrapbookplace.com) is a comprehensive site. Some, if not all, of the images on this site are 200 ppi. They have more CDs available than most other sites, offer a sizable collection of free material for downloading, and feature quite a few self-paced tutorials. The site is mounting a major effort to offer classes at what they call the Digital Scrapbook University.

- ✔ **Digital Scrapbooking Magazine** (www.digitalscrapbooking.com) is a really good site for digital scrapbookers — as its rapid growth seems to indicate.

- ✔ **Gauchogirl** (www.gauchogirl.com) has a couple of CDs for sale, but there's also a large freebie section containing a wide variety of digital embellishments. This site looks like it's really growing rapidly, so you may want to check in every week or so.

- ✔ **JASC/Corel** (www.corel.com) offers seven different software kits for various aspects of scrapbooking — including shabby chic, heritage, papers, and embellishments. Each kit costs $20 and you can see exactly what you will be purchasing by going through a series of screen examples. (If you use Paint Shop Pro, check out the scrapbook-specific material available for your program.)

✔ **Jeri's Digitals** (`www.littlehousetwo.homestead.com/index scrapbook.html`) sells a materials CD for $30 and also has several pages of downloads, fonts, and pictures (the pictures are low resolution but the scrapbook material is 300 ppi). If you want the downloads put on CD, Jeri will do that for you.

✔ **Mangels Designs** (`www.mangelsdesigns.com`) has an extensive library of frames and layouts. They offer free samples, so you can tell what quality to expect. If you pay $20 for a lifetime membership, you can download anything you want from the site. This site also has a huge links section.

✔ **Olivia and Company** (`www.oliviaandco.com`) offers a few free images along with some downloads and CDs for sale. These images could be defined as frilly and feminine. This site is worth looking at to see if its artwork fits your style.

✔ **Raggedy Scrappin'** (`www.raggedyscrappin.com`) offers you a whole site of ragdoll design backgrounds and embellishments. This site has a raft of CDs and other items for sale. There's also a section of free material you can download. If "cute" is your thing, you'll love this site.

✔ **Scrap Elegance** (`www.scrapelegance.com`) is a new site that's still growing, and a place where free downloads are as good or better than the material you can buy — the kind of site you want to support. The material you can get is softly elegant and colorful.

✔ **Scrap Girls** (`www.scrapgirls.com`) sells digital paper collections, digital embellishments, and predesigned pages they call *easy pages*. They also have video tutorials that show basic digital scrapbook techniques. You can either download the material you wish to purchase or have your selections saved to CD and mailed to you. Images are 300 ppi resolution and descriptions of the items offered are very clearly pictured and properly described. This site also offers a newsletter and some freebies if you subscribe.

✔ **Scrapoetry** (`www.scrapoetry.com`) offers little poems to put into your scrapbooks. While most of their poems aren't free, they don't cost very much. The site also advertises free clip art. They have over 400 nice images you can choose from, but many are low resolution.

✔ **Shabby Princess.com** (`www.shabbyprincess.com`) lets you download nice page backgrounds and embellishments for free. (This site also features contests you can enter to showcase your work.)

## Be a smart site shopper

Digital scrapbooking is a relatively new activity. Demand for digital scrapbooking material is just now becoming strong enough to justify offering it for sale. Sites that advertise digital scrapbook paper, embellishments, and templates may list links to other sites that do the same thing, and the newest sites frequently offer better deals on materials in an attempt to get business and to start word-of-mouth advertising.

Before you purchase any of these materials, determine what resolution you need when you place these images in your scrapbook-building program. You should also understand how many various designs you're getting for your money. Most of these offerings have coordinated material (which is nice), but some offer as few as seven different designs. The price for each offering also varies. Be certain you totally understand what you're getting before you spend your money.

# *Locating Clip Art and Images on the Web*

The Internet is a great place to find digital graphics — which people from a wide variety of different sectors (besides scrapbooking) have been putting into Web sites for many years now. Some of these are free and some aren't. (You usually have to pay for high-quality images.)

To help you in your efforts to mine the Internet for first rate clip art and images, we've collected a list of some sites for you to visit. There are undoubtedly many more, but these will give you a good start in searching for images for your scrapbooks.

When you find material you want to download from the Web, it's important to find out what publication rights come with it.

- **Barry's Clip Art Server** (www.barrysclipart.com) offers one of the nicer selections of free clip art images on the Web. Some of the images are as large as 3-x-4 inches at 200 ppi. To get the largest possible image, select the largest file size listed under the thumbnail listing. When the large image comes up on your screen, save it to your computer.

- **Corbis Stock Photography and Digital Images** (www.pro.corbis.com) is one of the largest stock photo services. You have to register with this service to view their images. Then you can either download the individual images or purchase image CDs. Single images usually cost about $40 each and the whole CD costs about $400. The nice thing here is that you know exactly what rights you're purchasing.

- **Dreamstime** (www.dreamstime.com) is a cheaper (although more complicated) stock photo site. If you use these images for scrapbooking, you pay about $1 per image. If you used the image for publication, the cost would be more, but it's unclear just how much you'd be charged.

- **Freeimages.co.uk** (www.freeimages.co.uk) allows you to find images either by looking through the gallery section or by typing in a request with their search option. After you see a thumbnail you like, choose the image to get a large version of the image to come up on your screen (sometimes this takes a long time). When you see the large image, run your cursor over the image and activate the little toolbar that lets you save the image to your computer.

- **Gifworld** (www.gif.com) offers the same material you can get at barrysclipart.com.

- **Image*After** (www.imageafter.com) offers a collection of images similar to the one at morguefile.com. Click on the thumbnail to get a larger image. Place your cursor on the larger image and click your right mouse button if you want to save the image to your computer.

- **morgueFile** (www.morguefile.com) offers an outstanding selection of digital images free for download. Click on Image Archive. The file size for each image is listed in the information under the thumbnail of the photo. Click on the image and a larger version will appear. When you drag your mouse across the larger image, a small toolbar lets you save the image to your computer.

- **Pixel Perfect Digital** (www.pixelperfectdigital.com) offers several categories of free images when you select the gallery option on the top Menu bar. The free images on this site aren't as large as those on some of the other sites, but you may find an image you need. The site's other photo listings are all fee-based.

- **Totem Graphics, Inc.** (www.gototem.com) features some of the better clip art on the Internet market.

If you want to use a downloaded image as a background, save it in the largest possible size. Naturally, the smaller images will download faster, but they will only be good for small embellishments or photo accents.

---

# U.S. government public domain images

Images collected or taken for the United States government can't be copyrighted, and are therefore in the public domain. This means you can use them without having to worry about copyright issues. If you type in "U.S. government photo archives" in your Web search engine, you get an extensive list of government-supported photo archives. You should find one site entitled Public Domain Images. If not, type

in http://mciunix.mciu.k12.pa.us/~spjvweb/cfimages.html. This takes you to a huge archive that contains everything from current military images to old civil war photographs. Some of the images are very small or low resolution, but some of them are high- or super-high-resolution digital images. This is a site that will continue to get better as more old images are scanned for use.

# Finding Fonts Images on the Web

We explain in Chapter 9 that brand name fonts (which you have to pay for) usually work better than the inexpensive or free fonts (these are often artsy, wild, and fun-looking) you find on the Internet. To help you see the difference, we have included some examples of both types of fonts in the following list. While many free or inexpensive fonts are perfectly okay, just keep in mind that when you use them, you're doing so at your own risk.

Here are some good sites to start with:

- **Adobe** (`www.adobe.com`) offers top quality fonts for sale.

- **Berthold** (`www.bertholdtypes.com`) also sells high-quality fonts.

- **Fontifier** (`www.fontifier.com`) can make a custom font for you for about $9. This is very easy to do by utilizing a special template provided by the Fontifer company.

- **freewarefonts.com** (`www.freewarefonts.com`) offers a listing of many sites where you can download free fonts. This listing is so good, it deserves to be saved in the Favorites section of your Web browser. Other good free front sites include:

  - `www.acidfonts.com`

  - `www.fontfreak.com`

  - `www.1001freefonts.com`

- **High Logic** (`www.high-logic.com/index.html`) sells software for making fonts (Creator). This software vendor will also allow you to "try" their software for 30 days prior to making the decision to purchase.

- **Scrap N Fonts** (`www.scrapnfonts.com`) offers a wide variety of fonts including CK's fonts.

# Checking Out the Chat Rooms

Chat rooms are online "meeting rooms" — virtual "locations" where people with common interests meet to talk digital talk and exchange information. Chat rooms have many advantages for the beginning digital scrapper, including the following:

- Some chat rooms allow you to post a few of your scrapbook pages so that other people can comment on them. These critiques can be very useful for beginners.

- You can find lots of info on programs, resources, and other digital scrapbooking interests.

✔ Samples of other people's work may give you some great ideas.

✔ Many chat rooms let you visit and watch the interchange without requiring you to sign up, so you can eavesdrop before you decide whether this group chat stuff is for you (other chat rooms do require you to join by registering a username).

# Posting Your Pages

If you're interested in posting your pages on the Web, go to the Gallery or Members Gallery section of a digital scrapbooking Web site. Follow the site directions for the resolution, file format, and downloading of the image to the right section of the Web site.

The process isn't difficult. You may need a savvy friend to help you with the procedure the first time you try it — but after that, you can easily do it by yourself.

The following sites (by no means an exhaustive list) let you post your scrapbook pages so that they can be seen by others on the Internet. These suggestions give you an idea of what to expect for sites of this type:

✔ www.scrapbookit.net

✔ www.scrapbookeronline.com

✔ www.scrapbook.com

✔ www.twopeasinabucket.com

# Specialty Programs

The following list includes the names of some programs that can be very helpful when you want to start making digital scrapbook albums. You may or may not want to take advantage of these specialty programs, but take a look before you say yay or nay:

✔ **Creative Scrapbook Assistant** (www.hp.com) offers free scrapbook resources to those that own the program. The problem is that this material can be difficult to find. The easiest way to get to the proper location on the huge HP Web site is to first locate the search box and type in "HP creative scrapbook assistant." Doing this will take you to the Web page with all the links for the various materials. HP adds new scrapbook-specific materials to their site constantly. If nothing else, you may want to visit this site just to get some ideas.

- ✔ **Foto Scraps** (`www.fotoscraps.com`) features FotoFusion v3, a program designed to help you automatically place several photographs on a page. You select your page size and your photographs, and the program automatically places them on your layout. If you don't like the arrangement, you can hit a computer key and a new arrangement appears. You can select one image for the background and the program places it there and reworks the page design. You can also create some special effects and use filters on your images with this program.

- ✔ **Picasa** (`www.picasa.com`) lets you download a nice PC album program for free. The great thing about this program is that it finds and shows you all the images you have on your computer. This is a great feature for those of us who periodically lose images.

- ✔ **Storyteller** (`www.epson.com`) is a new kit from Epson. This is a PC-only offering that includes software and special inkjet papers. You use the software to bring your photos into a program that walks you through the process of making a book using your images. You print out the pages and clip them in a special binder that's included in the kit. You then have a completed hard copy book to share with family and friends. (The material comes in various sizes so you can choose the size that best meets your scrapbooking needs.)

- ✔ **Triscape FxFoto** (`www.fxfoto.com`) advertises another specialty program — basically a high-end photo album program that includes some nice photo-editing tools. If you're looking to get a good photo album, you might want to give this software a look-see.

# Index

## • *Numerics* •

3-D items
  digitizing, 114
  flattening, 162
  mixing traditional and digital, 301
  scanning, 173–174

## • *A* •

accessories, 236–237, 253–254
ACDSee Power Pack (photo-editing
    software), 45
Acrobat Distiller (software), 278
Acrobat (viewer) program (Web site),
    278, 303
adhesives, 301
Adobe Acrobat Reader (software), 277
Adobe Illustrator (photo-editing software),
    136, 150, 186
Adobe InDesign (photo-editing
    software), 150
Adobe Photoshop Elements (photo-editing
    software)
  for advanced photo-editing, 150
  audio/video features of, 201
  colorizing illustrations and drawings
    with, 129
  cost of, 14
  described, 43–44
  filter plug-ins for, 168
  importing digital graphics, 122
advantages of digital scrapbooking, 9–10
advertisements, 183
after-market products, 29
"aging" photographs
  adding spots, folds, and tears, 232–234
  dodging and burning tools for, 154
  heritage style, 66–67
  shabby chic style, 72

airbrushing, 155–157
album program (picture-viewing
    program), 32
animated flipbook software, 45
anti-aliased outlines, 130
archival quality prints, 29, 266
arrow keys, 74
art
  books, 183
  "non-art," 252–253
Art Explosion Scrapbook Factory Deluxe
    (scrapbooking software), 41, 46
artist style scrapbook, 76
ascenders and descenders, 136
asymmetrical design, 104
audio/video editing software
  authoring programs, 202–203
  PowerPoint, 199, 200, 201
auto-leading, 136

## • *B* •

baby scrapbook, 77
baby shower scrapbook, 256
background
  blurring out, 170, 171
  categorizing and storing, 178
  classic style, 223
  colors for, 181–182
  crafty style, 68
  drawing or painting look for, 171
  dropping out (erasing), 158
  foreground and, 172, 250–251
  heritage style, 67, 239–240, 241
  inspiration for new ideas, 183–184
  magazine ads and, 183
  monochromatic (single color)
    images, 250–251
  montaging, 162–163
  opaquing, 181

background *(continued)*
overview, 176–177
photos as, 117, 177–178
pop style, 250–252
selling to papermakers, 179
shooting photographs for, 177–179
text and, 197
texturing with, 179–181
wallpaper effect, 177
washing out, 252
watermarked images for, 182–183
backing up files. *See* copying files;
saving your work
balance, 104, 109–110, 221–222
base page, creating, 58–59
battery backup for computer, 290
battery life, 32, 290
beginning a digital scrapbook. *See also*
page layout
beginners scrapbooking software, 40–42
design library materials for, 54–55
page size choices, 55
project folder for, 58, 288
selecting photos and images, 57–58
sketching pages for, 55–56
starting too many projects and, 296
style choices for, 15–16
type of scrapbooks for, 54, 285
workstation for, 20–21
writing the story, 56–57
binding the pages, 267–268
birthday party scrapbook, 257
black-and-white images
color photos converted to, 152
converting to color, 153, 166, 167, 235
old photographs and, 237
blocky (pixelated) images, 95
blurring out a background, 170, 171
books and magazines
advertisements, 183
art books, 183
clip art in, 126–127
comic books, 249
pop style, 249
scanning, 28, 115, 219
scrapbooking, 15

borders and frames, 76
branded products, 29
Brightness/Contrast tool, 99, 166, 223
"brush" tools, 155
Burn tool, 233
burning scrapbooks to CDs and
DVDs, 18, 19, 280–281
business scrapbooks, 263–264

**• C •**

callouts, 198
camera case, 36
camera, digital. *See* digital camera
candid shots, 87
Canon digital Elph camera, 32
cartridges for printers, 268
cast shadow, 175
cataloging. *See* organizing and storing
your work
CD or DVD burner, 36
CD or DVD player/writer unit, 17
CD/DVD drives, 17–18
CD/DVDs
burning scrapbooks on, 19, 280–281
photo collections on, 133, 219
photos and scrapbook files stored on,
17–18, 64
printing labels onto, 281
viruses protection and, 288
chair for computer, 21
Chambers, Mark (*Scanners For
Dummies*), 27
chat groups/rooms, 15, 316–317
children
comic books for, 249
digital camera for, 306
favorite possessions scrapbook, 307–308
scanning illustrations and drawings by,
130–131
scrapbooking with, 305–309
classic style scrapbook, 73–75. *See also*
Wedding Album (classic style)
cleanup
computer disk check, 287
defragmenting the computer, 25, 287

discarding or relocating leftover files,
    62–64
reorganizing morgue files, 295
clip art
    CD collections of, 47
    children and, 306
    choosing, 47–48
    coloring in, 68
    described, 125
    printed, 126–127
    travel bureau and, 48
    using, 127–128
    Web sites, 48, 127, 314–315
cloning images, 102, 151–152
Cloning tool, 151
clustering or grouping images, 61–62
collages (montages), 119, 162–163
color palette
    advanced adjustments, 152–154, 166–167
    for backgrounds, 181–182
    black-and-white photos, converting to
        color, 153, 166, 167, 235
    choosing, 107
    classic style, 219–220
    converting color images to grayscale, 166
    converting color photos to
        black-and-white, 152
    duotone, 166–167, 235
    filling letters with, 191–192
    heritage style, 234–235
    hot and cool, 181
    light and dark, 182
    opaquing a background, 181
    RGB color mode, 234, 235
    saturating and desaturating images,
        154, 166
    sepia tone, 235
    text and, 143
    texture and, 152
    tinting an image, 166–167
color printers, 268
color wheel (by EK Success), 52
colored paper, 296–297
comic books, 249
commercial printing service, 92

completing a scrapbook
    classic style and, 224–225
    mock ups for, 216, 254
    pop style scrapbooks and, 254
    support for, 298
tips for, 296
computer. *See also* software programs
    CD/DVD drives, 17–18
    crashing, 17, 25, 26, 141
    defragmenting, 25, 287
    determining your need for,
        11–12, 24–27, 286
    discarding or relocating leftover files,
        62–64
    disk check for, 287
    extended warranty for, 25
    hard drive, 25–27
    laptop, 12, 26, 290
    maintenance and repair, 25, 26, 287–288
    memory for, 25–27, 33, 286
    monitors, 33–34
    multimedia scrapbooks and, 203
    operating system (OS), 27, 38–39
    purchasing, 26–27
    researching, 25
    upgrading, 26, 33–34
    video editing and, 202
    viruses and, 141, 288
    Web sites, 25
computer platform, rolling, 20
computer stand, 20
consistency, 58
copy stand, 274
copying files. *See also* saving your work
    CD/DVDs for, 17–18, 64
    fonts and, 140
    generational loss, 28
    memory stick for, 288, 289
    original images and, 28, 94
    overview, 290–291
copyrights
    about, 124
    importance of, 295–296
    sharing fonts and, 141
    U.S. government public domain
        images, 315

Corel Draw Essentials (software), 44, 136, 137, 186, 196
cost
 Adobe Illustrator, 136
 of authoring programs, 202
 CD or DVD player/writer unit, 17
 Corel Draw Essentials, 136
 digital camera, 32
 font-creation software, 195
 ink and photo paper, 30
 PDF conversion program, 47
 for printing a color page, 306
 scanners, 27–28
 scrapbooking software, 14, 43
 surge protector/suppressor, 290
 universal power supply (UPS), 290
 virus protection software, 288
crafty style scrapbook, 68–69
Creating Keepsakes Scrapbook Designer Deluxe (software), 42
Creative Scrapbook Assistant (software), 14, 42, 46, 317
creativity, inspiration for, 297
cropping (or trimming)
 advanced techniques, 158–160
 described, 57, 96–97
 digital camera feature, 90–91
cross-platform program, 201
cutting out objects
 Cloning tool for, 151
 Eraser tool for, 158–159
 Magic Wand tool for, 159–160

## • D •

default settings for scanner, 92
defragmentation, 25, 287
descreening printed photos, 115–117
deterioration of photos, 234
digital camera. *See also* shooting digital photographs
 advantages of, 24, 289–290
 battery life, 32, 290
 carrying with you, 256, 294
 children using, 306
 collecting design materials with, 53
 cost of, 32
 cropping feature, 90–91

 extra memory cards for, 36, 290
 JPEG format of, 96
 lenses, 31, 35
 megapixels, 32
 picture viewing program, 32, 89–90
 purchasing, 13, 31–33
 size and durability, 32
 stabilizing, 86
 tripod for, 36, 273
 Web sites, 25, 31
digital design library
 choosing materials from, 54–55
 color palettes for, 52
 creating, 49–50
 embellishments for, 51–52
 organizing, 50
 photos for, 50–51
 resources for, 52–53
Digital Ice (scanning software), 34
Digital Images Suite (photo-editing software), 45, 150, 186
digital page, defined, 2
*Digital Photography For Dummies* (King), 31, 87
*Digital Photography Review* (Web site), 31
digital scrapbooking. *See also* planning a digital scrapbook
 advantages of, 9–10
 equipment for, 11–14
 popular styles for, 15–16
 saving your work, 16–19
 sharing digital files, 19
 standard terms, 2
 workspace for, 20–21
digitalization
 digital camera for, 114–115, 272–275
 scanning method for, 91, 268–272
discussion groups, 296, 298
display fonts (fancy title fonts), 47
distort filters, 176
documents and letters, scanning, 303
Dodge tool, 233
dodging and burning tools, 154–155
dots per inch (dpi), 92
drawing a free-hand line, 157
drawing a vector line, 157–158
drawing tools, 79. *See also* illustrations and drawings

Dreamweaver (Web page designing program), 279
drop cap letters, 78, 196
Drop Shadow function, 194
duotone (two-color) photos, 166–167
duplicating (cloning) images, 102, 151–152
dust spots, repairing, 151
DVD or CD burner, 36
DVD or CD player/writer unit, 17
DVD/CD drives, 17–18
DVD/CDs
  burning scrapbooks on, 19, 280–281
  photo collections on, 133, 219
  photos and scrapbook files stored on, 17–18, 64
  printing labels onto, 281
  viruses protection and, 288

● *E* ●

eclectic style scrapbook, 78
editing digital images, 66–67. *See also* photo-editing software; *specific techniques*
  "aging" techniques, 72, 154, 232–234
  brightness and contrast adjustments, 99, 166, 223
  cloning and healing, 102, 151–152
  color adjustments, 152–154
  cropping (or trimming), 57, 90–91, 96–97, 158–160
  cutting out objects, 151, 158–160
  filters and plug-ins, 167–171, 172
  flipping photos, 98
  generational loss and, 93
  red eye reduction, 100
  repairing scanned photos, 102
  retouching, 154–158
  rotating photo positions, 98
  saving the original image and, 93
  sharpening photo images, 101
  size and resolution adjustments, 93–96
  software for, 43–45
  stitching photos together, 164
  tiling, 118–119
e-mail address, 125
e-mail attachments, 19, 275–278
e-mail, viruses and, 288
embedding fonts into the file, 277–278
embellishments
  binding the pages and, 267
  classic style, 218
  collecting, 51–52
  combining real and digital, 72
  described, 300
  filtering, 176
  found objects as, 173
  hand drawings as, 172–173
  heritage style, 240
  iron-ons, 302–303
  light and shadow for, 174–175
  pop style, 253–254
  "real" look for, 174–175
  sizing to fit the layout, 175–176, 237–238
  "stickers," digital, 173, 301
  for texturing, 176
  3-D items, 114, 162, 173–174, 301
embossed page elements, 72
emphasis, 113
enlarging an image
  copying original images and, 94
  described, 94, 95–96
  Sizing tool for, 74
Epson brand, 28, 29, 266
equipment and tools. *See also* computer; digital camera; printer; scanner
  CD/DVD player/writer unit, 17
  computer chair, 21
  computer stand, 20
  connectors, 21
  copy stand, 274
  extenders for, 104
  memory stick (flash drive), 288, 289
  for multimedia scrapbooks, 199–200
  music stand, 273
  outdated, 11
  overview, 11–12
  photo-grade lights, 36, 86, 275
  purchasing tips, 21, 293–294
  rolling computer platform, 20
  surge protector, 290
  tripod, 36, 273
  Web sites, 294

Eraser tool, 158–159, 233
ethnic history scrapbooks, 82
events scrapbook, 82, 306
extenders for traditional scrapbooks, 104
Eyedropper tool, 52, 68, 102, 157

## • *F* •

family album (heritage style)
  assembling, 238–241
  color palette for, 234–236
  layout for, 236–238
  photographs for, 230–234
  writing the story, 227–230
family scrapbooks, 261–262
family tree scrapbook, 307
fantasy style scrapbook, 77–78, 79–80
favorite possessions scrapbook,
  307–308
feathering (fuzzing or fringing) effect,
  155, 159
Feathering tool, 160
file formats. *See also* PDF (portable
  document format)
  choosing, 267
  JPEG, 18, 96, 267, 279
  printing digital pages and, 267
  for saving digital images, 96
  for saving your work, 267
  TIFF, 18, 96, 267
file transfer protocol (FTP), 279
files. *See also* copying files; file formats
  converting to PDF format, 47, 278
  defined, 2
  discarding or relocating leftovers,
    62–64
  size and resolution issues, 291
  transferring to the Web, 279
filing system. *See also* organizing and
  storing your work
  project folders for, 58, 288
  setting up, 288–289
fill-in images, 57
films/movies, 183

filters
  backgrounds and, 252
  benefits of using, 167–168
  blurring out a background with, 170
  classic style, 224
  for drawing and painting looks for
    background, 171
  embellishments and, 176
  foreground and background balanced
    with, 172
  fuzzy images improved with, 170
  for heritage-style images, 229–230
  motion effect with, 248
  neon photo-processing, 178
  over background material, 178
  pop style images and, 246
  posterization, 246, 300
  saving filtered images and, 17
  tips for using, 169–170
  undoing, 170
finishing a scrapbook
  classic style and, 224–225
  mock ups for, 216, 254
  pop style scrapbooks and, 254
  support for, 298
  tips for, 296
flash drive (memory stick), 288, 289
flattening an image, 18, 59, 162
flipbooks, animated, 45
flipping photos, 98
floppy disks, 16
focal point, finding, 110–111, 220
folds, adding to photos, 233
fonts. *See also* text
  basics of, 138–139
  body and display types, 139
  classic style, 214–215
  conversions, 142
  customized, 195
  embedding into files, 277–278
  fancy title, 47
  handwriting made into, 145, 195
  origins of, 137
  problem prevention, 140–141
  pseudo, 143–144

purchasing collections of, 142
sending copies of, 141
sources of, 141–142
storing and copying, 140
Web sites, 142, 195, 316
Fott, Galen (*Photoshop Elements For Dummies*), 44
found objects, 173
framing, 76, 225
free stuff
  illustrations and drawings, 128
  photo-editing software, 150
  photographs, 219
  scrapbooking materials, 311
  software (freeware), 39–40, 311
  spyware protection software, 125
friend scrapbooks, 260–261
FTP (file transfer protocol), 279
fuzzy images, improving, 170

### • *G* •

Gaussian blur, 171
genealogy heritage scrapbook, 230
generational loss, 28, 93
geography scrapbooks, 82
geometrical shapes, 76
getting started. *See* planning a digital scrapbook
gift scrapbooks, 308
golden mean, 220
Gookin, Dan
  *Laptops For Dummies*, 26
  *PCs For Dummies*, 24
grandparent scrapbooks, 261–262
graphics, digital. *See also* clip art
  bitmapped image, 122
  copyrighting issues, 124
  illustrations and drawings, 79, 128–131, 302
  Internet photos, 131–133
  overview, 121–122
  resolution for, 123–124
  stock images, 132–133
  vector-based, 122–123, 127

graphics, traditional, 121
grayscale images, 166
grid buttons, 59
grid, tic-tac-toe, 2, 108–109. *See also* positioning items on a page
group scrapbooks for kids, 309
grouping or clustering images, 61–62
Guide Line tool, 108–109
Gutenberg, Johannes (printing press inventor), 137

### • *H* •

hand-drawn embellishments, 172–173
hand-drawn letters, 68, 69
handmade/traditional albums
  collecting materials for, 121
  converting to digital form, 268–275, 303
  digital scrapbooking and, 10, 297
  digital tools for, 23
  embellishments used in, 174
  extenders for, 104
  sharing, 303
handwriting, fonts for, 145, 195
handwritten text, 144–145, 302
hanging indent, 196–197
hard drive, computer, 25–27
harmony, 60, 105
Hart, Russell (*Photography For Dummies*), 247
headlines and titles, 190, 198, 301–302
healing damaged images, 152
heritage style scrapbook, 66–67, 162. *See also* Family Album (heritage style)
high-resolution (hi-res) image, 86
historic style scrapbook, 78–79, 82
history of digital imaging, 38
hobby scrapbooks, 264
home page, 280
hot and cool colors, coordinating, 181
HP Creative Scrapbook Assistant (software), 14, 42, 46, 317
HTML format, 207, 279
Hue button, 235

## • I •

illustrations and drawings
  colorizing, 129–130
  fashion-style, 79
  scanning, 302
  sources of, 128
*Illustrator For Dummies* (Wiley
    Publishing), 186
image interpolation **program, 28**
iMovie (audio-video software), 201
indoor photography, 114–115, 274–275
ink
  author's recommendations, 266
  choosing, 29–30
  cost of using, 30
  Epson brand, 29, 266
  quality issues, 29
inkjet printer, 30, 266
inspiration for new ideas, finding, **297**
instruction manuals, 267, 287
Internet. *See also* Web sites
  downloading photos from, 131–132
  using safely, 125
interpolation component, 94
iron-ons, 302–303

## • J •

journaling. *See also* text
  classic style, 213–215
  defined, 142, 244
  heritage-style, 227–**230, 238–239**
  incorporating into a scrapbook,
    57, 195–198
  length of story and, **244–245**
  multimedia and, 204
  overview, 56–57
  pop style, 244–246
  word processing software for, **12, 143, 186**
JPEG format
  of digital cameras, 96
  image quality of, 18
  photography stores' preference for, 267
  for Web site graphics, 279
justified text, 197

## • K •

kerning, 137
King, Julie Adair (*Digital Photography
    For Dummies*), 31, 87

## • L •

laptop computer, 12, 26, 290
*Laptops For Dummies* (Gookin), 26
large items, scanning, 114, 270–272
laser printer, 30, 266
layering page elements, 59
layering text onto images, 58
layout. *See also* background; editing
    digital images
  balance for, 104, 109–110, 221–222
  classic style, 220–222
  heritage style, 236–238
  layering and, 59
  as one- or two-page spread, 2, 104
  panoramic, 163–165
  pop style, 250–254
  positioning items on, 59–61
  template page for, 58–59
  for theme scrapbooks, 258
  visual design principles for, 104–107
leading, 196
legal issues (copyrights)
  about, 124
  importance of, 295–296
  sharing fonts and, 141
  U.S. government public domain
    images, 315
lenses, 31, 35
letters. *See also* text
  drop cap, 78, 196
  outlining and filling, 191–192
LeVitus, Bob (*Mac OS X For Dummies*), 39
library, digital
  choosing materials from, 54–55
  color palettes for, 52
  creating, 49–50
  embellishments for, 51–52
  organizing, 50

photos for, 50–51
resources for, 52–53
light and dark areas, retouching, 154–155
light and dark colors, balancing, 182
light and shadow, 174–175
light table, 173
lighting
  automatic flashes and, 86
  for background photos, 178
  photo-grade lights, 36, 86, 275
  shooting indoors and, 114–115, 274–275
  shooting outdoors and, 114–115,
    272–273
lighting filters, 224
lines
  creating on a computer, 173
  darkening the edges of, 130
  drawing a vector line, 157–158
  page design and, 111–113
  spacing or leading adjustments, 136
  tic-tac-toe grid, 2, 108–109
linking your Web pages, 280
Lopuck, Lisa (*Web Design For
    Dummies*), 279
Lowe, Doug (*PowerPoint For Dummies*), 201
low-resolution (low-res) image, 86

• *M* •

*Mac OS X For Dummies* (LeVitus), 39
Macintosh computers, 14, 39, 201
Macintosh OSX operating system, 27, 39
*Macs For Dummies* (Pogue), 24
magazines and books
  advertisements, 183
  art books, 183
  clip art in, 126–127
  comic books, 249
  pop style, 249
  scanning, 28, 115, 219
  scrapbooking, 15
Magic Wand tool, 159–160
Magnifying tool, 130
maintaining and repairing computers,
    25, 26, 287–288

McClelland, Deke (*Photoshop Elements
    For Dummies*), 44
megapixels, 32
memorabilia
  heritage style, 236–237
  pop style, 253–254
memory cards, 36, 290
memory, for computers, 25–27, 33, 286
memory stick (flash drive), 288, 289
Microsoft PowerPoint (audio/video
    software)
  background templates with, 200
  beginners and, 199
  creation of, 201
Microsoft Web site, 150
Microsoft Word (software), 12
Microtek scanners, 28
mirror image, 98
mock up of scrapbook, 216, 254
modern style scrapbook, 75–76
moiré pattern, 115
monitors, 33–34
monochromatic (single color) images
  backgrounds as, 250–251
  heritage style, 235
  Hue control bar for, 153
montages (collages), 119, 162–163
morgues, 53, 295
Move tool, 74
movement, showing, 247–248
movies/films, 183
multimedia scrapbook
  equipment for, 199–200
  image size and resolution for, 205
  organizing, 203–204
  paying someone to create, 208
  pop style albums and, 254
  sharing, 207–209
  software for, 199, 201–203
  sound and video for, 205–207
  writing the story and, 204
music stand, 273
My Scrapbook (software), 41

### • N •

native format file, 18
negative space, 106–107
neon photo-processing filter, 178
"non-art," using, 252–253

### • O •

Obermeier, Barbara (*Photoshop Album For Dummies*), 122
old photographs
  color variations in, 237
  restoring, 66
  scanning and, 230–234
Olympus digital cameras, 32, 33
one point perspective, 190
Opacity Adjustment feature, 166
opaquing a background, 181
operating system (OS)
  described, 27
  identifying, 38
  Macintosh OS X, 27, 39
  Windows XP, 27, 38
optimization programs for computers, 25
organizing and storing your work. *See also* saving your work
  background photos, 178
  CD or DVD backups for, 17–18, 64
  filing system for, 288–289
  frequency of, 17
  overview, 304
  photographs, digital and, 16–17, 51, 289
  photographs, hard-copy and, 50, 51
  project folder for, 18–19, 58, 288
  pros and cons of digital storage, 16
original images
  copying, 28, 93, 94
  scanning, 303
  types of, 246
OS (operating system)
  described, 27
  identifying, 38
  Windows XP, 27, 38
OS X Macintosh operating system, 27, 39
outdated equipment, 11

outdoor photography, 114–115, 272–273
oversized photos or documents, scanning, 115, 270–272

### • P •

page layout. *See also* background; editing digital images
  balance for, 104, 109–110, 221–222
  classic style, 220–222
  collecting materials for, 49–53
  color variations, 166–167
  embellishments, 172–176
  heritage style, 236–238
  layering page elements, 59
  marking out a grid, 108–109
  montages (collages) for, 119, 162–163
  as one- or two-page spread, 2, 104
  panoramic, 163–165
  pop style, 250–254
  positioning items on, 59–61
  structure, depth, dimension, 111–113
  template page for, 58–59
  for theme scrapbooks, 258
  visual design principles for, 104–107
page size
  choosing, 222–223
  classic style scrapbook and, 222–223
  heritage-style scrapbooks and, 238–239
pages. *See also* page layout; printing digital pages
  binding, 267–268
  "stitching" together, 164, 270–272
Paint Shop Pro (photo-editing software), 44, 129, 168, 186, 224
Paintbrush tool, 157
painting filters, 171, 224
"painting" tools, 154–158
panoramic photos, 163–165, 248
paper
  author's recommendation, 266
  colored, 296–297
  customized, 300
  for handwritten text, 145
  posterizing, 246, 300
  for printing digital pages, 266
  specialized, 34

PC (personal computer), 38
*PCs For Dummies* (Gookin), 24
PCWorld (Web site), 25
PDF (portable document format)
  for burning scrapbooks to CDs/DVDs, 281
  converting files to, 47, 278
  fonts and, 140
  reading files in, 277–278
  saving files and, 275–276, 291
  for sharing digital files, 47, 275–277, 291
Pen tool, 157–158
Pencil tool, 157Perfect Scrapbook Maker
    (software), 14, 41
personal computer (PC), 38
personal Web site
  linking your pages, 280
  page size and format for, 279
  remounting or reinstalling, 278
  saving, 278
  transferring files to, 279
  Web space for, 279
pet scrapbooks, 263
photo archives, 133
photo paper, 19, 29–30, 115
photo printers, 30, 268
photo-editing software. *See also* editing
    digital images; *specific software*
  advanced, 150–151
  file formats and, 96
  native format file of, 18
  upgrading, 34
photo-grade lights, 36, 86, 275
photographs, digital. *See also* editing
    digital images; printing photos;
    shooting digital photographs
  as background, 241
  classic style, 216–219
  color quality and, 32
  digital photo album software for, 17
  downloading from the Internet, 131–132
  enhancing, 35–36
  flattening into one layer, 18
  heritage style, 230–234, 240–241
  interplay with the text, 57–58
  organizing and storing, 16–17
  originals of, 246
  photographic paper and, 115

pop style, 246–249
sources of, 51, 133, 219
texturing with, 119
time-lapse, 248
photographs, hard-copy. *See also*
    photographs, digital; printing photos
  descreening and scanning, 115–117
  native format file, 18
  organizing, 50
  preparing for storage, 18–19
  protecting from deterioration, 234
  repairing, 231–232
*Photography For Dummies* (Hart), 247
photography store
  for archival quality color prints, 266
  file formats preferred by, 267
  hard-copy prints from, 50
  preparing digital images for, 92, 266
PhotoImpact (photo-editing software), 45
photo-processing filters, 178
*Photoshop Album For Dummies*
    (Obermeier), 122
*Photoshop Elements For Dummies*
    (McClelland and Fott), 44
Photoshop Elements (photo-editing
    software)
  for advanced photo-editing, 150
  audio/video features of, 201
  colorizing illustrations and drawings
    with, 129
  cost of, 14, 43
  described, 43–44
  filter plug-ins for, 168
  importing digital graphics, 122
Picasso, Pablo (artist), 253
Picture It! Premium (photo-editing
    software), 45, 150
picture-viewing program (album
    programs), 32
pitfalls to avoid, 293–298
pixelated (blocky) images, 95
pixeled map, 122
pixels per inch (ppi)
  adding pixels, 94
  printing digital graphics and, 123–124
  resolution and, 86, 291
  scanner and printer settings and, 92

planning a digital scrapbook. *See also* organizing and storing your work; page layout
  materials for, 54–55
  page size choices, 55
  project folder for, 58, 288
  selecting photos and images, 57–58
  sketching pages for, 55–56
  starting too many projects and, 296
  style choices for, 15–16
  type of scrapbooks for, 54, 285
  writing the story and, 56–57
plug-ins, 168
Pogue, David (*Macs For Dummies*), 24
point size, 135
pop style scrapbook, 70–72. *See also* reunion album (pop style)
portable document format (PDF) See PDF
positioning items on a page. *See also* page layout
  clustering, 61–62
  overview, 59–60
  sizing and resizing, 60
  tic-tac-toe grid for, 2, 108–109
  using arrow keys for, 74
  varying the shapes, 60
positive and negative space, 106–107
Poster Edges tool, 246
posterization, 246, 300
power surges, 290
PowerPoint (audio/video software)
  background templates with, 200
  beginners and, 199
  creation of, 201
*PowerPoint For Dummies* (Lowe), 201
ppi (pixels per inch)
  adding pixels, 94
  printing digital graphics and, 123–124
  resolution and, 86, 291
  scanner and printer settings and, 92
presentation programs/software, 200, 201. *See also* audio/video editing software
preserving (saving) your work. *See also* copying files; organizing and storing your work
  archiving digital pages, 19
  file formats for, 96, 267
  ink and photo paper quality and, 29
  original images and, 93

  in PDF format, 275–276, 291
  renaming your file and, 266
Print Explosion Deluxe (photo-editing software), 43
The Print Shop Deluxe (photo-editing software), 42–43
printer. *See also* printing digital pages; printing photos
  authors' recommendations, 266
  cartridges for, 268
  choosing, 12–13, 30
  color, 12, 268
  image resolution and, 64
  inkjet and laser, 30, 266
  long-lasting images and, 266
  manuals for, 267
  photo prints and, 30, 268
  printing labels onto CD/DVDs, 281
  resolution settings, 18–19, 92
  settings for printing, 18–19, 92, 267
printer font, 139
printing digital pages. *See also* printing photos
  archival quality, 29
  best ink and paper for, 266
  binding the pages and, 267–268
  flattening images for, 18, 59
  Internet photo services for, 300
  photography stores and, 266, 300
  resizing and saving, 266–267
  resolution for, 18–19, 266
  tips for, 266, 299–300
printing photos. *See also* printer
  commercial printing, 29–30, 34
  home-printing, 29–30
  ink and photo paper for, 29–30
  specialized, 34
printing press, 137
problems
  discussion groups help with, 296, 298
  pitfalls to avoid, 293–298
product license numbers, 40
project folder, 58, 288
proofing pages, 74–75
proportion, 60
pseudo font, 143–144
public building project scrapbooks, 264
public domain images (Web sites), 315

## • *Q* •

quotes and phrases, finding, 67

## • *R* •

RAM (random access memory),
    25–26, 33, 286
"real" look embellishments, 174–175
red eye reduction, 100
reducing the size of digital images, 94–95
reinstalling software, 40
remodeling project scrapbooks, 264
removing objects
    Cloning tool for, 151
    Eraser tool for, 158–159
    Magic Wand tool for, 159–160
repairing and restoring photos, 66, 151–152
repairing computers, 26
repairing images, 102, 158
resolution
    adjusting, 93–94
    camera settings for, 18–19
    copying original images and, 94
    creating a PDF file and, 276
    for digital graphics, 123–124
    photo paper and, 19
    printer settings for, 18–19, 92, 266
    scanner settings for, 92
    shooting digital photographs and, 86–87
retouching images
    airbrushing, 155–157
    dodging and burning tools for, 154–155
    pen tool for, 157–158
    pencil tool for, 157
retro-pop images, 248
reunion album (pop style)
    color palette for, 249–250
    completing, 254
    layout, 250–254
    overview, 243–244
    photos and images for, 246–249
    writing the story, 244–246
RGB color mode, 176, 234
rhythm, 105–106
Rotate tool, 98, 192–193
ruler, displaying on computer, 59, 74, 75

## • *S* •

saturating and desaturating images,
    154, 166
saving your work. *See also* copying files;
    organizing and storing your work
    archiving digital pages, 19
    file formats for, 96, 267
    ink and photo paper quality and, 29
    original images and, 93
    in PDF format, 275–276, 291
    renaming your file and, 266
scanner. *See also* scanning
    cleaning, 91
    cost of, 27–28
    enhancing, 34
    hardware and software settings, 91–92
    large size, 270
    Microtek and Epson, 28
    purchasing, 13–14, 27
    resolution settings, 92
    software program of, 13–14, 91–92
    transparency, 28
*Scanners For Dummies* (Chambers), 27
scanning. *See also* scanner
    descreening hard-copy images for,
        28, 115–117
    documents and letters, originals, 303
    drawings, 302
    generational loss and, 28
    hand-drawn embellishments, 172–173
    handwritten text, 302
    items with rough surfaces, 115
    large flat items, 114
    old photographs and, 230–234
    oversized photos or pages, 115, 270–272
    protection needed for, 115
    real life texture items for, 179
    reflective, 28
    repairing scanned images, 102
    slides and, 28
    small photos or pages and, 269
    3-D items, 114, 173–174
    traditional scrapbooks and, 268–272
school-related scrapbooks, 259–260
Scrapbook Factory Deluxe (software),
    14, 186

*Scrapbooking For Dummies* (Wiley),
    19, 65, 87, 96, 103
scrapbooking software. *See also*
    software programs
  advanced-level, 43–46
  authors' recommendations, 46
  beginning-level, 40–42
  choosing, 39–40
  extras for, 46–48
  freeware, shareware, and trial, 39–40
  images and, 63
  intermediate-level, 42–43
  PDF format and, 47
  product license numbers and, 40
  reinstalling, 40
scrapbooks. *See* digital scrapbooking;
    multimedia scrapbook; traditional
    scrapbooking
scratches, repairing, 151
screen font, 139
selling digital background photos, 179
sepia tone, 235
setting up (beginning) a digital scrapbook.
    *See also* page layout
  beginners scrapbooking software, 40–42
  design library materials for, 54–55
  page size choices, 55
  project folder for, 58, 288
  selecting photos and images, 57–58
  sketching pages for, 55–56
  starting too many projects and, 296
  style choices for, 15–16
  type of scrapbooks for, 54, 285
  workstation for, 20–21
  writing the story, 56–57
shabby chic style scrapbook, 72–73
shadow
  adding with airbrushing, 157
  embellishments with, 174–175
  text and, 194
shapes of page elements, 60, 111–113
sharing your scrapbook
  CD/DVDs for, 19, 280–281
  converting traditional scrapbook to
      digital form, 268–275, 303
  as e-mail attachments, 19, 275–278

  heritage materials and, 229
  PDF file format for, 291
  as printed scrapbook pages, 266–268
  Web site for, 278–280, 317
Sharpen filter, 170
sharpening feature, 101
shooting digital photographs. *See also*
    digital camera
  automatic flash and, 86
  for background images, 177–181
  extra photos and, 89
  indoors session, 114–115, 274–275
  new angles and candid shots, 87–88
  outdoor sessions, 272–273
  for panorama layouts, 163–165
  of pets, 263
  resolution and, 86–87
  saving originals and copies of, 93
  setting up shots, 87
  stabilizing the camera, 86
  of textures, 180–181
  3-D items, 114
  time estimates for, 88–89
  of traditional scrapbooks, 272–275
single color (monochromatic) images
  backgrounds as, 250–251
  heritage style, 235
  Hue control bar for, 153
single-page layouts, 258
size adjustments
  of embellishments, 175–176
  enlarging and reducing on a page, 60
  increasing the size of digital images,
      94, 95–96
  photo-editing software for, 93–96
  for printing digital pages, 266–267
  reducing the size of digital images, 94–95
size and opacity features, 161
size of page
  choosing, 55, 269
  scanning large scrapbook pages, 270–272
  scanning small scrapbook pages, 269
Sizing tool, 74, 221–222
sketching your pages, 55–56
skewing text, 190
slide show presentations, 200

slides, scanning, 28
small scrapbook pages, scanning, 269
Smudge tool, 233
Snap to Grid feature, 109, 221
software programs. *See also* photo-editing
    software; scrapbooking software;
    *specific software*
  animated flipbook, 45
  audio/video, 199, 201–203
  beginning-level, 14, 40–42
  for CD/DVD labels, 281
  choosing, 14, 286–287
  digital photo album programs, 17
  for fonts, 195
  freeware, 39–40, 311
  image interpolation program feature, 28
  learning about, 287
  operating system (OS), 27, 38–39
  PDF conversion program, 47, 275
  picture viewing, 32
  problem prevention, 294
  purchasing tips, 293–294
  reinstalling, 40
  for scanners, 13–14, 91–92
  specialty, 317–318
  spyware protection, 125
  templates created with, 58–59
  text created with, 185–186
  trial downloads, 14, 150
  upgrading, 34
  virus protection for, 141, 288
  for Web page designing, 279
  word processing, 12, 143, 186
sound, 205–207
space, positive and negative, 106–107
special/important events scrapbook,
    82, 307
sports style scrapbooks, 80–81
spots, adding to photos, 232
spyware protection software, 125
starting (planning) a digital scrapbook. *See
    also* organizing and storing your work;
    page layout
  materials for, 54–55
  page size choices, 55
  project folder for, 58, 288

selecting photos and images, 57–58
sketching pages for, 55–56
starting too many projects and, 296
style choices for, 15–16
type of scrapbooks for, 54, 285
writing the story and, 56–57
state archival photos, 133
stickers, digital, 173, 301
"stitching" pages together, 164, 270–272
stock graphics, 132–133
story, writing. *See also* text
  classic style, 213–215
  heritage-style, 227–230, 238–239
  incorporating into a scrapbook,
      57, 195–198
  length for, 244–245
  multimedia and, 204
  overview, 56–57
  pop style, 244–246
  word processing software for, 12, 143, 186
streaming video, 207
stretching the text, 189–190
styles. *See also* themes for scrapbooks
  artist, 76
  baby scrapbooks, 77
  choosing, 15–16
  classic, 73–75
  crafty, 68–69
  defined, 65
  eclectic, 78
  ethnic history, 82
  fantasy, 77–78
  fashion, 79–80
  geography, 82
  getting into a rut, 297
  heritage, 66–67
  historic, 78–79, 82
  modern, 75–76
  pop, 70–72
  shabby chic, 72–73
  special/important event, 82, 307
  sports, 80–81
  vocational, 80
  Western, 82
sugar paper, 34
symmetrical design, 104

## • T •

teaching scrapbooking, 309
tears, repairing, 151
templates
  creating, 55, 58–59
  ready-made, 257
text. *See also* fonts; journaling; letters
  alignment on a page, 136
  ascenders and descenders, 136
  in columns, 197
  curvy or wavy lines for, 189
  filters for, 194
  handwritten, 144–145, 302
  inserting into a layout, 143
  interplay with photos and images, 57–58
  kerning, 137
  line spacing or leading, 136
  outlining and filling letters, 191–192
  placing on images, 58
  point size for, 135
  pre-made special effects, 186
  quotes and phrases, finding, 67
  rotating, 192–193
  shadowing, 194
  skewing, 190
  software programs for, 185–186
  stretching, 189–190
  vertical, 193
  wrapping, 186–188, 287
texture
  background and, 179–181
  contrasting, 181
  embellishments and, 176
  photographs and, 119, 180–181
themes for scrapbooks. *See also* styles
  birthday party, 257
  business, 263–264
  choosing, 54, 255–257
  family, 261–262
  family tree, 307
  favorite possessions, 307–308
  friend, 260–261
  grandparents, 261–262
  group scrapbooks for kids, 309
  hobbies, 264
  layout and, 258
  pets, 263
  public building projects, 264

remodeling projects, 264
school, 259–260
special/important events, 307
vacations, 263
3-D items
  digitizing, 114
  flattening, 162
  mixing traditional and digital, 301
  scanning, 173–174
thumbnails of photos, 289
tic-tac-toe grid, 2, 108–109. *See also*
    positioning items on a page
TIFF file formats, 18, 96, 267
tiling, 118–119
time, 10, 88–89
time-lapse photos, 248
tinting an image, 166–167
titles and headlines, 190, 198, 301–302
tools and equipment. *See also* computer;
    digital camera; printer; scanner
  CD/DVD player/writer unit, 17
  computer chair, 21
  computer stand, 20
  connectors, 21
  copy stand, 274
  extenders for, 104
  memory stick (flash drive), 288, 289
  for multimedia scrapbooks, 199–200
  music stand, 273
  outdated, 11
  overview, 11–12
  photo-grade lights, 36, 86, 275
  purchasing tips, 21, 293–294
  rolling computer platform, 20
  surge protector, 290
  tripod, 36, 273
  Web sites, 294
topics for scrapbooking. *See* styles;
    themes for scrapbooks
torn photos, 233
tracing a fashion photograph, 79
Tracking feature, 137
trademarks (copyrights)
  about, 124
  importance of, 295–296
  sharing fonts and, 141
  U.S. government public domain
    images, 315

traditional scrapbooking
  collecting materials for, 121
  converting to digital form, 268–275, 303
  digital scrapbooking and, 10, 297
  digital tools for, 23
  embellishments used in, 174
  extenders for, 104
  sharing, 303
training programs (online), 15
translucent images, 152
transparency adapters, 28
transparency scanner, 28
travel bureau graphics, 48
trial software, 40
trimming (or cropping)
  advanced techniques, 158–160
  described, 57, 96–97
  digital camera's feature for, 90–91
tripod, 36, 273
true photograph, 115
T-shirts, images for, 303
two-page spread, 258. *See also*
    page layout

• *U* •

unfinished projects, 296
unity, 105
UPS (universal power supply), 290
URL address, 280
U.S. government public domain
    images, 315
USB connection, 21, 24

• *V* •

vacation scrapbooks, 263
vanishing point, 190
vector line, drawing, 157–158
vector-based graphics, 122–123, 127
vertical text, 193
video editing, 202
video-only scrapbooks, 285
video, streaming, 207
virus, computer, 141, 288
visual design principles
  balance, 104, 109–110, 221–222
  color, 107

harmony, 60, 105
  positive and negative space, 106–107
  rhythm, 105–106
  unity, 105
vocational style scrapbook, 80
voice-over recording, 204

• *W* •

wallpaper effect, 177
washed out look, 252
watermarked images, 182–183
Web animations software, 45
*Web Design For Dummies* (Lopuck), 279
Web sites. *See also* personal Web site
  Acrobat (viewer) program, 278, 303
  caution for using, 125
  chat rooms, 316–317
  clip art, 48, 127, 314–315
  computer research, 25
  creating your own, 278–280
  digital camera, 25, 31
  digital photo album programs, 17
  discussion groups, 296, 298
  equipment shopping, 294
  fonts, 142, 316
  for free stuff, 128
  freeware (software), 311
  galleries, 15
  HP Creative Scrapbook Assistant, 317
  illustrations and drawings, 128
  Internet photo services, 300
  Microsoft, 150
  multimedia album services, 208
  PDF conversion program, 47
  photo-editing software, free, 150
  photos and images, 219
  posting your pages on, 317
  printers/ink and paper, 266
  public domain images, 315
  scrapbook-specific, 311–313
  security issues, 125
  specialty software, 317–318
  stock images, 132–133
  style galleries, 15
  training programs, 15
  trial software, 150
  video editing, 202

wedding album (classic style)
  assembling, 222–223
  choosing photos, 216–219
  color palette, 219–220
  finishing, 224–225
  layout, 220–222
  story for, 213–215
Western style, 82
white space, 106
Windows Movie Maker (audio-video
  software), 201
Windows XP (operating system), 27, 38
wireless connections, 21
WMF format (windows file format), 122

Word (Microsoft word processing
  software), 12
word processing software, 12, 143, 186
workstation, creating, 20–21
wrapping the text, 186–188, 287
writing the story. *See also* text
  classic style, 213–215
  heritage-style, 227–230, 238–239
  incorporating into your scrapbook,
    57, 195–198
  length for, 244–245
  multimedia and, 204
  overview, 56–57
  pop style, 244–246

## BUSINESS, CAREERS & PERSONAL FINANCE

0-7645-5307-0

0-7645-5331-3 *†

**Also available:**

- Accounting For Dummies †
  0-7645-5314-3
- Business Plans Kit For Dummies †
  0-7645-5365-8
- Cover Letters For Dummies
  0-7645-5224-4
- Frugal Living For Dummies
  0-7645-5403-4
- Leadership For Dummies
  0-7645-5176-0
- Managing For Dummies
  0-7645-1771-6

- Marketing For Dummies
  0-7645-5600-2
- Personal Finance For Dummies *
  0-7645-2590-5
- Project Management For Dummies
  0-7645-5283-X
- Resumes For Dummies †
  0-7645-5471-9
- Selling For Dummies
  0-7645-5363-1
- Small Business Kit For Dummies *†
  0-7645-5093-4

## HOME & BUSINESS COMPUTER BASICS

0-7645-4074-2

0-7645-3758-X

**Also available:**

- ACT! 6 For Dummies
  0-7645-2645-6
- iLife '04 All-in-One Desk Reference
  For Dummies
  0-7645-7347-0
- iPAQ For Dummies
  0-7645-6769-1
- Mac OS X Panther Timesaving
  Techniques For Dummies
  0-7645-5812-9
- Macs For Dummies
  0-7645-5656-8

- Microsoft Money 2004 For Dummies
  0-7645-4195-1
- Office 2003 All-in-One Desk Reference
  For Dummies
  0-7645-3883-7
- Outlook 2003 For Dummies
  0-7645-3759-8
- PCs For Dummies
  0-7645-4074-2
- TiVo For Dummies
  0-7645-6923-6
- Upgrading and Fixing PCs For Dummies
  0-7645-1665-5
- Windows XP Timesaving Techniques
  For Dummies
  0-7645-3748-2

## FOOD, HOME, GARDEN, HOBBIES, MUSIC & PETS

0-7645-5295-3

0-7645-5232-5

**Also available:**

- Bass Guitar For Dummies
  0-7645-2487-9
- Diabetes Cookbook For Dummies
  0-7645-5230-9
- Gardening For Dummies *
  0-7645-5130-2
- Guitar For Dummies
  0-7645-5106-X
- Holiday Decorating For Dummies
  0-7645-2570-0
- Home Improvement All-in-One
  For Dummies
  0-7645-5680-0

- Knitting For Dummies
  0-7645-5395-X
- Piano For Dummies
  0-7645-5105-1
- Puppies For Dummies
  0-7645-5255-4
- Scrapbooking For Dummies
  0-7645-7208-3
- Senior Dogs For Dummies
  0-7645-5818-8
- Singing For Dummies
  0-7645-2475-5
- 30-Minute Meals For Dummies
  0-7645-2589-1

## INTERNET & DIGITAL MEDIA

0-7645-1664-7

0-7645-6924-4

**Also available:**

- 2005 Online Shopping Directory
  For Dummies
  0-7645-7495-7
- CD & DVD Recording For Dummies
  0-7645-5956-7
- eBay For Dummies
  0-7645-5654-1
- Fighting Spam For Dummies
  0-7645-5965-6
- Genealogy Online For Dummies
  0-7645-5964-8
- Google For Dummies
  0-7645-4420-9

- Home Recording For Musicians
  For Dummies
  0-7645-1634-5
- The Internet For Dummies
  0-7645-4173-0
- iPod & iTunes For Dummies
  0-7645-7772-7
- Preventing Identity Theft For Dummies
  0-7645-7336-5
- Pro Tools All-in-One Desk Reference
  For Dummies
  0-7645-5714-9
- Roxio Easy Media Creator For Dummies
  0-7645-7131-1

* Separate Canadian edition also available
† Separate U.K. edition also available

Available wherever books are sold. For more information or to order direct: U.S. customers visit www.dummies.com or call 1-877-762-2974.
U.K. customers visit www.wileyeurope.com or call 0800 243407. Canadian customers visit www.wiley.ca or call 1-800-567-4797.

## SPORTS, FITNESS, PARENTING, RELIGION & SPIRITUALITY

0-7645-5146-9

0-7645-5418-2

**Also available:**

- Adoption For Dummies
  0-7645-5488-3
- Basketball For Dummies
  0-7645-5248-1
- The Bible For Dummies
  0-7645-5296-1
- Buddhism For Dummies
  0-7645-5359-3
- Catholicism For Dummies
  0-7645-5391-7
- Hockey For Dummies
  0-7645-5228-7

- Judaism For Dummies
  0-7645-5299-6
- Martial Arts For Dummies
  0-7645-5358-5
- Pilates For Dummies
  0-7645-5397-6
- Religion For Dummies
  0-7645-5264-3
- Teaching Kids to Read For Dummies
  0-7645-4043-2
- Weight Training For Dummies
  0-7645-5168-X
- Yoga For Dummies
  0-7645-5117-5

## TRAVEL

0-7645-5438-7

0-7645-5453-0

**Also available:**

- Alaska For Dummies
  0-7645-1761-9
- Arizona For Dummies
  0-7645-6938-4
- Cancún and the Yucatán For Dummies
  0-7645-2437-2
- Cruise Vacations For Dummies
  0-7645-6941-4
- Europe For Dummies
  0-7645-5456-5
- Ireland For Dummies
  0-7645-5455-7

- Las Vegas For Dummies
  0-7645-5448-4
- London For Dummies
  0-7645-4277-X
- New York City For Dummies
  0-7645-6945-7
- Paris For Dummies
  0-7645-5494-8
- RV Vacations For Dummies
  0-7645-5443-3
- Walt Disney World & Orlando For Dummies
  0-7645-6943-0

## GRAPHICS, DESIGN & WEB DEVELOPMENT

0-7645-4345-8

0-7645-5589-8

**Also available:**

- Adobe Acrobat 6 PDF For Dummies
  0-7645-3760-1
- Building a Web Site For Dummies
  0-7645-7144-3
- Dreamweaver MX 2004 For Dummies
  0-7645-4342-3
- FrontPage 2003 For Dummies
  0-7645-3882-9
- HTML 4 For Dummies
  0-7645-1995-6
- Illustrator cs For Dummies
  0-7645-4084-X

- Macromedia Flash MX 2004 For Dummies
  0-7645-4358-X
- Photoshop 7 All-in-One Desk Reference For Dummies
  0-7645-1667-1
- Photoshop cs Timesaving Techniques For Dummies
  0-7645-6782-9
- PHP 5 For Dummies
  0-7645-4166-8
- PowerPoint 2003 For Dummies
  0-7645-3908-6
- QuarkXPress 6 For Dummies
  0-7645-2593-X

## NETWORKING, SECURITY, PROGRAMMING & DATABASES

0-7645-6852-3

0-7645-5784-X

**Also available:**

- A+ Certification For Dummies
  0-7645-4187-0
- Access 2003 All-in-One Desk Reference For Dummies
  0-7645-3988-4
- Beginning Programming For Dummies
  0-7645-4997-9
- C For Dummies
  0-7645-7068-4
- Firewalls For Dummies
  0-7645-4048-3
- Home Networking For Dummies
  0-7645-42796

- Network Security For Dummies
  0-7645-1679-5
- Networking For Dummies
  0-7645-1677-9
- TCP/IP For Dummies
  0-7645-1760-0
- VBA For Dummies
  0-7645-3989-2
- Wireless All In-One Desk Reference For Dummies
  0-7645-7496-5
- Wireless Home Networking For Dummies
  0-7645-3910-8

## HEALTH & SELF-HELP

0-7645-6820-5 *†

0-7645-2566-2

**Also available:**
- Alzheimer's For Dummies
  0-7645-3899-3
- Asthma For Dummies
  0-7645-4233-8
- Controlling Cholesterol For Dummies
  0-7645-5440-9
- Depression For Dummies
  0-7645-3900-0
- Dieting For Dummies
  0-7645-4149-8
- Fertility For Dummies
  0-7645-2549-2

- Fibromyalgia For Dummies
  0-7645-5441-7
- Improving Your Memory For Dummies
  0-7645-5435-2
- Pregnancy For Dummies †
  0-7645-4483-7
- Quitting Smoking For Dummies
  0-7645-2629-4
- Relationships For Dummies
  0-7645-5384-4
- Thyroid For Dummies
  0-7645-5385-2

## EDUCATION, HISTORY, REFERENCE & TEST PREPARATION

0-7645-5194-9

0-7645-4186-2

**Also available:**
- Algebra For Dummies
  0-7645-5325-9
- British History For Dummies
  0-7645-7021-8
- Calculus For Dummies
  0-7645-2498-4
- English Grammar For Dummies
  0-7645-5322-4
- Forensics For Dummies
  0-7645-5580-4
- The GMAT For Dummies
  0-7645-5251-1
- Inglés Para Dummies
  0-7645-5427-1

- Italian For Dummies
  0-7645-5196-5
- Latin For Dummies
  0-7645-5431-X
- Lewis & Clark For Dummies
  0-7645-2545-X
- Research Papers For Dummies
  0-7645-5426-3
- The SAT I For Dummies
  0-7645-7193-1
- Science Fair Projects For Dummies
  0-7645-5460-3
- U.S. History For Dummies
  0-7645-5249-X

# Get smart @ dummies.com®

- **Find a full list of Dummies titles**
- **Look into loads of FREE on-site articles**
- **Sign up for FREE eTips e-mailed to you weekly**
- **See what other products carry the Dummies name**
- **Shop directly from the Dummies bookstore**
- **Enter to win new prizes every month!**

**\* Separate Canadian edition also available**
**† Separate U.K. edition also available**

Available wherever books are sold. For more information or to order direct: U.S. customers visit www.dummies.com or call 1-877-762-2974.
U.K. customers visit www.wileyeurope.com or call 0800 243407. Canadian customers visit www.wiley.ca or call 1-800-567-4797.